THE DILEMMA
OF CANADIAN
SOCIALISM

THE CCF IN
ONTARIO

GERALD L. CAPLAN

McClelland and Stewart Limited

JL 209
A8
C633

CONTENTS

PREFACE

Ontarians instinctively identify their province with Canada as a whole. For them, Ontario is Canada, and the other provinces are merely extensions of Ontario. In consequence, the rest of Canada quite properly resents the citizens of Ontario.

Nonetheless, there is some objective substance (besides economic domination) to Ontario's conceit. Before the 1943 provincial election, the *Globe and Mail* editorially reminded Ontario voters of their singularly weighty responsibility: "Ontario is the key province in the Dominion. What is done on August 4 will not only affect every man and woman in Ontario but will be of vital importance to every Canadian."[1] Even should Quebec decide to secede, that proposition remains true. What Ontario accepts, the rest of the country must take seriously. What Ontario rejects can never achieve nation-wide significance. It is this reality which hopefully gives this book more than parochial interest.

Viewed from today's perspective, these pages evoke an eerie sense of *déjà vu*. So much of what happened between 1932 and 1945 feels so familiar. Parallels between then and now jump off the page. It is, to a partisan at least, rather chilling, for it is as if Canadian socialism were on a perpetually moving treadmill, going round and round and getting nowhere.

This is one lesson that can be drawn from this study. There are, I believe, others as well. I have attempted to present the situation fairly, so that the reader can draw his own conclusions. But I make no pretense to neutrality. The most any historian can do is to make his bias clear. I was an active and committed member of the CCF and remain active in and committed to its successor. For this reason, it would be highly satisfying if this book provoked some constructive debate within the democratic left in Canada.

[1.] *Globe and Mail*, July 24, 1943.

5

This study is a substantially revised version of a thesis I wrote a dozen years ago. That original work received much useful guidance from three upwardly-mobile young historians, and I happily acknowledge my debt to Professors John Saywell, Kenneth McNaught, and Ramsay Cook, whatever their present ideological predispositions. I am indebted too to Professor Gordon Vichert, formerly of the English Department at McMaster University and presently Provincial Secretary of the Ontario New Democratic Party, who took the trouble to scrutinize the present manuscript with meticulous care. I also want to thank my wife for her indispensable contribution to this work, some of which was practical but much of which was not.

Above all, however, this work owes its existence to my friend Stephen Lewis. It was he who introduced me to the CCF, to the study of history, and to the then Barbara Hill. His influence has profoundly influenced the direction of my life, and I therefore dedicate this book to him.

Gerald L. Caplan

THE FRINGES UNITE

I

"The difficulties are so vast," wrote the Bank of England's redoubtable Montague Norman. "It is too great for me."[1] The Great Depression of the 1930's was too great for most people to cope with. Throughout the western world they turned in frustration, in bewilderment, in hunger to a thousand and one bizarre panaceas. The decade was not one of radicalism of the left but of extremist movements of every shape and complexion. The sickest and most venomous was of course naziism. Among the most salutary was the Cooperative Commonwealth Federation, a peculiarly Canadian response to a universal phenomenon.

In those days, some people believed in politicians. Few politicians could fulfil their expectations. Foremost among these was Mackenzie King, who was unceremoniously dumped by the Canadian electorate in 1930. It needed about two years for the futility of his successor's policies to become evident. "Last year and the year before that," one columnist observed in April 1932,

> there was implicit faith in R. B. Bennett. . . . Enthusiasts proclaimed him a superman, the great engineer of politics and business who was going to conquer the depression. . . . [Now, however,] politicians and press have become querulous, sceptical, often cynical. . . . There is the suspicion of inconsistency, of a discrepancy between promise and performance.[2]

Nor was it yet psychologically time to re-invest one's trust in the egregiously cautious King. The failure of traditional politics increased the widespread sense of desperation and anxiety. As a result, many of the prevailing assumptions which Canadians had complacently taken for granted were rudely shattered. The conviction that industry and thrift brought their due material reward was profoundly shaken. The implicit belief that the existing system had produced the best of all possible worlds was severely undermined. Many Canadians, literally for the first time, began to challenge unstated dogmas and to examine first principles.

In their rage and despair, some of them turned to the philosophy of democratic socialism. In August 1932, a number of this group gathered together in Calgary to institutionalize their convictions. Independent members of parliament, radical intellectuals from Toronto and Montreal, representatives of powerful western agrarian groups and tiny parochial labour sects – these were the men and women who formally established the CCF, elected J. S. Woodsworth, the Winnipeg Labour M.P., as its first president, and adopted a vague but broadly socialist policy.[3] Woodsworth articulated the faith that brought the delegates together:

> We do not believe [he declared] that capitalism can survive much longer. We see the present system heading for the precipice, with anarchy, fascism, dictatorship, untold hardship and suffering as the probable consequences. That is why we formed the Federation. . . .
>
> Our idea is that the substitution of a commonwealth in which production was inspired by human need and not by private profit would end this anomaly of starvation in the midst of plenty, and would prevent a complete economic collapse, saving millions from want and misery.[4]

The new movement, it should be remembered, was a federation in fact as well as in name. The founders did not intend building a conventional political party with a centralized apparatus on the model of the old parties. Indeed, the organization was so structured that only its provincial sections were to have power to admit other bodies. The national organization would thereby remain essentially a federation of provincial affiliates, each of which might have its peculiar approach to socialism and politics. Each affiliating group was to retain its own identity and complete local autonomy, while agreeing to collaborate in general elections to achieve commonly held goals. As the second article in the constitution adopted at Calgary stated, "The object of the Federation shall be to promote cooperation between the member organizations and to correlate their political activities" in order to establish in Canada a cooperative commonwealth.[5]

The CCF quickly made a positive virtue of the federated principle, contrasting it with the bureaucratic and hierarchical operations of the old parties.[6] In truth, however, the movement's structure was one of its prime weaknesses, forced upon the leaders by the exigencies of the moment. The majority of the delegates at Calgary strongly opposed a unified political party which might limit the jealously guarded autonomy of the constituent units.[7] No mere prospect of success could convince the labour radicals to sacrifice one iota of a single sterile doctrine, while the historic antipathy between farmer and labour was barely submerged; it could only too easily re-assert itself if either element suspected the other was predominant.

Obviously then, there could be no alternative structure under the existing circumstances. It is, indeed, possible to argue that in no other way could organizational unity between the major factions have been achieved; without this unity, the new movement would probably have split into two conflicting parties. But the necessity proved to be anything but a blessing. In Ontario especially, the inherent weaknesses of a movement which refused to recognize any central decision-making body soon manifested themselves in a crisis which almost destroyed the CCF within two years of its creation.

II

As formed at Calgary, the CCF could not be considered a genuinely national party. With the exception of Aaron Mosher of the Canadian Brotherhood of Railway Employees, there was not a single delegate at the founding convention from east of Manitoba. This fundamental flaw was not lost on the movement's leaders. Immediately following the convention, Mosher was assigned to find contacts in urban Ontario, while William Irvine of Alberta and Agnes Macphail, both M.P.'s, began the CCF "invasion" of rural Ontario.

Macphail was the most prominent supporter of the CCF in Ontario. She was the only woman in the House of Commons. She had been first elected in 1921 as a Progressive candidate to represent a rural riding in south-western Ontario. Unlike most of the other Progressive M.P.'s, Macphail could not be seduced by Mackenzie King. Her attachment was to the two Labour M.P.'s, J. S. Woodsworth and Bill Irvine, and she later became part of the "Ginger Group" of those Progressives who remained independent of the Liberal party. She was re-elected in 1925, 1926, and 1930, by which time she had made herself an authentic spokesman of rural Ontario.

In her years in the Commons, Macphail earned a reputation

as a "cantankerous spinster," although her grave and severe manner hid genuine charm and warmth. "She was what she appeared to be," her biographers tell us, "a strong-minded country school-teacher." "She was proud of being farm-bred. She was proud of coming from pioneer stock. And she was proud of her Scotch blood. She considered her people – the farmers from the British Isles and particularly from Scotland – to be the backbone of Canada in a perfectly literal sense."[8] Now she was about to put her prestige on the line.

Late in August, Irvine and Macphail, who had been appointed Ontario CCF organizers, met with the executive of the United Farmers of Ontario and invited them to affiliate with the party. Macphail was the *grande dame* of the UFO and had considerable influence with its members. The executive expressed "very considerable sympathy" with CCF principles but informed the two M.P.'s that only a UFO convention had the authority to make the kind of decision they were requesting.[9] The executive did, however, undertake to submit a prepared statement to its local units, describing the new movement's aims and organizational structure.[10]

With this encouraging start, Irvine and Macphail began an extensive series of public meetings throughout rural Ontario. During September, October, and November, their meetings were frequent and well-attended, while more invitations than could be accepted "continued to pour in from across the province."[11] Their arguments must have been impressive, their listeners receptive. By the end of November, as UFO delegates began arriving in Toronto for their annual convention, the question of affiliating with the CCF was at the top of the agenda.[12]

It was reasonable that the CCF, as a third party, might look to the organized farm movement of Ontario for support. But it was predictable that the CCF as an avowedly socialist movement should fail to get it. The key variables in Saskatchewan's historical experience and socio-economic reality predisposed its farmers towards collectivist programmes and positive government; in Ontario, those factors functioned to reinforce orthodox political and social values. Even at its peak in the early 1920's, the UFO was far from being a notably reformist political movement. No ideological convictions had catapulted Ontario farmers into direct political action at the conclusion of World War I. Specific grievances were responsible for breaking the traditional agrarian attachment to one of the two major parties, among which resentment against conscription and high tariffs were uppermost.[13]

This was in no way a radical program, and the UFO's astonishing 1919 victory cannot be considered the victory of a radical political philosophy. The result was to be explained by the coincidence of several circumstances: resentment aroused by conscription, the Hearst government's opposition to farmer candidates, the prohibition issue, and the disintegration of the Liberal Party as a result of the formation of the Union government. As the historian of the Progressive Party cautions, "these were not circumstances likely to be repeated in conjunction."[14]

After the Farmer-Labour government's resounding and disillusioning defeat in 1923, the organized Ontario farmers never returned to independent political action with any enthusiasm. At its first post-election convention, the UFO voted to take no further political action as an independent party; the main activities of the organization were henceforth educational and commercial and increasingly irrelevant. From a high point of sixty thousand members in 1921, the UFO declined to a meagre seven thousand by 1932, and to five thousand by 1935.[15] It was difficult to see it as the authentic spokesman of Ontario's rural community.

Would the onslaught of the Depression disturb the historical political conservatism of rural Ontario? Certainly the economic catastrophe aroused in rural communities, as indeed everywhere, a desire to understand its causes and remedy its effects. Yet the farmers of Ontario were considerably slower than their western brethren in turning to radical doctrines in their search for practical solutions. At its annual meeting in December 1931, the deteriorating UFO passed major policy resolutions calling for a drastic reduction in road expenditures, reduced telephone rates to rural areas, and more temperance education.[16]

Such brazen escapism could not last. The Depression was no remote crisis to rural Ontario. In fact, the UFO's financial difficulties forced it to sell its official publication, the *Farmers' Sun*. As it turned out, the new owners, Graham Spry and Allan Plaunt, were close to the League for Social Reconstruction, Canada's own version of the Fabians. The change they wrought was not subtle. The *Sun* announced the imminent demise of the capitalist system and each issue was designed to expedite the blessed event.[17]

If the vanguard was too far ahead, conventional politics were falling too far behind. In the summer of 1932, the Imperial Economic Conference utterly failed to reduce tariffs or negotiate trade agreements favourable to agriculture. Then, on July 16, the

Prime Minister refused to address a protest delegation of 4,000 Ontario and Quebec farmers, and forbade his ministers to do so. The demonstrators were so infuriated they endorsed an anachronistic manifesto calling for lower tariffs and monetary inflation. Socialist solutions, the Depression and R. B. Bennett notwithstanding, were not on the agenda.[18] Nevertheless, the very existence of the protest movement indicated an increased receptiveness in rural Ontario to new forms of political activities, and perhaps even to new and relevant solutions.

It was at this juncture that William Irvine and Agnes Macphail began their organizing tour of Ontario farm districts. And it was two months later that the UFO met in annual convention in Toronto, where for two days they hammered out a most extraordinary manifesto. Radical in itself, the document was revolutionary when contrasted to its sterile predecessors. It called for the administration of financial institutions for the benefit of all, either under state or cooperative auspices; it advocated the reorganization of industry and commerce along cooperative lines; and it demanded an immediate and major increase of the tax on large incomes.[19] The emphasis on cooperative rather than direct governmental activity was less important than the general commitment to far-reaching reconstruction of the existing economic system.

The evening of November 30 had been reserved for a special political meeting, at which CCF leaders would address the citizens of Toronto. The newly-radicalized farmers officially adjourned their convention to attend the rally. It was an evening to shake the cramped elite of Tory Toronto.

> Packed into every seat available in Hygeia Hall, standing and even sitting in the aisles, strewn around the walls two and three deep, and overflowing in hundreds into a special meeting in Forester's Hall, a mixed audience totalling 3500 of UFO delegates, Toronto labourites, wellwishers, white collar people and obviously a sprinkling of Reds, listened to four speakers expound the principles of the newly-launched CCF political party last night.
>
> It was a meeting the numbers of which ... exceeded even the wildest dreams of its promoters, and one which ... displayed fervent enthusiasm for the cause, as it was propounded, of humanity as distinguished from "big interests," "profits," and "capitalism." At the conclusion the meeting enthusiastically carried a resolution expressing its approval of Cooperative Commonwealth Federation principles.[20]

It was no evening for waffling. That the new movement was frankly socialistic was openly, proudly proclaimed. The speakers, without exception, called for a revolution, Agnes Macphail urging her listeners to repeat the word hundreds of times if necessary to grow less fearful of it. Reverend Salem Bland insisted that "We must have a revolution ... a different kind of revolution to any the world has ever seen. But a revolution, mind you. Nothing less than that. Don't soften the word down!" "Attaboy!" came a cry from the crowded gallery. The chairman accurately predicted that the press would distort the use made of the word "revolution," and J. S. Woodsworth prudently pointed out that the CCF revolution would differ from the Russian variety in being "peaceful and orderly."[21] But there could be no doubt that the new movement had as its mortal enemy the entire existing order of society. Yet no less than one thousand members of the audience – a staggering total – agreed sufficiently to sign cards indicating their desire to join the CCF.

On the following day, the UFO convention re-assembled to determine its position vis-à-vis the new party. The euphoria of the previous evening remained evident. Scattered opposition to affiliation was quickly crushed. The clear feeling was that the UFO's new manifesto "was meaningless if it was not carried out. To do so, political action was commended."[22] Three impressive orations – by Robert Gardiner, president of the UFO, by William Irvine, and, above all, by Agnes Macphail – carried the day. "With one final impassioned address – so fervently spoken that her voice broke with emotion – Agnes swept the UFO convention ... into declaring for affiliation with the CCF." On the final vote on the key resolution, no more than six hands were raised in opposition among the three hundred delegates.[23] The UFO was once again "in politics."

There were, however, to be three severely limiting qualifications to its affiliation, without which the resolution might not have passed. The UFO, it was made perfectly clear, would retain its identity and all its privileges and powers unimpaired. The principle of constituency autonomy prevailing within the UFO with respect to direct political activity was retained. And finally, "the affiliation of the UFO with the CCF was to be limited by the declared policies of the UFO."[24]

This gain was far from negligible. Yet did the decimated UFO any longer represent rural Ontario? In fact, the answer seemed to be in the affirmative – attitudinally at least, if no longer directly. The UFO had been quite as conservative as its putative constituency and this gave its endorsation of the socialists an even greater significance. The UFO was seen as the advance guard of a mass movement of radicalized Ontario farmers. Despite all the constraints, then, the UFO's affiliation with the CCF came as an unexpected blow to the old parties. "Such goings-on," noted a labour journal, "might be expected of the farmers in the Wild West, but not in respectable Old Ontario."[25] It was one more reflection of the severe dislocation of the status quo which the Depression was producing.

The CCF was determined to facilitate the process. At the Hygeia Hall meeting, a thousand persons had signed cards signifying their support for the new movement. Moreover, it was evident that numerous men and women throughout the province, members of no organized farm, labour or socialist organizations, shared this desire. Since, under the CCF constitution, membership in the party was possible only by joining an affiliated organization, how could the CCF accommodate these scattered and unorganized individuals?

Immediately after the Hygeia Hall rally, Woodsworth asked Professor Frank Underhill to head a temporary organizing committee to resolve this dilemma. Mr. Donat M. LeBourdais, who had previously been associated with the Liberal Party, was chosen for the vital post of committee secretary. With two rooms in a small office building provided by a music teacher named Sam Marks, LeBourdais set up the first Ontario CCF office; his resources consisted of a typewriter, also lent by Marks, and the money and cards collected at Hygeia Hall. The responsibility for finding a method of incorporating independent persons into the party now devolved upon LeBourdais. "So," as he put it, "I invented the CCF Clubs."[26]

On December 14, Woodsworth announced the formation of the Clubs, to which any citizen not associated with an organized group might belong. Organization of the Clubs would be undertaken immediately by a committee of eight persons headed by Underhill and LeBourdais, and that "vast unattached body of Canadians" who supported CCF principles would form the third of three proposed sections which were to comprise the Ontario CCF: the Clubs, the UFO, and Labour and Socialist groups organized in a "Labour Conference." The Clubs were expected to attract a "vast body of clerical and professional workers . . . which only now has realized it has been exploited. . . . For them alone was the Club Plan conceived."[27]

The chartering of the first CCF Club in Toronto on December 22 meant that, within three months of its entry upon the provincial scene, two-thirds of the proposed Ontario CCF organization had formally been established. The Labour Conference was not officially set up until early in the new year, though tentative beginnings had been made in 1932. On November 27, "over a score" of labour and socialist bodies had convened in Toronto and "decided unanimously to recommend to their constituent bodies affiliation with the CCF."[28] At a second conference, two weeks later, addressed by Woodsworth, Agnes Macphail, and Salem Bland, the delegates again "indicated their willingness to join the CCF." Represented at this gathering were most of the province's politicized labour elements, including Independent Labour Party branches from five cities; two Labour Party units; two units of the National Labour Party; four branches of the Socialist Party of Canada; two units of the Christian Social Order; two Workers' Association branches; the South-Wellington Progressive Labour Party; the Jewish Socialist Verbund (Farbund); and the League for Social Reconstruction.[29]

No better indication can be given of the lack of class solidarity within the Ontario labour movement. Radical labour was weak, divided, and largely inconsequential to the lives of most working people. Nor did it have substantial influence within the organized labour movement. Martin Robin has deftly characterized the ambience in which this multiplicity of impotent sects existed: "Remoteness from power ... contributed to schism; doctrinal differences lengthened the distance from power; and distance from power aggravated doctrinal schism."[30]

Yet it was precisely upon such elements that CCF ties with "labour" were dependent. From the first, its relations with the more established labour movement were ambivalent at best. At a regular meeting of the Toronto Labour Council on December 15, for example, the CCF had friends enough to have a motion for affiliation debated, but not enough to have it passed.[31]

Nevertheless, despite this set-back, one fact stood out: the new movement had made an unprecedented impact upon Ontario in the year 1932. "No political organization," reported *Saturday Night*, "ever had so much free advertising. People are discussing it everywhere, regarding it with growing respect...."[32] On the whole, its anticipated supporters had not disappointed; nor had its anticipated enemies. As early as November 9, Prime Minister Bennett paid the new movement the tribute of a vigorous denunciation before a Conservative convention. "What do these so-called groups of socialists and communists offer you?" he asked. "We know that throughout Canada this propaganda is being put forward by organizations from foreign lands that seek to destroy our institutions. Now, ladies and gentlemen," he exhorted in a memorable phrase, "we ask every true Canadian to put the iron heel of ruthlessness to a thing of that kind."[33]

One month later, Attorney-General Price of Ontario devoted an entire speech to exhorting the churches to organize against communism "with its partner, atheism," as represented by such reverend gentlemen as Woodsworth, Salem Bland, A. A. Heaps, and A. E. Smith. In a subsequent interview with *The Varsity*, Price stated that the CCF was "probably directed from Moscow."[34]

The newspapers were quick to follow the politicians' example. After the UFO endorsement of the CCF, papers across the province began developing a profound interest in the movement they had virtually ignored from August to the end of November. In Toronto, both the Liberal *Globe* and Conservative *Telegram* reminded their readers of Woodsworth's role in the 1919 Winnipeg Strike, which the former described as a "post-war product of bolshevism."[35] The *Telegram* declared that the attempt by Woodsworth and Bland

> to fasten the Soviet system upon Canada thirteen years ago purported to be for the benefit of the masses. The masses rejected them. Today, in their proposal to wreck capitalism, they still profess to be animated by a desire to serve the masses. But, *although they want to have section 98 of the Criminal Code repealed*, they declare that they are not aligned with those who aim at economic revolution through force.[36]

Such was the prevailing attitude of the vast majority of Ontario dailies and weeklies. When the *Financial Post* assembled editorial comments on the CCF from over a dozen Ontario newspapers, it discovered that the most characteristic phrases attached to the party included "wreckers," "twaddle," "wild-eyed agitators," "tremendous taxation," and "a threat to British institutions."

Clearly the young movement was doing very well indeed.

References

1. Cited in F. L. Allen, *Since Yesterday* (New York, 1940), p. 74.
2. "Politician With a Notebook," *Maclean's,* April 1, 1932.

3. See Kenneth McNaught, *A Prophet in Politics* (Toronto, 1959), pp. 255-61; S. M. Lipset, *Agrarian Socialism: The CCF in Saskatchewan* (Anchor edition, New York, 1968), ch. 4; and Walter D. Young, *The Anatomy of a Party: The National CCF, 1932-61* (Toronto, 1969), ch. 2.

4. *Toronto Star*, August 30, 1932.

5. *The Cooperative Commonwealth Federation (Farmer-Labour-Socialist) – A Call to the People of Canada* (Calgary, 1932), a pamphlet issued by the United Farmers of Alberta; Dean McHenry, *Third Force in Canada* (Berkely, 1950), p. 26.

6. See, for example, *The CCF in Ontario*, a pamphlet, early 1932.

7. George H. Hougham, *Minor Parties in Canadian National Politics, 1867-1940,* Ph.D. thesis, 1954. An abstract of this thesis may be found in Mrs. Margaret Stewart's collection of Agnes Macphail Private Papers (hereafter Macphail Private Papers), volume 2, *The UFO and Politics.*

8. Margaret Stewart and Doris French, *Ask No Quarter* (Toronto, 1959), pp. 18, 26-27, 64.

9. *Farmers' Sun*, September 1, 1932.

10. *Ibid.*, September 15, 1932.

11. *Ibid.*, September 29 and November 10, 1932.

12. Toronto *Star*, November 29, 1932.

13. W. L. Morton, *The Progressive Party in Canada* (Toronto, 1967), pp. 72-4; John D. Hoffman, *Farmer-Labour Government in Ontario, 1919-1923,* unpublished M.A. thesis (University of Toronto, 1959), pp. 4-11.

14. Morton, *op. cit.*, pp. 212, 83-4.

15. Marion Hebb, *The Political Heritage of the United Farmers of Ontario*, unpublished undergraduate research paper (University of Toronto, 1961), pp. 14-15, 18, 24.

16. *Canadian Annual Review,* 1932, p. 157.

17. *Farmers' Sun*, February 4, 1932 and March 3, 1932.

18. *Ibid.*, July 21, 1932.

19. *Ibid.*, December 1, 1932.

20. Toronto *Globe*, December 1, 1932.

21. Toronto *Star*, December 1, 1932.

22. *Farmers' Sun*, December 1, 1932.

23. Toronto *Globe*, December 2, 1932.

24. Stewart and French, *Ask No Quarter*, p. 166; *Farmers' Sun,* December 8, 1932.

25. *Canadian Unionist,* December 1932.

26. Interview with D. M. LeBourdais.

27. Toronto *Star*, December 14, 1932.

28. *Ibid.*; *Canadian Forum*, January, 1933.

29. Toronto *Star*, December 14, 1932.

30. Martin Robin, *Radical Politics and Canadian Labour* (Kingston, 1968), pp. 279-80.

31. Toronto Trades and Labour Council Meeting Minutes, December 15, 1932.

32. *Saturday Night,* December 17, 1932.

33. Cited in *Canadian Unionist,* December 1932

34. Toronto *Star*, December 16, 1932. When informed of Price's speeches, Agnes Macphail explained that "A. E. Smith is of course an avowed Communist. The others are not, but what they do want to see is the practical application of Christian ethics to our economic system."

35. Toronto *Globe*, December 2, 1932.

36. Toronto *Telegram,* December 2, 1932; emphasis added.

2 PROSPECTS AND PROBLEMS

The relentless raging of the Depression during the year 1933 was accompanied in Canada by the spectacular growth of the young CCF movement. Although gravely affecting every area of the nation, the Depression's impact was most widely felt in industrial working class areas; unemployment among trade union members was 22 per cent.[1] CCF leaders took for granted that such areas provided fertile soil for cultivating socialism. Electoral success in Ontario obviously depended upon obtaining the support of labour as well as farmers. Having secured the endorsement of the UFO, the party now turned its attention to the other crucial element.

Organized labour represented only a small minority of Ontario's working people. Still, 125,000 potential voters constituted a not unattractive base from which to build. In 1932, the two major trade union bodies were the conservative Trades and Labour Congress of Canada, affiliated with the American Federation of Labor, and the smaller, more radical and unstable All-Canadian Congress of Labour. The two were bitter rivals. There were also, in Ontario, several numerically insignificant labour and/or socialist political parties, which have already been introduced. Clearly the important prize was recognition by the two congresses.

The Trades and Labour Congress of Canada was the nation's largest and most influential trade union organization. The social and economic unrest which followed World War I led the T.L.C. in 1918 to urge its affiliates to form the Canadian Labour Party, a moderate body designed "to promote legislation in the interests of the wealth-producers of the nation."[2] Yet it maintained thereafter only a perfunctory relationship with the party it had created. In the cherished tradition of the American Federation of Labor, the T.L.C.'s sacred policy was to "act as the legislative mouthpiece for organized labour . . . independent of any political organization."[3]

The absence of any mention whatever of the CCF from the official journal of the T.L.C. until early in 1933 usefully reflects the thinking of Congress leaders. After the 1932 T.L.C. convention, its journal reprinted, with obvious pride, a Toronto *Mail and Empire* editorial congratulating it "upon its conservative attitudes and its determination not to be led astray by agitators"; in other words, it had declared against a parliamentary labour party.[4]

Not even the Depression could shake the Congress. A resolution at its 1933 convention endorsing the CCF was, after a lengthy debate, withdrawn when it became clear it had no chance of passing.[5] Although the T.L.C.'s legislative programme – including public ownership of all utilities and the nationalization of the banking system – was strikingly similar to the CCF's, the Congress succeeded in retaining its vaunted independence unimpaired for another quarter of a century.

Thus the new party lost its largest potential source of support. The second largest labour congress in Canada, the All-Canadian Congress of Labour, seemed a more fruitful prospect. The A.C.C.L. was formed in 1926 as a central congress for wholly Canadian and industrial unions which the T.L.C. refused to admit. Under the leadership of the aggressive A. R. Mosher, president of the powerful Canadian Brotherhood of Railway Employees, the new congress accepted as part of its purpose the need "to come to grips with Canadian capitalism and to overthrow its political and economic power ... "; its original program was correspondingly radical, calling for public ownership at the municipal level, nationalization of mines, minerals and railways, and, of course, improved wages and working conditions. These goals would be achieved by economic action on the part of strongly organized workers in the industrial field, and by educating workers to realize the need for independent political action.[6]

In the industrial field, the new Congress met with considerable early success, claiming in 1933 to represent 92,000 Canadian workers, though the large majority belonged to Mosher's Canadian Brotherhood of Railway Employees.[7] Politically, the Congress's position appeared to be straightforward. The two major parties were scornfully regarded as completely identical since both continued to uphold the "private ownership of the means of production and distribution." What was needed therefore was a workers' party, so that labour's interest could "cease being the shuttlecock in the exhibition games of Tweedledum and Tweed-ledee."[8]

Why, asked the A.C.C.L.'s official organ, the *Canadian Union-ist*, was there no strong labour party in Canada after two years of Depression? This failure it laid at the conservative and complacent feet of the rival T.L.C. And rather than devote its time to building such a party, the A.C.C.L. preferred to dissipate a large part of its energy in violent denunciation of the T.L.C. and its contemptible policy of "Yankee unionism." In article after article, month after month, the *Unionist* waged bitter and implacable war against this foul perversion; not even the Bay Street capitalists, it sometimes seemed, were more insidious and destructive of "genuine," "Canadian-controlled" trade unionism. T.L.C. counterattacks, through its official journal, were comparably fatuous in content, if less frequent. One typical editorial branded the A.C.C.L. leaders as opportunists and revolutionaries who wanted to destroy all the gains the T.L.C. had achieved for Canadian workers.[9] It was this kind of incident which understandably led Frank Underhill to moan: "As for Canadian labour, the energy its various factions spend fighting one another would suffice for several social revolutions; in the meantime, most of them vote Liberal or Tory."[10]

This was palpably true. Nevertheless, Aaron Mosher accepted an invitation to attend the conference of Western Labour Parties in Calgary in July 1932, and remained to become a delegate to the founding convention of the CCF. And, in January 1933, the Canadian Brotherhood of Railway Employees, of which Mosher was also president, was accepted as an affiliate of the Ontario section of the CCF.

The contribution of the CBRE to the party was, however, sorely disappointing. Although Mosher had been appointed in Calgary to the provisional national CCF executive, he appears to have played a negligible role in introducing the CCF into Ontario. In his sole article in the *Canadian Unionist* after the creation of the CCF, Mosher's obsession with nefarious "foreign-controlled" unions remained paramount; labour unity in the interests of the new party was clearly a marginal concern. More important was his declaration – one month *after* the CCF was formed – that the objective of the "nationally-organized workers" was "*to organize*" a political labour party. Its goals, as he outlined them, were precisely those of the CCF. Yet the CCF was never once referred to in this article, and indeed, his tone clearly implied that no labour party yet existed.[11] Nor was Mosher or the CBRE to play any role of importance in the crisis which soon confronted the Ontario party, a fact which suggests that their interest in its affairs was peripheral at best. Despite its strength of numbers, then, as well as its pugnacious radicalism, it seems that the leaders of the All-Canadian Congress of Labour, like those of the other major congress, played an inconsequential role in the early affairs of the CCF. This fact spelled electoral doom for the young socialist movement from the outset, although it was not fully appreciated at the time.

What was apparent from the first was the wildly disproportionate amount of time and energy which the CCF expended in dealing with all the ineffectual and unrepresentative labour sects. Most of them seemed to have more leaders than followers. The one which nearly became a major movement was the Canadian Labour Party created in 1918 by the T.L.C. During the 1920's, the desire for a united labour movement induced the C.L.P. to admit the newly-formed Workers' (Communist) Party to its ranks, and to accept the cooperation without affiliation of the Independent Labour Party. At the same time, the expanded movement adopted a radical program calling for "a complete change in our present economic and social systems," as a result of which its relationship with its founder became increasingly tenuous.[12]

At its peak in 1926, the C.L.P. represented ten thousand Ontario workers who belonged to trade unions, local labour parties or the Communist Party. Leaders of the C.L.P. included such labour notables as Tim Buck, James Simpson, Reverend A. E. Smith, Bert Robinson, Arthur Mould, and Jack MacDonald,[13] all of whom we shall have occasion to meet again. By the following year, however, the party, now known as the Ontario Labour Party, suffered a grievous division over the question of permitting Communists to remain within the organization. When the Communists convinced the C.L.P. to remove the name of James Simpson, a rabid anti-Communist, as the party's nominee for controller in a Toronto municipal election, Simpson, James Conner, John Bruce, David Goldstick, and sixteen followers resigned in disgust.[14] This small band thereupon formed yet another local labour organization, the Toronto Labour Party, which would embrace only non-Communist labour and radical groups of that city.[15] At the same time, the Ontario Independent Labour Party dissolved its ties with the

C.L.P. and it too became an independent "non-Communist labour political organization."[16]

There have been three different Independent Labour Parties in Ontario's history. The first began in 1899 and was virtually defunct before World War I. The second was created in 1917. It unexpectedly elected eleven members to Queen's Park in the provincial election two years later and became the "Labour" element in the Farmer-Labour administration which was defeated in 1923. Under I.L.P. pressure, that government passed so many pieces of welfare legislation that it earned for labour the undying resentment of economy-minded rural Ontario. After 1923, what remained of the I.L.P. cooperated with the Canadian Labour Party and, by 1927, had so deteriorated that it had but one branch, Hamilton East, still functioning.

At the conclusion of the C.L.P. convention of 1927, fifty-three delegates from fifteen organizations, all of whom opposed the extremely radical resolutions adopted by the convention, met in caucus and unanimously agreed to revive the Ontario I.L.P. A conservative platform was tentatively adopted, and the decision unofficially made to reject any forthcoming overtures of the C.L.P. The I.L.P. would shun the C.L.P., "leaving the Communists with the shell" it presumptuously believed would alone remain after the departure of I.L.P. supporters.

The I.L.P. was a fringe offshoot of a marginal group. The advent of the Depression did little to improve this status. No exact statistics are available, but the size of the party may be inferred from its revenues of a paltry 292 dollars in 1930, of which it spent only one-third, and fifteen hundred dollars the following year. It was this shadow of a movement which brought its several tiny units into the Ontario CCF Labour Conference early in 1933.[17]

A similar group which the CCF was reduced to courting was the Socialist Party of Canada. Begun in 1904, the S.P. of C. retained a consistent ideological orientation closer to Lenin than to Keir Hardie. Its membership probably never reached one thousand, a large percentage of whom left to join the Workers' Party in 1922; only a tiny, faithful doctrinaire remnant remained.[18] They survived the 1920's in glorious isolation, remaining absolutely loyal to the concept of "scientific socialism," and reminding each other of the bitter and relentless class struggle which history predetermined would be won by the proletariat. The dictatorship of the proletariat, the general strike, and the likely need for violent revolution were weighty items in their ideological baggage.[19]

To the s.p. of c., the CCF was but one of several instruments to be used in expediting the arrival – inevitable in any case – of a socialist society. When it chose to affiliate with the CCF through the Ontario Labour Conference, then, clearly it was to obtain a fresh platform from which to propagate its chiliastic creed, and hopefully to bring the new organization around to more correct policies.

Since it had been ignored or dismissed by the T.L.C. and A.C.C.L., it was presumably through the likes of the Socialist Party of Canada and the Independent Labour Party that the CCF believed it could resurrect labour as a political force in Ontario.

II

With the True Believer's blinkered faith in the righteousness and irresistibility of his creed, the CCF set out early in 1933 to organize the various representatives of labour into a distinct section within the movement to work in conjunction with the CCF Club section and the UFO. Apparent success came rapidly. On February 26, 164 delegates from sixty-six organizations throughout the province, meeting in closed session, decided to work within a single Labour Conference which would be affiliated with the CCF. The groups represented included labour parties, socialist parties, and trade union locals from ten cities and towns across the province; it is impossible to determine the number of persons they represented. Affiliation having been agreed upon, a resolution voicing confidence in J. S. Woodsworth was passed, as were others demanding the repeal of Section 98 of the Criminal Code and the immediate release from prison of Tim Buck, who had been convicted of having engaged in a "seditious conspiracy to overthrow the state."[20]

Such ostensible harmony was in fact deceptive. An earlier conference of the Toronto Labour Party, for example, had split broadly into two opposing camps – those who supported affiliation as a means of increasing labour's political power, and those who saw in the CCF what one speaker called "white collar pinks masquerading under the name of labour." The "pinks" were the members of the CCF Clubs, whose section was clearly becoming the largest and most influential of the three sections of the Ontario party. George Watson, president of the T.L.P., denounced those who were joining the Clubs "because they think they are too 'respectable' to join Socialist or Labour groups. We're not good enough for their standing in the community." James Connor, t.l.p. secretary, challenged the right of D. M. LeBourdais, Club section organizer, to represent a socialist organization, since the latter was secretary of the Canadian Mental Hygiene Council, "an organization largely supported by . . . capitalists, and studying people's minds, particularly those of the working class." Rose Henderson, another prominent member, asserted that "the tragedy of the working classes today is middle class rule, and we are being asked to sink our own interests for the benefits of a glorified middle class party."

In rebuttal, one delegate from the floor accurately pointed out that "As soon as Woodsworth has got the whole thing together, the rank and file of labour want to pull back and paddle their own canoe. . . . I'm ashamed of Labour for not doing more in twenty years than the ccf has done in two months." Another emphasized that "the ccf Clubs are doing glorious work by educating the people we'd never get to our meetings." In the end, affiliation was approved,[21] but the episode reveals the kind of paranoid hostilities endemic to the ccf from the very outset.

While internecine conflict thus threatened the very existence of the labour section of the Ontario ccf before it even began to function, the *bêtes noires* of that section, the ccf Clubs, were growing with extraordinary rapidity throughout the province. Under LeBourdais and E. A. Beder, a non-Communist Marxist who became ccf Club Committee chairman upon Underhill's resignation, and then under Elmore Philpott, about fifty clubs had been formed across Ontario by July, about half of them in Toronto, with a membership of some six thousand persons.[22]

Activity had begun in Toronto late in 1932. From the Hygeia Hall cards and from letters of support from across the province, names were divided by federal riding, a hall hired in one particular riding, and a notice of meeting sent out. LeBourdais or Beder would attend this meeting, have a *pro forma* constitution accepted, and a club executive elected. Then, with a new unit officially established, the Club would begin conducting regular meetings, rallies, educational sessions, and membership drives in its area.[23]

Thus, for example, at the first general organizational meeting in Toronto's Lakeshore district in March, nearly 200 persons listened to LeBourdais outline ccf principles and policies, and then decided to form three units, in Mimico, New Toronto, and Humber Bay. Provisional committees were elected, and additional clubs were planned for Long Branch and other districts.[24] One week later, both the New Toronto and Mimico clubs held meetings at which executives were elected, with forty persons signing membership cards in the former group, sixty in the latter.[25]

In this manner, fifty clubs were formed by the middle of 1933. The response from white collar and professional people was proving quite phenomenal. Yet the club section suffered from a dangerous weakness: it was less a coherent organization than a large number of uncoordinated, individual units. "We had," one member later recalled, "a loose mass of clubs. Nobody knew what the other was doing. The organization was full of people who had their own crank ideas. Sectionalism was rampant."[26] There was no central body authorized to direct the activities of the various units into one main channel. The continued successes in creating new groups would be meaningless if they did not form a truly unified section; for this, some type of central coordinating council was clearly necessary.

It was for this reason that club delegates from across the province attended a special convention in May to establish the Ontario Association of CCF Clubs, a single province-wide section to complete the "triple alliance" which constituted the Ontario CCF. John Walter, a Kitchener businessman, was elected the Association's first vice-president, LeBourdais became general-secretary, and Sam Marks was chosen treasurer. The executive committee, based on geographic representation, included Graham Spry, William Dennison, Dr. Lorna Cotton, Alice Loeb, and Herbert Orloff (later Orliffe). And as its first president, the Association elected the 37-year old Elmore Philpott.[27]

Philpott was a fascinating personality. A badly-crippled war hero who walked with the aid of two canes, he was a dynamic romantic with immodest political ambition. An editorial writer for the Toronto *Globe*, he was soundly defeated by Mitchell Hepburn for the leadership of the Ontario Liberal Party in 1930. His defeat as a Liberal in a provincial by-election in 1931 not inconceivably expedited his conversion to less conventional politics. In February 1933, he grandly announced his resignation from the *Globe* in order to devote himself to bringing about "full and friendly team play between the Liberal Party and the CCF – in brief, a national people's movement for reconstruction and reform; not only to end unemployment but to write in Canada a new Magna Carta of human rights."[28] When, predictably, this scheme proved a non-starter, Philpott announced his momentous decision to join the CCF because he was

> convinced that no other political force in Canada is working whole-heartedly to reconstruct the social system on a basis of solid justice and human rights. The old parties are inex-

tricably linked to the old worn-out system which breeds wars and permits children to go to bed hungry in a land of plenty.

Furthermore, he announced, he would commence a new campaign on behalf of the CCF Clubs the following week in Toronto's Queen's Park.[29]

The new convert spoke not only the next week, but virtually every day thereafter for the CCF. He was an immediate success as a stump orator; another age would have characterized him as charismatic. On the platform, he paced continuously while speaking, though his crutches evidently caused him great pain; only his passionate dedication to the new cause made such torture endurable.[30] His martyrdom proved as effective with his party colleagues as with the multitudes who attended his meetings, for within three months of joining the party, Philpott was elected to head its largest section.

Thus, after six months, the CCF Clubs finally became part of an effective single section; when would the party as a whole do the same? For the Ontario CCF more nearly approximated three separate parties then it did one unified movement. Each of the three sections had its own spokesmen, its own interests and activities, its own interpretation of socialism. Though a few meetings had been held at which members of all sections had participated, until June 4, 1933 the Ontario party had no supreme, unifying provincial council on which all three sections were represented, and with the authority to make decisions binding on all.

One week after the Club section had been formally established, therefore, thirty-six delegates, twelve from each section, met to set up the Ontario CCF Provincial Council. The prelude was symbolic. The meeting had originally been planned for a Sunday, but after strenuous UFO objections to holding business meetings on the Sabbath, the convention was postponed until the Monday morning.[31] It was decided that the council should consist of twelve delegates from each section, and, when assembled, it

> shall be the final court of appeal in the case of disagreement as between the affiliated sections; its decisions on questions of policy shall be final, and it shall have control especially over all matters pertaining to elections; all candidates must obtain its endorsation.[32]

Agnes Macphail, the most prominent CCF'er in the province and the strongest link between the sections, was elected as the new

Council's first president. Other provincial officers included John Walter, LeBourdais, Philpott, Arthur Mould of the Ontario Labour Party, and H. H. Hannam of the UFO.[33]

Thus the Provincial Council of the Ontario CCF was born. It immediately settled down to a solid nine months of existence characterized by mutual distrust and strife. From the first, antagonism between the three sections was rife, and all contributed to the tensions which increasingly marked the Council's every meeting and activity. Labour representatives regarded the Club members as insincere opportunists whose conversion to socialism was prompted by the party's startling popularity, and they bitterly resented the manner in which Club leaders, especially Philpott, attempted to dominate the entire organization.[34] On the other side, the quaint labour custom of addressing all and sundry at CCF meetings as "Comrade" infuriated the UFO representatives. Agnes Macphail's face, we are told, "would get red with high blood pressure" whenever it was used.[35] Constant friction was generated as well over the question of holding council meetings on Sunday, the day favoured by the Labour representatives to the chagrin of the pious farmers.[36] As for the Club representatives, they considered themselves the elite of the Council, their education and middle class respectability ascribing for them positions of leadership. They thought theirs the only section of substance in the Triple Alliance, without which the party was but an empty form.[37] After all, they might justifiably have pointed out, the labour groups were ridiculously tiny, while by mid-1933 only two local UFO clubs had affiliated with the CCF.[38] All in all, it was difficult to see how long this precarious unity and fragile structure could remain intact.

III

And yet, how could mere organizational difficulties deflate the exhilarating buoyancy of CCF'ers given the promise of those early days? Moral indignation at the Depression plus the evangelical promise of a better world gave socialism its impetus and it spread across the province like a religious crusade. All the objective reasons for pessimism were submerged by the phenomenal response to the new faith. Throughout 1933, CCF meetings in every town and city in Ontario, addressed by Agnes Macphail, Salem Bland, William Irvine, Woodsworth, Philpott and other party leaders, drew enormous crowds to hear the gospel being handed down.

"Anybody who isn't socialistic isn't thinking," Macphail informed sixteen hundred excited people in Kitchener, after nearly as many had had to be turned away.[39] At a meeting in Toronto, after telling a thousand enthusiasts that Canada needed inflation and the nationalization and distribution of money, "so great was the crowd [unable to hear her], she was obliged to make a second address before an overflow meeting of several hundred in another part of the building."[40] In Toronto again the following month, Irvine and Bland denounced capitalism before an audience "that filled two auditoriums."[41] In Hamilton, Woodsworth and Humphrey Mitchell were "loudly supported" by "the largest audience given a political speaker since the 1930 campaign" as they denounced the dictatorship by financial interests of the federal government.[42]

In Toronto, the police force, supported by the provincial government, made frequent attempts to prevent the CCF from holding open meetings in public parks, and, on at least one occasion, a CCF Sunday meeting in a city theatre had to be cancelled because a police inspector warned the theatre owner his establishment would be closed if the meeting were held.[43] Yet even such set-backs the CCF turned to its own advantage. In May, after the police disrupted a Saturday afternoon meeting in Queen's Park, only a single announcement in the newspapers was necessary to induce three thousand loyal supporters "on a lovely spring evening from their gardens, sports and motor drives to sit in a hall and listen to speeches . . . protesting the infringement of the right of free speech in Toronto."[44]

The authorities notwithstanding, the CCF continued to sweep through the province. Throughout the summer, unprecedented crowds turned out in New Liskeard, in North Bay, in Palermo, Stouffville and Stratford to hear the faith's missionaries, led by their high priest Philpott, present the word of the new Christianity which would create for all a life of abundance and security, without war, without exploitation, without capitalism.[45] Truly it was bliss to be alive in that dawn, when a new social order did appear imminent, when a bloodless revolution did seem in the making. There was a sense of irresistibility about the whole process, an implicit belief that socialism was bound to come, that it must come. No wonder Woodsworth felt sufficiently optimistic to predict that his party's growing strength would compel the old parties to coalesce and wage a united counter-attack.[46] No wonder either that, although there was no formal coalition, just such a concerted drive against the CCF was launched early in 1933 from the floor of parliament, from the press, and from the stump.

It began in the House of Commons when "Government and opposition became as one party . . . united to present a solid front" to J. S. Woodsworth's resolution calling for "measures looking to the setting up in Canada of a cooperative common-wealth." The resolution was an annual event in parliament, but the attitude of the old parties to it was distinctly new. In the 1932 debate on the motion, the great number of empty seats attested to the general feeling that the proposal was "hopelessly visionary, outside the sphere of practical politics." In 1933, almost every member was in his seat, listening with great atten-tion, heckling, interjecting, rebutting the socialist analysis of the economic system.[47] One correspondent suggested this sudden interest "might well be regarded by the CCF as recognition of their new party and its policy in the political orientation of the country."[48]

The old party response to the resolution was put succinctly by Mr. Earl Lawson, a Conservative member from Toronto. "In its essence," he informed the House, "the CCF is Communism and Communism is CCF." Lawson's speech was greeted by a "bar-rage of applause," "twenty or thirty Liberals [joining] the Tories in the loud desk-banging. . . . "[49] Canadian newspapers took their cue from Lawson's approach. The Toronto *Telegram,* for exam-ple, agreed that CCF policies amounted to

> nothing less than a form of Communism. . . . Farmers would be treated as the Russian kulaks have been treated. . . . Pov-erty and slavery [would be] the accepted order. The Woods-worth scheme could only lead to chaos and misery. . . . The freedom and civilization of today would disappear . . . in its place a regime in which terrorism would take the place of order and bullets the place of ballots.[50]

Throughout the winter and summer, the image was assiduously cul-tivated of a party imported from Russia, dedicated to violent revo-lution and the confiscation of all private property. Whether such claptrap was believed can never be known. But the political threat was clearly being taken seriously. One writer, commenting upon the "National Government" proposals which were "the rage in Ottawa" during the spring of 1933, concluded that "the real spectre behind this movement [initiated "on behalf of St. James St."] is the CCF – the possibility of its holding the balance of power in the next parliament."[51]

Nor was Mackenzie King indifferent to the upstart young movement, which he saw as a real obstacle to his regaining the prime ministership. Having spent much of the previous decade consuming the Progressive Party, he had no intention of being once again at the mercy of an independent parliamentary group. The CCF threat to a renewed Liberal hegemony must be removed. King proceeded to his task in a peculiar manner. In one typical speech, he claimed "there is not one of them [CCF ideas] not taken from the Liberal Party. There is not one which is not in the Liberal platform." Yet the Liberals stood for individual liberty and "freedom to act," whereas the CCF – despite its plagiarized Liberal platform – was headed for a "system of regimentation by the State."[52]

Liberalism had rather more to offer than Mackenzie King, however. In 1930, the Ontario Liberal Party gambled on Mitchell Hepburn, a relatively obscure onion farmer and member of parliament for Elgin, as their new provincial leader. At this point, the Ontario party had been reduced to little more than "a rural Protestant splinter group, narrowly based on a dozen predominantly dry ridings, its policies bankrupt, its leadership pathetically weak."[53] The new leader had his work cut out for him.

He began by casting himself in the role of the reformer, who must attract to the Liberal banner those elements of agrarian and urban protest without which he knew a provincial Liberal renaissance was impossible. Even before the birth of the CCF, Hepburn had assumed his chosen guise. Addressing a Liberal rally in May 1932, he declared that

> I favour calling all the leaders together, Liberal, Progressive and Labour. I would have us discuss our common interests and see along the same lines. Let me repeat that I swing well to the left where even some Liberals will not follow me, but if it's necessary for me to travel alone, I will. I hope to see a complete re-alignment of political thought in this country.[54]

The founding convention of the CCF merely gave Hepburn an impetus to intensify his efforts in this direction. In February 1933, with the CCF drive in Ontario in high gear, D. M. LeBourdais was summoned to a secret meeting at a Toronto hotel, along with Graham Spry, Elmore Philpott, Samuel Proctor (an influential Toronto Liberal), and several other men he did not know. The meeting had been arranged by Hepburn in an attempt to form a Liberal-CCF coalition in opposition to the ruling Conservatives. Would the CCF accept such an arrangement? LeBourdais replied that he had no authority to speak for his party without consulting the membership, but suggested that any compromise of the CCF position was highly unlikely. Hepburn immediately dismissed the gathering.[55]

If the CCF itself could not be had, the simple alternative was to seduce its anticipated supporters. This Hepburn proceeded to do. His first objective was rural Ontario. To this area, Hepburn shrewdly offered "the old agrarian program" re-invigorated by his own personality. The Liberals thus came to represent "a dramatic revival of the traditional agrarian insistence upon simplicity, economy and honesty in government.... Farmers who had misgivings about the sweeping economic policies of the CCF could agree upon the reforms urged by the Liberals."[56]

As early as the end of 1932, Hepburn witnessed the first fruits of his strategy. In December, the Liberal leader and Harry Nixon, provincial secretary in the Farmer-Labour government and leader of the Ontario Progressive Party, announced an arrangement between them to cooperate as a united group against the Henry administration.[57] J. W. Freeborn, another former member of the Drury government, announced that he would stand as a candidate for Hepburn's party.[58] If a Hepburn swing should become apparent, was it not likely many other prominent farm leaders would offer their support to the rejuvenated Liberal Party?

On the other hand, the old agrarian shibboleths would clearly not satisfy the industrial areas of the province, the other key sector of the province crucial to the Liberals. Moreover, here the CCF would provide considerably stronger opposition than among the farmers. This was the reason Arthur Roebuck, Hepburn's chief adviser and popular Ontario labour lawyer, sent a private memorandum to leading party officials throughout the province.

> Democracy [he wrote] ... is working badly ... the results have driven many people to extreme policies. These, because the capitalist system, so-called, is not working equitably, have flown to the desperate conclusion that it should be scrapped.... The Canadian voter ... has been looking anxiously to the Liberals for some new and broad proposals. If they are disappointed, many of the best of them ... will go over in increasing numbers to the CCF.... [59]

How the Liberals would regain the electorate's confidence soon became clear. Roebuck proposed a Labour Code to humanize

PROSPECTS AND PROBLEMS 33

industry; Hepburn continued to employ the rhetoric of radical-ism – "I am not out to destroy capitalism ... but I condemn in no uncertain terms the abuses of the capitalist system as it has been practiced under the Tory administration";[60] and both men lent their vocal support to various unpopular strikes in the province before they took power. When, for example, a strike in Stratford resulted in Premier Henry calling out the militia and sending in tanks, Hepburn was conspicuous as one of the few old party M.P.'s to join Woodsworth and Agnes Macphail in protesting this outrage.[61] As the old farm leaders began sidling back into the Liberal fold, so the dominant figures of the power-ful 1919 labour group – Morrison McBride, Humphrey Mitchell, Peter Heenan – happily began the same process.[62]

By such means was the Liberal leader ingratiating himself and his party to the farmers and workers of Ontario. The struggle was clear: would reformed capitalism or democratic socialism prove more enticing to the forces of discontent created by the Depression? The outcome, however, remained very much in doubt.

References

1. *C.A.R*, 1933, p. 317.
2. J. F. Cahan, *A Survey of the Political Activities of the Ontario Labour Move-ment, 1850-1935*, unpublished M.A. thesis (University of Toronto, 1945), pp. 44-5.
3. Quoted in Harold A. Logan, *Trade Unions in Canada* (Toronto, 1948), p. 431.
4. *Canadian Congress Journal*, October 1932.
5. *Ibid.*, October 1933; Logan, *op. cit.*, pp. 432-3.
6. Logan, *op. cit.*, pp. 380-2.
7. *Canadian Unionist*, June 1932 and January 1933.
8. *Ibid.*, September 1931.
9. *Canadian Congress Journal*, September 1932.
10. *Canadian Forum*, September 1932.
11. *Canadian Unionist*, September 1932.
12. Cahan, *op. cit.*, pp. 58-64.
13. Report of C.L.P. Annual Convention, in Toronto Labour Council Minutes, April 15, 1926.
14. Toronto Labour Council Minutes, November 17, 1927.
15. Cahan, *op. cit.*, pp. 74-5.
16. Toronto Labour Council Minutes, November 15, 1927.
17. Cahan, *op. cit.*, pp. 75-7.

18. *Ibid.*, pp. 22-5, 26, 28, 30-1, 41.

19. Bernard and Alice Loeb Papers, *The Socialist Party of Canada (Ontario Section): Statement of Principles* (no publisher, no date, likely 1933), and S.P. of C., *Draft of Policy*, 1933.

20. Toronto *Mail and Empire*, February 27, 1933; Tim Buck, *Thirty Years, 1922-1952* (Toronto, 1952), p. 90. Among the organizations present, and some of the more important delegates, were the Railway Carmen, the Amalgamated Clothing Workers, Building Workers, C.B.R.E., Electricians' Union, and Painters' Union. Labour Party units: Ontario or Windsor, Toronto (George Watson, James Connor, Rose Henderson), Silverthorn (Harry Hatfield), and East Windsor. Socialist Party of Canada units: Ontario section (A. H. Downs, David Goldstick), Earlscourt, Central Toronto, Danforth, East York, London, and York Township. Independent Labour Party units: East Hamilton (Sam Lawrence), Central Hamilton, West Hamilton, Dundas, Wards One and Two Toronto (James Simpson), Ward Five Toronto, Long Branch, and Humber Bay. Workers' Associations: East York (Mrs. E. Morton, Arthur Williams), Canadian London (Arthur Mould). Miscellaneous bodies: Windsor Branch, Labour Section CCF; Perth Political Labour Association; Marxian Educational League (William Moriarity); Earlscourt Christian Social Order; Jewish Socialist Verbund; Branch 220 Jewish Workman's Circle; Mazzini Circle; United Women's Educational Federation (Mrs. Jean Laing). Minutes of the Emergency Convention of the Labour Conference of Ontario, October 29, 1933, in Loeb Papers.

21. Toronto *Star*, February 20, 1933.

22. *Weekly Sun*, May 18, 1933; Toronto *Star*, July 18, 1933.

23. LeBourdais interview.

24. Toronto *Star*, March 18, 1933.

25. *Ibid.*, March 23 and March 24, 1933.

26. Herbert Orloff, *New Commonwealth*, February 23, 1936.

27. Toronto *Star*, May 29, 1933.

28. *C.A.R.*, 1933, p. 133.

29. Toronto *Star*, March 2, 1933.

30. Interview with LeBourdais and Harry Hatfield.

31. U.F.O. Minutes, June 2, 1933, in LeBourdais Papers; *Weekly Sun*, June 8, 1933.

32. Public Archives of Canada, Agnes Macphail Papers (hereafter Macphail Public Papers), volume 3, *Cooperative Commonwealth Federation Council of Ontario Constitution.*

33. *Weekly Sun*, June 8, 1933.

34. Harry Hatfield interview.

35. According to Elmore Philpott in an interview with Mrs. Margaret Stewart, copy in Macphail Private Papers, volume 3, *Riding Relations.*

36. Stewart and French, *Ask No Quarter,* p. 175.

37. Interviews with LeBourdais and Hatfield.

38. These were the units in East and West Lambton. *Weekly Sun*, July 6, 1933.

39. Toronto *Star*, January 29, 1933.

40. Toronto *Mail and Empire*, February 6, 1933.

41. Toronto *Star*, February 27, 1933.

42. *Ibid.*, March 27, 1933.

43. *Ibid.*, March 24, 1933. The inspector told a protesting CCF delegation that "It is the Lord's Day. Sunday is a day on which people should go to Church. There have been far too many meetings on Sunday."

44. Toronto *Star*, May 29, June 3, 1933. On the various occasions when the police attempted to bar the CCF from public parks, of the city's five major dailies only the Toronto *Star* raised its editorial voice in support of civil liberties.

45. Toronto *Star*, May 3, July 3, July 22, and July 24, 1933; *Weekly Sun*, June 8 and June 15, 1933; Toronto *Mail and Empire*, July 7, 1933.

46. Toronto *Telegram*, March 13, 1933.

47. Grace MacInnis, *Alberta Labour News*, February 18, 1933, Dominion Archives, Woodsworth Papers, Scrap Book, Vol. 33.

48. E. C. Buchanan, *Saturday Night*, March 11, 1933.

49. Toronto *Mail and Empire*, February 3, 1933.

50. Toronto *Telegram*, February 21, 1933.

51. "Politician With a Notebook," *Maclean's*, May 15, 1933.

52. Quoted in *Weekly Sun*, June 8, 1933.

53. Neil McKenty, *Mitch Hepburn* (Toronto, 1967), pp. 301.

54. Toronto *Mail and Empire*, May 16, 1932.

55. LeBourdais interview. It was shortly after this meeting that Philpott joined the CCF.

56. Bristow, *Agrarian Interest in Ontario Politics*, pp. 150-1, 156.

57. *C.A.R.*, 1932, p. 108.

58. Larry Zolf, *The Emergence of Hepburn Liberalism in the 1930's*, unpublished graduate research paper (University of Toronto, 1960), p. 13.

59. Undated private memorandum, Arthur Roebuck Papers, cited by Larry Zolf in his uncompleted M.A. thesis on Mitchell Hepburn, which he kindly let me see in its unfinished form.

60. Quoted in *Farmers' Sun*, December 22, 1932.

61. Toronto *Star*, September 30, 1933.

62. McKenty, *op. cit.*, p. 49, and Martin Robin, *Radical Politics and Canadian Labour* (Kingston, 1968), p. 268.

3 SOCIALISTS AT WORK

I

In July 1933, twenty per cent of the labour force in Canada was
unemployed; one and a half million men, women and children
were on direct public relief; the Department of National Defence
had opened up its forty-fourth camp for single, unemployed
males; the price of farm products failed to meet the farmer's cost
of production.[1] The Toronto Conference of the United Church,
by a vote of 121 to 97, adopted a resolution opposing the
existing capitalist system, advocating a "Christian Social Order,"
and endorsing socialization of banking, transportation, and other
essential industries. Prime Minister Bennett announced that the
practice of granting titles to meritorious personages would be
re-introduced.[2] The Canadian intellectual left, as represented by
the *Canadian Forum*, feared that the prevailing mood of fear and
insecurity provided fertile soil for the growth of a powerful national
fascist movement. It believed only the CCF could counter such a
threat; hence the urgency of tone as it called repeatedly upon the
party to present to the nation "a positive concrete program of
action," "a clear and specific statement" of immediate aims which
would supplement the vague principles of social reconstruction laid
down at Calgary.[3]

CCF leaders were not unaware of this weakness in their program. For this reason, Professor Frank Underhill was asked to
draft a detailed statement of CCF policy and principle for presentation at the party's forthcoming national convention in
Regina. The manifesto Underhill produced, he later wrote, was
"an attempt to formulate in language applicable to Canadian
conditions a Fabian socialist policy such as the British Labour
Party had worked out for Great Britain."[4]

Of the 131 delegates at Regina in the third week of July 1933,
no fewer than forty-five had come from Ontario; of these,
although each of the three sections was entitled to equal representation, only five represented the Labour Conference, fourteen

the UFO, and twenty-six the Club section. Besides adopting a specific fourteen-point program and the hallowed Regina Manifesto, the convention re-affirmed its opposition to becoming a political party and adopted, largely to please the Ontario and Alberta farm delegates, a constitution preserving the autonomy of constituent organizations though providing for concerted action.[5] The provincial council in each province was made the primary membership centre, while the final authority in the party in matters of both discipline and policy was to be the annual provincial convention.[6]

For the Ontario party in particular, the events of the four days at Regina were most significant for the manner in which they exacerbated the already deteriorating relationship which existed among its three sections. Of these, the Club delegates were the most conciliatory. Although they preferred a unified structure for the party, they accepted the UFO's insistence on constituency autonomy and on maintaining the CCF as a mere federation of allied parties. Moreover, some of their views proved radical enough to satisfy the doctrinaire Labourites. Hence for a brief time it appeared that the natural distrust of the Labour men towards the new recruits brought in by the Clubs might be overcome.

The same was not true between Labour and the UFO; here the most discord and the least identity of purpose were evident. The Ontario delegates' table at the convention provided a weird spectacle: down one side, the fourteen conservative farmers, "impervious to social dogma and frankly antagonistic to the 'Comrade' with which each socialist delegate prefaced his remarks";[7] in one small corner, the five Labour Conference representatives, providing, with several Vancouver delegates, most of the extremist arguments of the sessions.

The first major clash was over the debate on the Manifesto presented by the provisional executive. Its very spirit and tone repelled the UFO. Although private ownership of the family farm was accepted, and although it called for little more public ownership than had some earlier western agrarian programs, the manifesto, as H. H. Hannam said, was more of a socialist than simply a cooperative document. The UFO delegates would reluctantly support it, although the language used "is not the language best understood by Ontario farmers." What was needed was "a few simple straight-forward reforms" expressed in "every-day language" to take back to rural Ontario.[8]

The greatest uproar concerning the manifesto was caused by an amendment to eliminate from it the declaration that "We do not believe in change through violence." Its two movers were Ernest Winch, a Vancouver Marxist, and William Moriarity of Toronto, a Trotskyite.[9] Moriarity, although claiming to favour constitutional methods wherever possible, believed "the methods suitable to capitalism are those of force," and asserted that "if the ruling class opposes the will of the people . . . we must use methods suitable to the occasion."[10] The amendment, of course, was overwhelmingly defeated, but not before the UFO delegates were stricken with something approaching a collective apoplectic fit.

After overwhelmingly adopting the Manifesto, the convention turned to the issue which provided the longest, most acrimonious debate during the four days. Once again it was Moriarity who presented the contentious amendment, demanding deletion of a plank promising fair compensation, not "outright confiscation," for private enterprises expropriated by a socialist government. Again Moriarity went down to a crushing defeat, but not before the debate revealed once more the vast, irreconcilable divergence of opinion between the Ontario Labour Conference representatives on the one hand and the Club and UFO delegates on the other.[11]

It was the second, but not the last, defeat for the extreme left. The Canadian Labour Defence League, a Communist organization, had asked the CCF to cooperate with it in securing the release from prison of "The Eight" – as the Communist leaders indicted for sedition are canonized in Communist Party scriptures. In an historically significant decision, the convention agreed almost unanimously on the following reply:

> We believe in constitutional methods to achieve this result [securing control of the government]. On that point there is a fundamental cleavage between us and the leaders of your organization, who maintain that civil strife is inevitable. This policy, in our opinion, would result in the intensification of political oppression. We therefore are unable to see that any useful purpose could be served by such joint . . . demonstrations as you propose.
>
> We propose to pursue our campaign for repeal of Section 98, the release of political prisoners, and the prevention of arbitrary deportations by methods approved and adopted by our organization.[12]

This account of the Regina convention has stressed only the divisions which occurred. These are especially apposite to this study since they all involved rancorous disputes within the

Ontario delegation. But it would be erroneous to conclude from the above – and as one might from reading the press reports of the convention – that it was constantly on the verge of secession and withdrawals. Although these disputes aggravated the tensions within the Ontario CCF, the convention otherwise was remarkable for its unanimity on matters of socialist principle, its determination to be honest and frank about those principles, and its affirmation of a devout faith in democratic, constitutional methods. Despite a national treasury which had received exactly $759.24 since August, 1932, a press entirely hostile but for the Toronto *Star*, and the acknowledged problem of implementing a program as radical as its own "by anything short of a united and thoroughly disciplined party"[13] – in the face of all this, the CCF was optimistic and enthusiastic. After Regina, its supporters knew, their party had ceased to be merely a collection of local protest groups and had become a fact of the nation's political life. How important a fact was yet to be determined.

II

In Ontario, the first immediate consequence of the Regina convention was an intensification of earlier activities both by a re-inspired CCF and by its increasingly nervous opponents. Innumerable party rallies throughout the province, in parks and halls and theatres, attracted crowds often numbering in the thousands and described even by an unfriendly press as "cheering," "enthusiastic," and "excited." One picnic-rally in Toronto's Lambton Park drew a phenomenal thirty thousand men, women, and children; of the city's four newspapers, only the Toronto *Star* covered the event.[14]

The revivalist quality of these gatherings was palpable. The new Manifesto was introduced and worshipped. It would bring salvation from capitalism, "the law of the jungle." In the promised land, depression would be unknown, "wage slavery" and irresponsible concentrations of wealth would be replaced by a planned economy, "people will come before profits," and all banks – but no farms – would be socialized. The CCF was described as the "first practical expression ever given to Christianity"; CCF'ers were not politicians but "crusaders for humanity."

Every city and town across the province was invaded by party organizers and speakers, usually followed by a new CCF Club if none had hitherto existed. Salem Bland wrote that it was impossible to pick up a newspaper without reading some news item that "indicates the widespread drift to socialism."[15] In October, LeBourdais asserted that, since January, CCF membership had increased by one thousand each month; there were 72 clubs in Ontario, one-third of them with ten thousand members in Toronto.[16]

The CCF's opponents, apparently, believed these claims; their attacks increased. Mackenzie King repeatedly charged that only by coercion and force could a socialist government maintain itself in power.[17] Premier Henry of Ontario wittily defined CCF as "Canada Crazy Federation," an organization which intended to "go as far" as the Russians "if they get the chance."[18] And the Toronto *Mail and Empire* offered its readers the following editorial scoop:

> ... it might as well be made known at once that Karl Marx and Louis Engels and others like them are the real authors of the "new era" rather than Miss Macphail and Mr. J. S. Woodsworth.[19]

In Ottawa, talk of a "national government" was once again rife. Initiated by Montreal financial circles, the objective was to halt the growth of radicalism in Canada while working towards a "solution of the railway problem" satisfactory to private enterprise, that is, amalgamation of the two major lines under C.P.R. control. Of course, it was noted, "That they [the CCF] would come into office there is no large apprenhension. That they might hold the balance of power and be a factor of great importance is within the province of possibility. A national government would stop . . . that. . . . "[20]

Montreal Catholics shared the antipathy to the CCF of Montreal capitalists. First the Archibishop of Montreal declared against the socialist movement. Then, in November 1933, the entire Quebec hierarchy issued a joint declaration which was generally interpreted as a warning to Catholics to remain outside the CCF.[21] The Church had spoken and its disciples proved generally faithful. For years thereafter, as one dissenting Catholic later wrote, "most Catholics I have met across Canada . . . are afflicted with a deep-rooted though unconscious prejudice against the CCF. . . . They are enslaved by the tyranny of a single word – 'socialism'. . . . "[22]

Catholics, like many other ordinary Canadians, had great difficulty distinguishing between socialism and communism. In fact, the CCF and the Communist Party were mortal enemies. The Regina Convention in July had rejected a Communist bid to cooperate with the CCF in fighting for specific common objectives. In August, Elmore Philpott raised publicly for the first time in Ontario the question of Communist-CCF relations at a mass rally. His speech was an emphatic warning to Communists, who he claimed were "trying to disrupt the CCF and ruin it," that he simply would not tolerate them in his party.

Philpott described the Communists' attitude toward the CCF as "run it or ruin it."[23] This was demonstrably true. In 1932, Communist parties in every country of the world were in the ultrarevolutionary phase of the party line. The distinguishing feature of this period outside of Russia was the designating of democratic socialism, not capitalism nor even fascism, as the main enemy. Fascism was the last stage of capitalist decay and consequently a transient period. Thus it could be disregarded as a serious obstacle to the onward march of Communism. The socialists, however, their rivals for working class support, had to be "exposed." Accordingly, the theory of "social fascism" was invented. Tim Buck later wrote that while his party sought, in the early 1930's, to bring about a united front between the CCF and the Communist Party, it was necessary simultaneously to "struggle against the illusion that the battle against monopoly capitalism" could be won by CCF policies and to "expose and combat the anti-working class ideology of the CCF leaders." The CCF, he charged, "systematically pursues policies which support monopoly capitalism against the working class."[24] This Canadian Communists brought themselves to believe, for Stalin declared it so, and it remained party policy until the Comintern peremptorily declared otherwise in 1935. Until then, the party continued in what an ex-member has called its "blind and mechanical application of a foreign line to Canadian conditions which were not analogous at all."[25]

The task became one of preventing the "social fascist" CCF from gaining political power in Canada, and specifically to prevent the Canadian trade union movement from supporting the CCF. This was the consistent Communist policy towards the CCF during its lifetime, pursued through tactics both straightforward and bewilderingly devious. Within the labour movement, the strong Communist group in the Trades and Labour Congress consistently supported the Gompers theory of political independence, thus enabling it, as it did in 1933, to support the Congress decision not to endorse the CCF.[26]

The attitude of CCF'ers to the Communists was somewhat more complex. In the first place, they took the problem of their relationship to the C.P. very seriously indeed. It was no mere question of tactics but one of integrity; it was about the soul of their party. It was the kind of problem which has perpetually bedevilled social democratic organizations, and the crisis of 1933 has an eerie ring of familiarity yet.

The CCF party line only barred active cooperation with the Communist party; it could not dictate CCF'ers, opinions of C.P.'ers. In truth, there was a striking dichotomy in socialist thinking on the subject. On the one hand, most CCF'ers genuinely repudiated the use of violence (at least for Canada), were more or less aware of the Communist attitude towards their party, and, perhaps most importantly, feared the Communists as their most significant rival for the leadership of the working class.[27] On the other hand, few socialists then saw in Russia a totalitarian regime ruled by a madman. While they criticized the absence of civil liberties in the Soviet Union, it was often rationalized as an "unfortunate necessity" of the early days; a revolution, after all, was not a picnic. On the whole, they believed that at least the economic foundations of a socialist society were being laid in Russia; democracy, hopefully, would follow. Consequently, Canadian Communists could be perceived as merely socialists in a hurry.[28]

Not all CCF'ers shared this perception. Elmore Philpott for one did not, and in August 1933 he warned Communists alleged to be in the Labour Conference that they would be tolerated no longer. Philpott and his supporters never documented their accusations. In fact, there is considerable reason to doubt that Communists in the Labour section ever gained any major positions of influence. Philpott's main antagonists were in reality a handful of uncontrollable doctrinaire radicals who insisted on their right to cooperate with anyone sharing similar ideals in order to achieve common aims.

One month after his initial outburst, the Provincial Council met and adopted two highly controversial resolutions submitted by Philpott. The first provided for a revamped organizational structure for the Ontario party, and the Council decided to submit it for a final decision to the forthcoming provincial convention. The resolution called for replacing the existing "complicated" and "confusing" structure with a single provincial unit; the federative principle would apply within each federal constituency rather than as a provincial super-structure. In each riding, one central Constituency Council would be established, and each CCF unit within the constituency would be entitled to representation on that Council *"in exact proportion to the numbers of their registered membership."* As for the critical and difficult problem of discipline, the resolution stated that since it is essential there be unity of purpose and action throughout the whole structure of the Ontario CCF, no individual, group or organization affiliated with the Ontario CCF shall pursue any course of action prejudicial to the welfare of the movement. The Provincial Council [chosen by the convention] shall have full power to discipline all members and local organizations, including the power of suspending, expelling or refusing any application for membership, subject only to the Provincial Convention.[29]

Not satisfied with the control this resolution, if effected, would give him, Philpott then set about to purify the party. In a disgraceful resolution, carried by a combined UFO-Club section vote over Labour objections, the Council recommended to all CCF units that no *former* officer of the Communist Party be accepted as a CCF member.[30]

The proposed organizational change was perfectly sensible. The tremendous growth of the Club section had been completely unforeseen when the original provincial structure was designed; now, equal representation for Labour and the UFO at conventions and on the Council actually discriminated against the Clubs. Nevertheless, many Labour delegates opposed the plan, and Arthur Mould, president of the Labour Conference, called an emergency meeting in Toronto for October 29.

Delegates representing forty-one organizations affiliated with the Conference were seated. They were addressed first by Reverend A. E. Smith of the Communist Party on the importance of a forthcoming united front congress for the repeal of Section 98 of the Criminal Code, then by Stratford alderman O. J. Kerr, a convention delegate, on the Stratford strike situation. Kerr paid tribute to the "splendid work" of the Workers' Unity League – a Communist organization – and the convention voted its endorsement of the strike.

The Executive then presented its report on the main business of the session. It declared that Philpott's proposed new structure, by trying to substitute proportional for equal sectional representation, was actually "aimed at eliminating the Labour Section from participating as a body in shaping the program and policy of the CCF. . . . " The convention agreed that any new structure "whereby the Labour Conference shall cease to exist as a provincial unit or . . . will be deprived of equality of representation with the other two sections . . . shall be regarded as a breach of trust on the part of the other two sections." Before adjourning, the meeting voted its strong opposition to the ban on former Communist officials recommended by the Provincial Council, then called for the resignations of Philpott and LeBourdais "on the ground that the statements made by them are fundamentally opposed to the principles of socialism and are detrimental to the advancement of the Labour movement as a whole."[31]

Philpott was unmoved by the indignation of the Labour group. He continued to insist that a reorganization of the CCF was necessary "so that Labour representation in the CCF would consist of genuine labour leaders and not irresponsible trouble-makers." Philpott sometimes confused trouble-makers with Communists, and began hinting publicly "of a coming storm he confidently expects to sweep out of the CCF all members of organized Communist groups."[32] Hints began developing into dangerous rumours. If the CCF were not purged of Communists, an anonymous "CCF leader" purportedly told a Toronto paper, "it will mean a smash-up of the organization in Ontario. It will be a fight to the finish."[33] Two newspapers reported there was a "grave possibility" that the UFO would "break away" from the CCF "if there is any compromise with Communism."[34]

At this critical juncture, Philpott and Agnes Macphail decided the issue finally had to be resolved. On November 17, a mass meeting at Massey Hall was organized in order to bring about a final "showdown" with the alleged Communists in the Labour Conference. The two leaders there served emphatic public warning to the radical element in the CCF to leave the party and join the Communist Party where it was said to belong. All but a handful of the sixteen hundred supporters present cheered Philpott's determination not to compromise "with those who advocate bloody revolution." He insisted that "either the noisy irreconcilable two per cent get out or the 98 per cent get out – and we don't intend to get out." Taking up the earlier statement by Macphail that the CCF must grow out of Canadian conditions and traditions, he asserted there could be no truck with the extreme radical element.

> Nothing could wreck the CCF sooner than a compromise with those who whisper about the inevitability of a revolution by force. . . . The most important purpose [of this meeting] is to inform the people of the province through the press that this noisy little minority has more noise than commonsense.[35]

That was probably true. Without its embarrassingly vocal fringe elements, the party would undoubtedly have been stronger and more attractive. And yet the moral pressure to avoid a split remained great. Suddenly, for a brief, deceptive moment, it appeared that an amicable settlement might be possible. A Provincial Council meeting on December 9 re-elected Agnes Macphail president, and chose an executive which included John Mitchell and LeBourdais of the Clubs, R. J. Scott and Hannam of the UFO, Edith Morton and Arthur Mould of Labour. (No one embarrassed the Labour delegates by pointing out that Mitchell of the Club Section was a leading Hamilton trade unionist infinitely more representative of Ontario workers than Mould or Morton.) The question of re-organizing the provincial structure was wisely postponed; it was placed in the hands of a joint committee of six members, two from each section, who would report to the next provincial convention. Equally important, the earlier resolution banning all former Communist officials from party membership was rescinded and replaced by the following resolution, introduced by three council members, again representing all sections:

> No person who is a member of any political party or organization not affiliated with the CCF shall be eligible for membership [in the CCF]; [they] shall include, for the purpose of this resolution, the Conservative Party, the Liberal Party, the Communist Party, and any organizations which are affiliated or related to these parties. . . . This resolution shall include members of existing or future organizations, Fascist or Communist in character which advocate social change by means of force.[36]

With this reasonable compromise, opposed only by three intransigent Labour Conference council members, the debilitating internecine strife seemed finally laid to rest.

It was – it could only have been – a delusory hope. No mere resolution, for example, could have assuaged the ever-increasing suspicions of the UFO. It was true such influential farm leaders as R. J. Scott and H. H. Hannam had spoken often on behalf of the CCF in rural Ontario, and that the recent UFO convention unanimously re-affirmed the 1932 decision to cooperate with the CCF. Moreover, the convention adopted a programme which, one farm leader explained, though perhaps more polite and respectable than the Regina Manifesto, certainly called for massive social and economic reconstruction. The programme, said the *Weekly Sun*, applied the "principles of the Regina Manifesto to the immediate and specific problems of Ontario agriculture."[37]

All of this was undeniably real. And yet for the UFO it is clear that there existed a greater reality. The CCF was not their party. There were all those "Communists" in it, for one thing. But it was more than that. The Ontario CCF was simply not a movement in which farmers could feel comfortable. Left-wing academics felt instinctively at home in the CCF. So did a small number of unusually politicized working-class activists. It was their party, a party of the cities, of an industrializing Ontario, which farmers were trying desperately to resist. It was, accordingly, largely irrelevant to rural Ontario, and it soon became clear that the UFO would have to sever its link.

As it happens, to withdraw from the CCF at this stage would demonstrate a nice sense of political timing, for the socialist tide was already beginning to roll out. Four major factors accounting for this decline can be isolated. They help explain why the Depression did not result in greater CCF strength. The slump began with the party's first taste of political defeat. On October 24, 1933, Judge L. S. Stubbs, running as the first federal CCF candidate in a Saskatchewan by-election, suffered a generally unexpected defeat at the hands of the Liberal Party. Nine days later, although the year-old party won a third of the popular vote, it elected only six members in the British Columbia provincial election as Patullo and his miniature New Deal swept the province for the Liberals. Both Stubbs and the British Columbia CCF had actually done remarkably well, but, as the *Canadian Unionist* percipiently observed,

> many CCF'ers have been so intemperate in their predictions of early success that anything less than victory with every attempt is a grievous disappointment to the overnight converts who form the bulk of their following.

As a result, the party had lost more than its first elections: it had "lost a good deal of the easy optimism which has been its chief stock-in-trade."[38] Moreover, CCF disillusionment was matched by a proportionate increase in renewed old party confidence, especially on the part of the Liberals. With the two defeats came an increased hope that the CCF, like all other protest parties, would eventually fade out of the political picture.[39] Voters rarely choose to ride a bandwagon which is standing still.

In the second place, the young party's image was already badly tarnished. Irresponsible statements of individual CCF members, some actually made, many terribly distorted, had been broadcast throughout the Dominion by the daily press. Just as the press had played up the extremist statements made at the

Regina convention out of all proportion to their actual significance, so it later selected particularly damaging statements ostensibly made by CCF'ers in the British Columbia election and used
these to damn the entire movement. Of course to very many
Canadians, even a reasonable and moderate socialist pronouncement was damning enough.

This situation was not helped by the lack of a national organization. This was the third major reason for the party's decline.
No adequate direction was forthcoming from the top. Although
Woodsworth was accepted as national leader, the multifarious
groups within the party took literally the concept of the CCF as a
federation rather than an integrated organism, and acted accordingly. Woodsworth himself admitted that "we have very little
real organization across the country. If I were to write to
Toronto with regard to the distribution of literature, I might or
might not get an answer, and if I got an answer it might not
result in any literature being distributed."[40] Moreover, aside
from the tiny parliamentary caucus, there was no centre which
could be said to represent the party as a whole. Any member
could legitimately be said to speak for the party, or at least a
section of it. And of course the press was more than happy to
exploit this divisive situation. In this manner, irrelevant and
unrepresentative denunciations by party members of the crown,
or religion, or the governor-general, had become, by the end of
1933, the basis of public discussion of the CCF; actual party
policies were virtually ignored.

The fourth factor in the CCF's fall from public esteem emerges
here. On the one hand, it was incapable of preventing titillating
gossip about its attitude to free love and the institution of the
family. On the other, it failed finally to communicate to Canadians what precisely and positively it did stand for. To be sure,
vague generalizations abounded about the inequities of capitalism and the glories of the coming socialist order. But it failed to
offer concrete, specific, and easily explainable solutions. There
was nothing really substantial and convincing for the average
voter to hang on to. People wanted to repudiate Bennett; that
much had become clear. They desperately needed something new
– a person, a movement, an idea – to give them a sense of
security during those dislocating times. The CCF's eschatology
was too remote and utopian to be comforting. Its well-publicized
internecine warfare was hardly reassuring. It was too far from
Canadians. "The consequence is," concluded one observer, "that
the expectancy of a Liberal government after the next election
has been strengthened."[41]

References

1. *Weekly Sun*, July 13, 1933.

2. *Ibid.*, June 15, 1933.

3. *Canadian Forum*, March and June 1933.

4. Underhill, "Political Parties and Ideas," in G. W. Brown (ed.), *Canada* (Berkeley, 1953), p. 345.

5. *Weekly Sun*, July 27, 1933.

6. McNaught, *Prophet in Politics*, p. 262.

7. *Saskatoon Western Producer*, quoted in *Canadian Unionist*, August 1933.

8. Toronto *Mail and Empire*, July 22, 1933; Toronto *Star*, July 22, 1933; *Weekly Sun*, August 3, 1933.

9. M. J. Coldwell, *CCF Twenty-Fifth Anniversary Souvenir Album* (Ottawa, 1957), p. 17.

10. Toronto *Mail and Empire*, July 20, 1933.

11. Weekly *Sun*, July 27, 1933; Toronto *Mail and Empire*, July 21, 1933.

12. Toronto *Star*, July 22, 1933.

13. Frank Scott, *Canadian Forum*, September 1933.

14. Toronto *Star*, August 8, 1933.

15. *Ibid.*, October 7, 1933.

16. *Ibid.*, September 1, 1933.

17. *Weekly Sun*, July 27, 1933; Toronto *Star*, July 24, 1933.

18. *Weekly Sun*, September 21, 1933.

19. Toronto *Mail and Empire*, July 29, 1933.

20. Charles Bishop, Ottawa *Citizen*, cited in *Weekly Sun*, September 21, 1933.

21. *Ibid.*, November 30, 1933.

22. Letter to S. M. Lipset from Rev. Eugence Cullinane, undated, cited in Lipset, *Agrarian Socialism,* p. 210.

23. Toronto *Star*, August 8, 1933.

24. Tim Buck, *Thirty Years*, pp. 111-115.

25. Interview with J. B. Salsberg, Toronto, 1961.

26. M. M. Armstrong, *The Development of Trade Union Activity in the CCF*, unpublished M.A. thesis (University of Toronto, 1959), pp. 17-35.

27. Interviews with Professor Underhill and I. J. Weinrot, Toronto, 1961.

28. The American Socialist Party maintained the same delusions. In 1932 its convention adopted a resolution urging the restoration of civil liberties in the Soviet Union, but still applauding "the efforts being made [there] to create the economic foundations of a Socialist society." Cited in D. A. Shannon, *The Socialist Party of America* (New York, 1955), p. 215.

29. Loeb Papers, CCF Provincial Council Minutes, September 9, 1933. Before then, local units alone held the power of expulsion.

30. *Ibid.;* Toronto *Star*, September 11, 1933. The *Star* quoted a "reliable source" as saying the action was taken because of criticism of the CCF for having William Moriarity, a former Communist official, as a delegate to Regina.

31. Loeb Papers, Minutes of the Emergency Convention, October 29, 1933.

32. Toronto *Star*, November 10, 1933.

33. Toronto *Telegram*, November 12, 1933.

34. *Ibid.;* Toronto *Mail and Empire*, November 13, 1933.

35. Toronto *Mail and Empire*, November 18, 1933.

36. Loeb Papers, Provincial Council Meeting Minutes, December 9, 1933; Toronto *Globe*, December 11, 1933; Toronto *Mail and Empire*, December 11, 1933.

37. *Weekly Sun*, December 15 and December 28, 1933.

38. *Canadian Unionist*, November 1933.

39. Ottawa correspondent, *Weekly Sun*, November 16, 1933.

40. Public Archives of Canada (P.A.C.), Woodsworth Papers, Correspondence, volume 3, Woodsworth to Underhill, February 27, 1934.

41. Ottawa correspondent, *Weekly Sun*, November 2, 1933.

4 DISSOLUTION OF THE TRIPLE ALLIANCE

I

On New Year's Day, 1934, the CCF in Ontario received its first bitter taste of political defeat. In municipal elections across the province save only in Hamilton, party candidates went down to inglorious defeat. In Toronto, only James Simpson, running for Controller and already a prominent civic figure, and Rose Henderson, campaigning for Board of Education, were successful; the other dozen candidates were swamped.[1]

From that point, the rest of the year was all downhill. For at the same time, a new issue arose which was destined, in one short month, to lead to the shattering of the entire CCF provincial structure. Early in 1933, Reverend A. E. Smith had returned from "seeing the dawn" in the Soviet Union, and had thrown himself into the campaign for the release of the eight Communist leaders imprisoned in 1931 as parties to a "seditious conspiracy" to overthrow the state. Working through a front group, the Canadian Labour Defense League, thousands of pamphlets were distributed, hundreds of meetings held. At one of these, on January 17, 1934, Smith accused the Bennett government of responsibility for the attempt that had been made on Tim Buck's life during the Kingston penitentiary riots of 1932. Two detectives who were present at the meeting later quoted Smith as stating that Bennett personally arranged the shooting. At the end of January, a grand jury indicted Smith for sedition.

Smith exaggerated very little when he later wrote that "hardly was the ink dry on the indictment, than the workers' organizations across Canada roused themselves into action.... In the next month, some of the largest mass rallies ever seen in Canadian labour history were taking place." Smith was accurate too when he wrote: "The CCF leaders could not stem the tide of united-front sentiment in their own ranks. CCF clubs sent delegates to our defence conferences in spite of the official [CCF] ban."[2] On March 5, a jury pronounced Smith innocent of the charge of sedition; he avoided a prison term, and his organization benefitted from the aura of martyrdom that resulted from his arrest and trial. To the Communists' undoubted delight the real victims of the Smith affair were the dreaded "social fascists" in the CCF.

The Canadian Labour Defense League's main tactic was to invite "progressive" organizations to unite with it in an unofficial united front. The question posed a profound dilemma for democratic socialists. On the one hand, Smith's indictment was unquestionably a flagrant violation of his civil liberties, and self-evidently had to be opposed. On the other hand, a united front presented two real threats to the CCF as a party. Such a close alliance could easily lead, in the public mind, to a confusion of basic principles between the two movements. Moreover, it would offer the Communists a singular opportunity to work their way into positions of influence within the CCF. It was a nice dilemma.

The C.L.D.L. began their united front appeals in the middle of February. On February 17, at a CCF provincial Council meeting in London, a long and unexpected debate was held on the question of participation in the protest rallies being held for Smith. The CCF Club and UFO delegates, although they opposed the "railroading" of any man to prison, felt that the party could not afford to be linked up with "left wing" bodies in any joint action. The Labour Conference representatives could not accept this position. They strongly advocated cooperation with the C.L.D.L. in the Smith meetings, and went so far as to move non-confidence votes in the existing CCF leaders. On the vote, the UFO and Club delegates combined to make their position official Council policy. Labour angrily indicated its determination to do "whatever it pleased, regardless of Council rulings." The UFO delegates were so exasperated and concerned they appointed a committee consisting of Robert Scott and Herbert Hannam to "take whatever action they may find necessary in view of the events of the next few weeks."[3]

The following day, February 18, the C.L.D.L. held a mass protest rally in Massey Hall with Smith himself the main speaker. After attacking the Conservative leaders, Smith launched a savage attack upon Woodsworth, charging him and his colleagues in the House with the responsibility for the sedition charge against him. On the same platform were several CCF members, including Wilfrid Jones, secretary of the St. Paul's CCF Club, who joined in the criticism of his party and thereby immortalized his name.[4]

An outraged Woodsworth immediately branded Smith's accusations "baseless and fantastic." He warned CCF members that those who ignored the provincial and national council rulings on cooperation with the C.L.D.L. faced "only one course . . . and that is that they be expelled from the CCF."[5] Thus encouraged, Philpott affirmed that any member of the Club section who "espoused" protest meetings in Smith's interests would be "summarily ejected from the Clubs."[6]

On February 20, Edith Morton, secretary of the Labour Conference, announced at a public meeting on behalf of Smith that she and the rest of the Labour Section would defy the Council's decision. The following day, Philpott replied that "drastic action" could be expected "at an early date" in view of this challenge. "The entire CCF has either got to get in line with its official policy or the rebels will have to get out. . . . " In turn, Mrs. Morton publicly reminded Philpott that expulsion could be authorized only by the section involved, and the Labour Section was hardly about to expel a member working for Smith. In fact labour, she declared, "fully intends to continue protesting" Smith's indictment.[7]

Here was the CCF's dilemma laid bare. How could the right of freedom be reconciled with the need for order? At what stage did minority rights of dissent nullify the majority's right to rule? When did democracy slip into anarchy? As rebels and civil libertarians, did socialists have unfettered freedom to repudiate their party's official policies – especially if the party was not being "left" enough? "Socialist parties," Walter Young claims, "suffer from this misunderstanding of democracy,"[8] and the CCF was certainly suffering.

On February 23, Scott and Hannam of the UFO sent Agnes Macphail a telegram notifying her of their decision to withdraw from the CCF.

> Efforts at constructive cooperation in CCF during past year rendered futile. Situation looks hopeless. Left Wing labour made name [of CCF] repulsive to Ontario farmers. Feel strongly we can best serve people and promote reconstruction independent of Federation. . . .[9]

Macphail wired back immediately, attempting to placate the two farm leaders. She assured them the "pro-Communists" would be expelled, leaving the UFO "and others" in control of the party. Realizing time was of the essence, she then wrote Philpott suggesting a Council meeting on March 3 to "read out the organizations that won't conform to the constitution drawn up at Regina. There is no use fooling about this thing any longer."[10]

In Ottawa, the party's national leaders had arrived at the same conclusion. On February 25, the four Labour M.P.'s – Woodsworth, McInnis, Heaps, and Humphrey Mitchell – wrote Agnes Macphail, reminding her of Smith's outrageous accusation against them, and that various CCF members

> have cooperated with those bitterly opposed to the CCF and themselves have denounced CCF principles and stated they would not be bound by the decisions of the duly constituted CCF organizations. In view of this situation, we call upon the provincial council of Ontario to take immediate steps to rid the CCF of individuals or organizations who are not in sympathy with the program of the CCF or who refuse to support loyally its constitution.[11]

No compromise seemed possible. The rebels had continued to rebel. The St. Paul's CCF Club refused to expel Wilfrid Jones as ordered. The Socialist Party of Canada replaced Tom Cruden as president because he supported the expulsion of "Communist infiltrators."[12] Many believed a complete "house-cleaning," as the press described it, aimed at expelling Communist elements and simplifying the provincial constitution, was immediately necessary.

On February 26, the UFO and Club sections, acting separately but likely in collusion, petitioned the national executive to expel the Labour Conference from the provincial party. This, declared Philpott, was to be "the final showdown." But "Labour as a whole," he explained, was not the object of the expulsion; after the reorganization, most of the labour groups would be welcomed back to the CCF fold. This would give "real labour organizations" some voice in running the party, which they hitherto lacked. Certain labour groups, as he pointed out, had unfairly monopolized Labour's representation on the Provincial Council. The Socialist Party of Canada, for example, with a meagre forty-eight members, incredibly occupied no fewer than eight of Labour's twelve council seats; this organization, Philpott promised, would certainly be among the groups expelled. The other great need was to replace the "cumbersome" existing provincial structure with a single cohesive unit. Unions and other bodies would still maintain their identities, but it was vital that there be one central council "which will actually control, instead of being laughed at by anyone who wanted to go his own way."[13]

It was becoming increasingly uncertain that anyone would remain in the party for Philpott to control. On March 1, Scott and Hannam, who had been empowered by the UFO to decide on its future course of action, informed LeBourdais of their decision.

> The recent action of certain members of the Labour Section in associating themselves with the activities of groups communistic in character has brought matters to a head [they wrote]. Such activities and the sympathetic support which those individuals received from other Labour representatives in the Council demonstrated to us the futility of continuing our association with them.
>
> Feeling that we can best serve the farm people of this province . . . independently of the CCF we have decided to withdraw officially from the Federation.[14]

This was clearly irrevocable. But Agnes Macphail, whose own position in the CCF became untenable once the UFO withdrew, persuaded the two men to keep their statement absolutely secret for ten days when a Provincial Council meeting would be held; reluctantly, they agreed.[15]

The March 10 meeting had been necessitated when Woodsworth and the National Executive refused to take action on the expulsion of the Labour Conference, referring the matter instead back to the Provincial Council with the expressed hope it could settle its own differences. This was probably impossible even had the UFO delegates appeared at the meeting. When they failed to do so, all hope was lost. Predictably, with equal representation, an absolute deadlock occurred between the representatives of the Labour and Club Sections.

The UFO's absence, it appears, came as a surprise even to Agnes Macphail and Philpott. Presumably, Scott and Hannam simply – and correctly – decided that the meeting could not possibly repair all the damage already done. On their own initiative, the two men issued a statement on the day the Council met, affirming the official withdrawal of the UFO from the CCF.[16]

The decision was long anticipated. The fact was that the alliance was essentially incongruous. To an Ontario farmer, the editor of the *Weekly Sun* once wrote, "The mere mention of control or socialization brings to mind visions of slavery and provokes an emotional opposition."[17] Already the latent fear of the ultimate socialization of land prevented a real identification with the aims of the CCF. The five per cent of Ontario farmers who belonged to the UFO largely shared these views. In short, as Agnes Macphail later recalled, given the UFO's prime loyalty to agriculture and the disdain of urban CCF'ers for rural problems, there was little to hold the farmers in the party.[18]

In Saskatchewan, where the CCF grew strongly and steadily, the circumstances were exactly the opposite. There local CCF leaders were also the province's "normal" community leaders; hence the CCF was no alien, radical import but the authentic spokesman of the rural community.[19] In Ontario, in profound contrast, the CCF was clearly an urban-oriented party motivated by an ideology both unfamiliar and essentially foreign to the rural experience and temper. And so the UFO left, to begin the inexorable drift back to the more comfortable Liberalism which Mitch Hepburn had shrewdly moulded. In Hepburn's conquest of rural Ontario in the 1934 and 1937 elections, those ridings in which UFO strength had been greatest formed the bedrock for his support; and to this day, those same areas keep the Ontario Liberal party alive. The brief alignment of the UFO was probably more of a tribute to Agnes Macphail than anything else.

All in all, then, it was perhaps inevitable that the UFO would some day simply not appear at a scheduled CCF meeting. As it happens, the Provincial Council meeting of March 10 was the most crucial in the CCF's short history. In the absence of the UFO delegates, neither of the other sections could gain control. The hopelessness of any accord was realized by the Council members, who asked the national executive once again to assume responsibility. Members of the executive present, however – Woodsworth, E. J. Garland, and Angus MacInnis – urged further discussion by the Council. Although the delegates did go through the motions again, the conclusion was obviously anticipated; Woodsworth finally produced a detailed statement prepared in advance by the national executive outlining the problem and its proposed solution:

> a) The Labour Conference [Woodsworth read] was an attempt to establish a working arrangement between rival Labour parties. Instead of providing common ground for cooperative effort, it became a new field for the struggle of party advantage. The provision for affiliated organizations lent itself admirably to well-known Communist tactics. The difficulty of maintaining discipline within such a structure was too great.
>
> b) UFO – The conditional affiliation was not satisfactory. With little sense of corporate responsibility; with a great fear of being associated with Communists, many members were influenced by considerations of temporary and local expediency . . . .
>
> c) The Clubs were hurriedly set up to provide for the needs of hundreds who desired to associate themselves with

the new movement. The organization and education of such large numbers who had been swept into the movement on a wave of emotional enthusiasm proved too heavy a task for a new organization without trairfed local membership or financial resources. The Clubs, too, became a "happy-hunting ground" for various types of cranks and for Communists. To escape from the interminable bickerings, many members withdrew in disgust.

d) The Provincial Council, erected on the basis of such organization, has proved incompetent to unify and control and direct the activities of the affiliated bodies.

Woodsworth allocated no blame for this situation. To him, the important fact was that with economic conditions as pressing as ever, the need for the CCF was greater than ever. "Thousands" still sympathized with the party's program. In Ontario, as he properly stressed, outside of Toronto and perhaps London and Stratford, the movement was in a comparatively healthy condition. Two steps, the national executive had concluded, were urgently needed: each CCF local must rid itself completely of Communist influence, and a complete reorganization of the party in Ontario must be undertaken. For this reason, Woodsworth informed a stunned meeting, it had been decided to take the most drastic action possible: the immediate suspension of the Provincial Council and the reorganization of the provincial party by the National Council. The new structure would be based on a single cohesive unit, with actual control in a central council, instead of three autonomous groups joined in a loose federation.[20]

That was all. In ten short minutes, much of the original CCF was destroyed. Leadership went as precipitately as structure. Agnes Macphail automatically ceased being a CCF member when the UFO withdrew its application. Then on March 12, Elmore Philpott announced his resignation from the party. He explained that he was the candidate in the next provincial election of UFO supporters in Halton County and felt bound to follow the UFO withdrawal. His intention, he declared, "is to work as a straight independent, particularly in the rural ridings of Ontario, to promote the same object as the CCF has in view."[21]

As usual, Philpott's firm decision was short-lived. In July, he announced his "indefinite, and perhaps permanent, withdrawal from political activity. I simply couldn't go on without some sort of income."[22] In March 1935, Philpott, who only twenty months earlier had described the capitalist system as "insane . . . murderous [and] bloody,"[23] announced he had rejoined the Liberal

Party. Since all parties had accepted social reform, he explained, any obstacle to his rejoining the Liberals had been removed.[24] In the federal election of October 1935, he was defeated as the Liberal candidate in York South.

In the eyes of the Labour Conference, Philpott's machinations vindicated their view of him and his allies. "The opportunist leadership of the CCF Clubs," in their judgement, "felt our socialism should be toned down so the CCF could be made safe for endorsation by the Toronto *Star* and other capitalist newspapers."[25] The analysis was far from unconvincing. But it tells as much about the Labour representatives as of Philpott. They refused to acknowledge the fact that the Clubs had more working class members than the Labour Conference, and refused to consider the possibility that the Club leaders authentically spoke for their members. Nor were they prepared to expel two of their prominent members who came to epitomize the general perception of the Labour section. William Moriarity was the Trotskyite who had gained national notoriety for advocating violent revolution if necessary at the Regina Convention; he was on the executive of the Labour Conference's Toronto Council. The other was Jack MacDonald, a Lovestonite, a believer in the theory of "American exceptionalism."

So far as is known, these were the only members of other formal groups who belonged to the Labour Conference. The charges of Communist infiltration were untrue; Bert Robinson and Arthur Mould became Communists after the crisis was ended. The problem was not Communists, or even Trotskyites. The problem was those who considered themselves radical socialists, CCF'ers in a hurry. They were a destructive crew: inflexible, uncompromising, utterly dogmatic, elevating intransigence to the level of a sacred principle. They held a conviction of their righteousness and a delusion of their self-importance which were totally unshakeable. Frank Underhill told of visits he and Woodsworth made to several tiny socialist and radical labour sects in Toronto and Hamilton; they found such groups instinctively suspicious of being absorbed by the larger CCF and losing their own sense of unique worth.[26] This, of course, is precisely what happened as "bourgeois reactionaries" like Macphail and Philpott rose to dominate "their movement" – as Labour's spokesmen always considered it. The psychological blow was too great to be endured. In the end, everything took precedence over the good of the cause.

But it is also tempting, in the light of this analysis, to suggest that the enemies of the Labour Conference were in fact conducting a gratuitous witchhunt to rid the CCF of non-existent Communists. It is hard to say. LeBourdais claims he only wished to expel disruptive elements.[27] It would be invidious to attempt to disentangle Philpott's motives. Agnes Macphail's position was in a sense most politically significant. Not even her radical liberal philosophy enabled her to distinguish clearly between doctrinaire Marxists and pro-Soviet Communists. But how many Ontario citizens could?

II

> There have been plenty of parties without a platform but the CCF is practically unique in being a platform without a party.[28]

The general opinion outside of CCF circles, wrote an unfriendly newspaper immediately after the suspension of the Provincial Council, was that this development "spelled the beginning of the end for that organization in Ontario .... With Miss Macphail and the gallant captain Philpott out, what remains of the CCF in Ontario?"[29] Another agreed that it would take several years to recover the ground just lost, for the stigma of disunion would be difficult to erase.[30] Who could believe there was worse to come?

In the absence of any strong leaders remaining in that province, and until a new executive was elected, the National Council took command of the vital task of the immediate rebuilding of the Ontario section of the party. On March 18, a tentative new provincial constitution was agreed upon at an informal gathering of some members of both the Labour and Club sections meeting with Woodsworth in Toronto. The plan, based on individual membership to the provincial party through constituency organizations and the election of the provincial council from the convention at large, was generally approved by those present. It would, of course, have to be ratified by the provincial convention called for the following month. With individual membership as the keystone, the new council would have complete disciplinary powers over each member; further, no longer would there be affiliation by group, with the inherent danger that a member of the group, though belonging to another political party, would be entitled to represent himself as a CCF'er.[31]

In the meantime, however, groups still existed, and the Labour Conference, as usual, was in opposition to whatever was put forth by any leaders other than its own. On March 30, its executive "bitterly assailed" the proposed new constitution. With the old charges that "opportunists and canny politicians" were plotting to "rule out of the CCF all those who would make it a working class movement," it declined absolutely to depart from the original principle of federation as a group and join the reconstructed party as individuals. Of the eight Labour delegates elected to attend the CCF convention in April, at least five were considered more or less unfriendly to the new proposals; and despite all that had previously transpired, William Moriarity and Jack MacDonald were among the eight selected.[32]

The convention opened on April 14, with Woodsworth in attendance. From the first, most delegates believed it would see a power struggle between those supporting the new draft constitution and the representatives of the Labour Conference. In this they were wrong only to the extent that what occurred was far too decisive to be considered a struggle. It was soon evident the Labour delegates would be impotent except in creating confusion and wasting time. And, inevitably, the more their impotence was revealed, the more vociferous and objectionable they became. Through the tumultuous fifteen-hour session – it ended well after midnight – not a single matter was greeted with accord by the delegates: not the adopting of the constitution, not the electing of new officers, not even the unexpected appearance of Agnes Macphail on the convention floor, which elicited scattered boos as well as wild cheers.

The National Executive's proposed constitution, by basing representation on council and to conventions on numerical strength, would effectively eliminate the tiny Labour Conference as a significant entity within the CCF. Similarly, with affiliation possible only through individual membership in a constituency unit, the Labour Conference as such would lose its *raison d'être*. Furthermore, article three of the document demanded not only acceptance by members of the CCF's program and principles, but "strict adherence" to its constitution. Obviously this was totally unacceptable to the Labour section's leaders, and the question of its adoption gave rise to a bitter and sometimes violent debate.

In a lengthy statement circulated in the convention hall by Edith Morton on behalf of the Labour Conference, the delegates were assured that it was not Labour's refusal to accept Council decisions which had been the cause of strife.

> All differences of opinion have centred around the working class policy and socialist approach of the Labour Section as against the reformist policy of the Club and Farmer Sections. . . . It is quite all right for Agnes Macphail and Elmore

Philpott to champion a "Christian Revolution," but it is a horse of another colour when others, *with more accuracy and sounder judgment,* advocate a Socialist revolution as the only way out for workers and farmers.

Reiterating Labour's opposition to a party based on individual membership, the statement concluded with a belligerent demand for the retention of the Labour Conference within a federated party structure.[33] In the end, the National Executive's constitution was adopted with only a few minor changes, with the minority continuing its opposition until the final word received endorsement.

The debate on the constitution lasted an entire morning and afternoon. The entire evening was needed to elect a new slate of provincial officers. The same Labour techniques characterized the elections. While certain of its nominated members declined to run on principle, Labour delegates continued to use every possible excuse to disrupt and delay the proceedings. Finally, after rousing choruses by the small band of dissidents of the "Internationale" and "The Red Flag," the new officers were duly elected.[34] John Mitchell, the new president, was a Hamilton trade unionist and alderman; his election was clearly a compromise aimed at gaining the support of moderate labour people. The Labour Conference delegates achieved a certain revenge when they helped Graham Spry defeat LeBourdais for the vice-presidency. The remainder of the Council included Herbert Orloff as secretary; three labour representatives (Arthur Williams of the East York Workers, Ben Levert of Windsor, and Thomas Cruden, former president of the Socialist Party of Canada); a United Church minister, a dentist and a businessman.[35]

It was a body which well illuminated the CCF's new character. Significantly, there was no single leader in the entire group who could stir party members and sympathizers as Agnes Macphail and Philpott had done. John Mitchell, who was to remain president through most of the decade, was an honest, God-fearing, moderate Christian socialist, with great integrity and a burning social conscience. He was able to evoke mild respect, but little love and no passion. Graham Spry certainly played a leading and often dominating role in the party until his sudden resignation in 1937, but he too lacked the personal qualities to become the CCF's motivating force. Until 1942, the Ontario CCF was destined to suffer the serious handicap of having no single outstanding personality to assume the role of provincial leader, an office which did not exist until that time.

Moreover, the Provincial Council's composition revealed the narrow scope of the CCF's following in Ontario. Glaringly conspicuous by their absence were any members who could have been considered even remotely as rural representatives. Council membership provided, too, an accurate mirror of the party's geographical strength and weaknesses. Virtually its entire membership was drawn from the major urban areas of Toronto, Hamilton, London, Windsor, and Peterborough. Even then there was no representation from the two major labour congresses. The only redeeming feature of the Council was the number of members who represented middle class elements in the community – a businessman, a dentist, a newspaperman, and a minister; indeed, during its entire existence, about half of the CCF's leaders at any given moment were derived from the middle class. The party always had a disproportionately large share of Rhodes Scholars who belonged to the United Church.

Finally, the Council indicated that the party had successfully eliminated the "troublemakers." Except for Arthur Williams, none of the labour representatives had been identified previously with the extremist wing of the Labour Conference; and Williams had accepted office against the express wishes of the East York Workers' Association which he represented.[36] The day after the convention, Edith Morton announced on its behalf that the Labour Section as a unit considered itself excluded from the CCF under the new constitution. Asked if the majority of the Conference's members would rejoin the CCF as individuals, she replied that it would likely be a close division, with the anti-CCF group probably forming a small majority.[37] On the following day, the Socialist Party announced the withdrawal of its five branches (four in Toronto, one in London), from the CCF, since with the new constitution and council, the "socialists" had been eliminated from the party.[38] In the end, however, it appears that only a minority of labour bodies remained irrevocably alienated from the party.[39]

Nevertheless, the CCF had certainly suffered severe damages. The months of strife and the final crisis had taken their toll in terms of a shattered image, disrupted organization, and reduced membership. Indeed, the party avoided announcing its membership total, though it was clear many members had quit during the preceding year. Consequently, although harmony seemed to have been restored, the CCF's condition was in reality far worse than it had been during the first year of its existence. Then, although with neither financial resources nor a party newspaper, it at least had recognized leaders and a favourable climate of opinion. By the spring of 1934, it still had no paper; it still had no money – exactly forty-five dollars had been expended in the previous year (the provincial convention was financed entirely by the delegates);[40] it no longer had compelling leaders such as Philpott and Agnes Macphail; and the tide of public opinion had clearly ceased what had once appeared as its inexorable flow towards the cooperative commonwealth. And worst of all, it abruptly found itself – almost totally unprepared – in the midst of its first major election campaign.

References

1. Toronto *Mail and Empire*, January 2, 1934. In Hamilton, Sam Lawrence was elected controller and five CCF candidates were chosen aldermen. Toronto *Star* December 28, 1933.

2. A. E. Smith, *All My Life* (Toronto, 1949), pp. 163-8.

3. Macphail Private Papers, volume 1, Philpott to Macphail, February 19, 1934.

4. Stewart and French, *Ask No Quarter*, p. 177.

5. Toronto *Star*, February 19, 1934.

6. Toronto *Mail and Empire*, February 20, 1934.

7. *Ibid.*, February 22, 1934.

8. Walter Young, *Anatomy of a Party: The National CCF, 1932-61* (Toronto, 1968), p. 234.

9. Macphail Public Papers, volume 1, Correspondence, Scott and Hannam to Macphail, February 20, 1934.

10. Macphail Private Papers, volume 1, *Rise of the CCF,* Macphail to Philpott. February 23, 1934.

11. Toronto *Mail and Empire*, February 26, 1934.

12. Toronto *Star*, February 26, 1934.

13. Toronto *Mail and Empire*, February 26, 1934.

14. Macphail Public Papers, volume 1, Correspondence, Hannam and Scott to LeBourdais, March 1, 1934.

15. Margaret Stewart interview with Philpott, copy in her collection of Macphail Private Papers, volume 1, *Rise of the CCF*.

16. *Ibid.*, March 12, 1934.

17. D'Arcy Marsh, *Canadian Forum*, July 1934.

18. Stewart and French, *Ask No Quarter*, p. 266.

19. Lipset, *Agrarian Socialism*, pp. 180-3, 187.

20. Loeb Papers, Woodsworth's Memorandum to the CCF Provincial Council, March 10, 1934.

21. Quoted in letter from LeBourdais to CCF Clubs, March 12, 1934. Loeb Papers.

22. P.A.C., Woodsworth Papers, volume 3, Philpott to Woodsworth, July 23, 1934.

23. *Weekly Sun*, June 8, 1933.

24. *New Commonwealth*, March 9, 1935.

25. Loeb Papers, Labour Conference executive to all affiliated organizations, undated.

26. Underhill interview, 1961.

27. LeBourdais interview, 1961.

28. Hal Frank, *Saturday Night*, March 24, 1934.

29. Toronto *Mail and Empire*, March 13, 1934.

30. *Saturday Night*, March 24, 1934.

31. Toronto *Mail and Empire*, March 19, 1934.

32. Toronto *Star*, March 31, 1934; Toronto *Globe*, March 31, April 2, 1934.

33. Loeb Papers, Labour Conference Statement to Special CCF Convention, April 14, 1934.

34. Toronto *Globe*, April 16, 1934; Toronto *Star*, April 16, 1934; Toronto *Mail and Empire*, April 16, 1934.

35. Loeb Papers, Report of the Annual Provincial Convention, April 20, 1935.

36. Toronto *Globe*, April 16, 1934.

37. *Ibid.;* Toronto *Mail and Empire*, April 16, 1934.

38. Toronto *Mail and Empire*, April 17, 1934.

39. Harry Hatfield recalled that many labour people returned to the CCF either by transforming their organizations into constituency clubs or by joining established CCF Clubs.

40. Toronto *Globe*, April 30, 1934.

5 THE FIRST MORAL VICTORIES

I

The historical significance of the Ontario election of June 19, 1934 lies in Mitch Hepburn's victory, not in the CCF's defeat. For Hepburn, the election was the climax of a brilliant four-year campaign to rebuild the provincial Liberal party, and when he finished he was unbeatable. To no avail did Premier George Henry brand him as an irresponsible, impractical radical with "dictatorial ambitions" who aimed to become "the Dolfuss, the Lenin, the Stalin and the Trotsky of Ontario business."[1] Not even the Toronto *Telegram's* startling revelation of a "Papist plot" between Hepburn and the Catholic Taxpayers Association could stand in the way.

On the hustings, Hepburn was incomparable: colourful, vigorous, mocking, intuitively exploiting those fears and anxieties which the Depression raised everywhere. At the same time, his well-publicized alliances with Harry Nixon of the rural Progressive Party and a number of prominent labour personalities – Arthur Roebuck, Sam McBride, David Croll, Sam Factor – served greatly to increase his party's appeal.

Hepburn concentrated most of his attacks against the Conservative government. The poor CCF he largely ignored. This treatment was warranted. Initially, after all, the party intended not to enter the election. Bert Robinson reflected the attitude of many party members when he declared that "the CCF is interested primarily in federal politics. We must not be turned away for any side-show like provincial politics. . . ."[2] According to Hepburn's biographer, three issues beside the Depression constituted "the stuff of politics in Ontario during the early 1930's"; these were "liquor, religion and electricity,"[3] and the CCF had no official policy on any of them.

As for its attitude towards provincial elections, after the initial decision against any participation, the party decided to contest seats only where it was "reasonably sure of success." Once the election was called, however, enthusiasm was such as to justify an announcement that the CCF would nominate in every riding but two which already had UFO canadidates.[4] Finally, thirty-seven CCF candidates were nominated – there were 90 seats – five of them in rural ridings. The party could not manage the lofty ambition of running a full-slate any more than it could carry out, where there was a candidate, the sophisticated canvassing techniques which were considered the ideal.[5] In fact, few ridings outside of a handful in Toronto and Hamilton conducted any serious campaign. Most of them simply lacked the manpower.[6] In a few, the conviction that a socialist triumph was ultimately inevitable no doubt militated against the mundane work of election organizing. Nor was there effective direction from the centre; the total expenditures of provincial headquarters during the campaign came to 80 dollars.[7]

Despite all these insuperable obstacles, however, observers found the CCF campaign to be driven by a "militant, crusading spirit."[8] According to one reporter, "vilification and self-praise are keys to the campaign [of the old parties]. In the absence of issues personalities have become paramount. . . . There are . . . only vague and contradictory generalizations."[9] In contrast, noted another, CCF candidates "everywhere refrained from indulging in personalities or innuendo,"[10] The CCF, the Winnipeg *Free Press* correspondent explained, was not basing its campaign "on special interests. The CCF stands on its manifesto. The general campaign consists of attacks on the capitalist system and the two old parties."[11]

Three days before the election, the CCF held a mass rally in Toronto, addressed by E. J. Garland, the Alberta Labour M.P. To the three thousand cheering enthusiasts who crammed Massey Hall, Garland predicted that the continued Depression in Canada would result in a "period of chaos" followed by a "type of dictatorship." To prevent this, he called for economic planning in general, and socialization of the banks as the first immediate step in bringing about improved conditions. "We aren't aliens; we aren't anarchists; we aren't going to take the farmers' farms," he promised, clearly on the defensive. Describing a system which permitted suffering and privation in a land of plenty as "un-Christian" and "sacrilegious," Garland declared that "the law of the jungle" existed in Canada.

> Our children [he warned] are being trained in it. Our capitalistic system belongs in an age of barbarism. . . . It doesn't matter whether you vote for Hepburn or Henry, you'll get

the same result from both. This movement is the only one that stands for the definite retention of private ownership. It stands for a man owning his home, his own goods, his own farm. You don't get that under capitalism.[12]

Yet not even as the defender of private property could the CCF influence the results; "seldom had there been so decisive a reversal in Canadian political history."[13] Of Henry's eighty-four members, only seventeen were returned. The Liberals' fifteen incumbents mushroomed into sixty-five, but four Liberal-Progressives and the Liberal-Labour victory gave them seventy out of the ninety seats.[14] Hepburn received a majority vote from virtually all elements and in all areas of the province, amassing a total vote 150,000 greater than that of the hapless Henry.[15] The northern and western areas of the province fell completely before the Liberal onslaught, as did every rural riding in Ontario with the exception of a few in the Orange-dominated east.

For the CCF, the 1934 election was a disaster. Sam Lawrence in Hamilton East was the only successful CCF candidate, and, in fact, Lawrence was the only Ontario socialist to sit in either Ottawa or Queen's Park during the ten long years from 1932 to 1942. The party polled 108,961 votes, or 7.1 per cent of all votes cast. Only six thousand of these were in agricultural ridings. In metropolitan areas (as opposed to urban ridings with small cities or towns), its percentage was a barely respectable 14.5; of the total CCF vote, 71 per cent was polled in sixteen ridings which fell within five major industrial centres. Of these, Toronto and Hamilton were the most important. In Toronto, CCF candidates made strong showings in half a dozen ridings, although coming second only in one, and rolled up a city vote of 49,000. The Hamilton vote was even more impressive: Liberals 28,400 (three seats), Conservatives 28,000 (no seats), CCF 20,242 (one seat).[16] In Hamilton East, Sam Lawrence faced no Liberal opponent, and, had the CCF accepted a Liberal offer not to oppose John Mitchell in Wentworth if the CCF stayed out of the other two Hamilton constituencies, it is very likely Mitchell would have won.[17]

The CCF also consoled itself with the encouraging delusion that its supporters had been "serious and enthusiastic," since they had not voted in response to a high-powered and slick campaign. At least half the argument was sound, and on this basis the party delivered itself of a classic statement of groundless optimism. Its support represented, according to the new party paper,

> not a passing protest that will ebb if the depression ebbs but a solid group in Ontario who believe in the CCF policy. That vote is a foundation on which the CCF can build for power.... In both the candidate elected and the total vote polled, the CCF in Ontario has grounds for enthusiasm.[18]

It was the CCF's first moral victory. Yet party spokesmen seemed undisturbed that potential CCF supporters had been successfully attracted by a non-radical, progressive alternative. Hepburn's radicalism may have been confined to his rhetoric, but many were convinced that it was genuine; after all, both Henry and Hepburn himself had repeatedly stressed that only minor differences separated the Liberals and CCF. In rural Ontario, Hepburn was widely considered the inheritor of Drury's cloak, and received his greatest support from ridings won by the UFO in 1919. The sweeping Liberal victories in urban areas resulted from the support of a majority of working class and ethnic elements. That most workers supported Hepburn's progressivism rather than the CCF's socialism testified, of course, to their lack of class consciousness. But it was a fact of Ontario's political life.

It is no doubt true that few people knew precisely what programmes Hepburn might implement. But he had succeeded in communicating a more useful message: he had made himself credible as a New Dealer. One must distinguish between Hepburn's political image and rhetoric and the specific proposals he laid before the public. His was the radicalism of the demagogue, a red-necked populism that seemed plausible and appealing to a people who longed during the Depression for strong and positive leadership. Hepburn offered few constructive, meaningful policies. One of the his most consistently effective techniques was his promise to slash "ruthlessly" the administrative costs of government. He attacked the "luxurious limousines" driven by members of the Henry cabinet, and pledged that no members of a government he headed would drive cars bought with the taxpayers' money. He promised to eliminate the office of the Lieutenant-Governor until the Depression was ended. His party would give Ontario Hydro "courageous and economical" direction, in contrast to Henry's management which "reeked of graft, corruption and maladministration." He "endorsed" unemployment insurance and "reasonable" wage scales and hours of labour, and declared for "the British principle of free speech and the right of assembly."[19] This, surely, was the form of radicalism without its substance. In the United States, this same kind of appeal was winning great support for the Huey Longs, Francis Townshends, and Father Coughlins. In Ontario, it had propelled a crafty onion farmer from the back hustings to an astonishing victory.

In social as well as political terms, Hepburn's Liberals were more palatable to most Ontario voters than was the CCF. In certain ways, the CCF represented the worst of all worlds. Its enemies characterized it as an alien import. Ideologically this was more valid than not. Though its Christian socialist and British Labour roots gave it some respectability in the Ontario community, ultimately it was beyond the political culture's mainstream.

Ethnically, the picture was more complex. So far from being alien, the CCF was dominated by the United Church. Its leaders were Anglo-Saxon, Protestant, middle class, and highly educated; many belonged to the Orange Lodge. Its membership was overwhelmingly of British descent. Herbert Orloff (later Orliffe) was the only senior officer in the Ontario CCF from a minority group.[20] This traditional ethnocentricity hardly made the party more appealing to Ontario's growing number of Italians, Poles, and Jews. Ironically, however, the CCF's Waspiness was not representative either. It had too many Oxford graduates. It had too many social gospellers. It had too many extremists even among its Christians; a substantial section within the party, represented by William Temple and Reverend Ben Spence, was always intransigently prohibitionist – and usually on the party's left. Another group, which included Jimmy Simpson, mayor of Toronto, was fanatically anti-Catholic. Almost from the beginning, then, there was something about the CCF to alienate just about everyone.

It was, in consequence, not unconvincing for the press to begin sounding the death-knell for the CCF. As third parties had always done, this Depression-produced aberration was bound to fade in the face of good Canadian common sense.[21] Only the CCF disagreed. Their spokesmen described the results as providing a strong foundation for the coming federal campaign. To the hundred thousand faithful would be added "thousands" more as the party pursued its educational and organizational activities. The quintessential election eve comment came from Reverend Stanley Elliot, the CCF candidate who had eked out second place in Toronto-Beaches, and who felt "we have made a great start." He reminded his supporters that his campaign had run only three weeks and on a meagre 350 dollars. "We don't feel a bit discouraged. Remember the beginnings of the Labour Party in Britain. . . . "[22]

The doom-sayers and Mr. Elliot could not both be right; but events were soon to prove that they both could be wrong.

II

Hepburn began his Premiership in high style. Cabinet ministers' salaries were reduced. Government automobiles were sold at a huge public auction. The entire civil service was overhauled in "Operation Broom."[23] A group of two hundred "Hunger Marchers" which the Toronto Chief of Police had banned as being part of a Bolshevik plot, was received warmly at Queen's Park by Hepburn and Roebuck.[24] Following this, Roebuck announced, to the expressed delight of Aaron Mosher, Tom Moore of the T.L.C., and the Toronto *Star*, that the government intended to introduce legislation establishing industrial standards or codes for all industries in Ontario. The codes were designed to abolish sweat-shop conditions, and any firm violating them, Roebuck promised, would be fined.[25]

Whatever other effects Hepburn's actions were having, they had successfully begun to undermine the appeal of the CCF. This had the salutary result of awakening many socialists to the difficulties that faced them. The facile illusion common only a year earlier of accomplishing great things with little effort was dispelled. "Their experience with practical politics evaporated most of their naive optimism and brought some realization of the amount of spade work to be done by those who would dig the foundations of a new social order."[26]

An official party organ, the *New Commonwealth*, was introduced. Though it rarely transcended its origins as a hack sheet for the converted, it soon had 5500 subscribers. Soon the paper launched the first of an infinite series of special financial appeals to enable the party to hire more organizers, buy radio time, "flood" the province with free literature, and build up an election fund. Throughout the province, street-corner meetings, rallies, and picnics were the order of the day. The inevitable youth section was formed, the CCYM. With Felix Lazarus and Murray Cotterill as itinerant organizers, and taking themselves very seriously indeed, it was these 500 splendid men and women – with their adolescent idealism and naive optimism – who helped create the romantic myth of the 1930's as the radical or "Red" decade.[27]

It was far from that. Troubled, anxious, and groping as Canadians were, serious radicalism was too unnerving and threatening. More reassurance was necessary, and in Ontario the Liberals found the right formula. To test the political climate, Bennett called by-elections in six Ontario federal seats for September 1934. Hepburn ran much of the show for the Liberals, while Mackenzie King entered the ring to announce that a Liberal victory would bring "a great cooperative commonwealth in this country even better and greater than ever Mr. Woodsworth dreamed."[28]

The Liberals easily won five of the six by-elections. The one they lost, Toronto-Broadview, was the only one the CCF contested. Graham Spry's vote, a respectable twenty per cent, probably cost the Liberals a clean sweep. It was a disastrous outcome for the federal Tories, and not less so for the CCF. The party was confident, of course, that when people realized that "the only change is a change to socialism ... then our day will come."[29] That day would be a long way off. The bitter truth was that Hepburn's swing to the left had clearly out-manoeuvred the inexperienced young movement. Success in Ontario depended upon convincing the electorate that both old parties were wholly the puppets of Big Business. At least with the Liberals, this was now impossible. Many people in Ontario had begun to identify Liberalism with the Hepburns and Roebucks, "men that appeared not only devoid of business domination, but indeed radical and even anti-capitalist. Thus, in one stroke, the Hepburn forces had destroyed the premise upon which the success of the CCF in Ontario depended."

That the CCF had the ability to improve its position seemed doubtful. As the *Canadian Forum* pointed out, the movement had failed hitherto to exhibit any competent strategy; it had yet to bring forth a strong group of leaders; its existing leaders lacked, and were known to lack, administrative capacity; Woodsworth and his colleagues, though brilliant in Parliament, still demonstrated an opposition mentality. There was much cause for pessimism.[30]

Suddenly, for one brief moment, there appeared grounds for renewed hope. On New Year's Day, 1935, to the list of Canadian cities that had just elected socialist mayors – Vancouver, Lethbridge, Calgary, Winnipeg, and Windsor – Toronto was added. Jimmy Simpson was the CCF-Labour mayoralty candidate. Both old party organizations and Toronto dailies except the *Star* supported Simpson's only opponent, Alderman Harry Hunt, a known Conservative; the Toronto *Star* endorsed Simpson. Hunt and the newspapers charged that the CCF was under Communist influence, and Toronto's voters were urged to rally to the defence of sanity, order, and British principles. Percy Parker, head of the Toronto Liberal organization, took to the radio on Hunt's behalf to declare that "the bells of Moscow will ring when Simpson is elected mayor."[31]

The *Star*'s support, the strong organization developed by CCF'ers and trade unionists, and Simpson's personal popularity provided a most significant victory for the CCF. Toronto was the largest city in North America ever to have elected a socialist mayor. This triumph in itself gave the CCF considerable added respectability, the potential mass support with which to construct a powerful Toronto election machine, and the renewed enthusiasm to begin preparing for the federal election.

Only one day later, however, a new blow fell from a wholly unexpected source. In a series of six successive broadcasts, Prime Minister Bennett announced that the capitalist system, as it operated in Canada, must be overhauled from top to bottom, and that he was the man for the job. In order to prevent the victory of a socialist or Communist government, he promised to introduce legislation which would remove "the abuses and inequalities in the capitalistic system in order that it might survive"; his proposed reforms included limiting working hours, enforcing minimum wage laws, introducing unemployment insurance, and eliminating unfair business practices.[32]

Extreme frustration often manifests itself in perverse ways. Bennett's extraordinary *volte-face* was likely to undermine CCF support even further, and the party lashed out with irrational fury. It would show the nation what "real" radicalism was. Those CCF'ers who were swayed by Bennett's speeches, it was announced, were mere reformers who never actually believed in "real" socialism. Their defection would aid, not injure, the CCF. For with the reformers gone, the sides were neatly polarized between "reforming and preserving the capitalist system" and "establishing a socialist state."[33] How this policy of purity would attract those disdained reformers without whom no CCF victory was remotely conceivable, was never explained. But this was the party's election year policy; and in adopting it, the CCF was being uncompromisingly honest. It was to be a highly virtuous movement when it was crushed in the vital 1935 election.

The immediate task at hand was to develop an organization in preparation for the forthcoming debacle. With the impetus of the Toronto and Windsor mayoralty victories, party activities were marked by a renewed vigour and enthusiasm in all urban centres of the province. Concerts for the unemployed, distributing literature, building an election machine, attending meetings to hear Woodsworth or M. J. Coldwell, the party's new national secretary – there was always something to keep one busy.

Moreover, the suffering which the Depression – and therefore, the capitalist system – had brought in its wake continued with little abatement. Those Canadians on relief and unemployed during the 1930's were always a minority of the population, but a hideously large minority. In 1935, more than a million people in the country were on relief, a quarter of them in Ontario.[34] To the CCF's credit, it did more than just exploit this tragedy for political gain. When, in February, the Hepburn government reduced maximum relief grants for single unemployed women from eight to four dollars a week, the Toronto CCF established a special Welfare Committee to coordinate party relief and eviction protest activities throughout the city. By June, the Committee had dealt with more than one hundred eviction cases, and had aided about 150 families on relief. This work, on the whole, was done quietly, unostentatiously, and successfully.[35]

The most famous incident occurred in August when Hepburn, in order to cut "unnecessary" expenses, cancelled all relief for single, unemployed men, and had eleven hundred persons ejected from Toronto hostels into the city streets. The CCF took charge immediately and made all its organizational facilities available to feed and shelter the men. Handbills were printed and circulated, radio time purchased, and sound trucks secured, all used to publicize the location of its committee rooms and to appeal to Toronto citizens for assistance. For two days, the CCF's fifteen city club houses fed and housed from six to eight hundred of the evicted men. So great was the outcry against Hepburn's "economizing" that within forty-eight hours of issuing the eviction order he relented and instructed the hostels to re-admit the men. The CCF, noted *Saturday Night*, reaped incalculable prestige from the entire affair.[36]

Welfare work, then, combined with regular unit meetings, public rallies, study groups, social functions, euchres, and educational forums, assured that few CCF members had an inactive moment in the hectic, enthusiastic months that characterized the pre-election period. Through the spring and summer months the mood of the party was one of reasoned optimism, and when Bennett called the election for October 14, the CCF considered itself ready. The party had waited long for its first crucial general election, and it was determined to make the most of it.

III

Four national parties contested the 1935 election, and all based their appeal to a greater or lesser extent on programmes of reform. The Reconstruction Party of H. H. Stevens, a former senior colleague of Bennett, like the flexible old parties, offered a reformed capitalism. The CCF showed little flexibility, and received a decent amount of attention from Bennett and King. Nevertheless, if the prodigious energy spent discrediting Harry Stevens is any evidence, they both regarded him as a greater political threat than they did the CCF.

Most attacks on the CCF were notably straightforward. A Toronto Liberal candidate caught the spirit admirably: "A Vote for the CCF is a vote for Communism."[37] More spectacular, however, was the bold accusation of "a secret and sinister conspiracy to effect a united front between the Communist Party in Canada and the CCF." The accuser was Captain Elmore Philpott, in his capacity as a Liberal candidate in York South, and his evidence was a pamphlet issued by the National Communist Election Committee. The pamphlet called for a "united front . . . to elect a majority of Communist and CCF candidates."[38] This was the full extent of Philpott's proof that the CCF was in collusion with the Communists.

Yet the charge succeeded in re-opening the CCF's most unbridgeable internal gap. Shortly after Philpott's speech, William Douglas, a trade union official speaking on behalf of Fred Fish, CCF candidate in West York, told an election meeting that "There is no great line of differentiation" between the CCF and the Communists. "The methods they apply may be slightly different but they have in common the welfare of the common people. . . . At heart I am absolutely a Communist and proud of the fact. . . . [Both parties] are opposed to the capitalist system which prevails today." Fish, in turn, stated that all groups – Communists, socialists, "even vivisectionists" – who stood by the principles he upheld were "very, very welcome."[39]

Fish and Douglas may well have represented the views of many CCF members, but the fact remained that they were deliberately repudiating official party policy. This of course suited the Communists perfectly. They, apparently, had been surprised at the CCF's relatively strong vote in the Ontario and British Columbia elections. They believed their twin objectives of gaining the support of the Canadian workers while destroying the democratic socialist movement had suffered a distinct set-back. This problem had been discussed in considerable detail at the party's annual conference in December 1934. Stewart Smith, party theorist, told the gathering that "We must on no account allow the CCF to step forward as the working class alternative to the two old parties, as it was able to do in the provincial elections up to now. We must make such an application of our revolutionary mass policy as to prevent the CCF from appearing in the eyes of the masses as the only alternative to the two old parties.''[40]

In an election, this meant publicly offering united fronts in some ridings in order to discredit the CCF candidate, while in others opposing the CCF in order to split the labour vote. Nor, strangely, did this tactic change on August 20, 1935, when Stalin's declaration that Social Democrats were ''the moderate wing of fascism'' was officially dropped from the Communist interpretation of history. In its stead, the Communist International adopted the famous resolution based on the report presented by Georgi Dimitroff.

> In the face of the towering menace of fascism to the working class and all the gains it has made . . . it is imperative that unity of action be established between all sections of the working class, irrespective of what organization they belong to. . . . The Communists . . . must strive to secure joint action with the Social Democratic Parties, reformist trade unions and other organizations of the toilers against the class enemies of the proletariat on the basis of short- or long-term agreements.[41]

Once the Soviet Union adopted a policy, of course, it was to be applied automatically and mechanically everywhere. Yet it would seem that, on this occasion at least, implementation in Canada took an unusually long time. The Communist Party ran thirteen federal candidates; in only two of these was no CCF candidate running. Surely ''working class unity'' against the ''fascist menace'' should have meant no ''working class'' candidates opposing one another.

The official Communist program reiterated the proposal for electoral cooperation with the CCF ''on the basis of the common economic and political interests of the masses in this fight.''[42] But the defeat of as many CCF'ers as possible still seemed a prime objective. J. B. Salsberg's Toronto committee room window was adorned with a banner calling for his election in Spadina riding, but adding: ''Fight for the unity of the working class. Elect a majority of CCF or Communist candidates.'' Yet Salsberg was being opposed by the CCF. The Toronto *Mail and Empire* captioned its picture of Salsberg's committee room, ''Communist Links Party with CCF.'' Under the photograph was the pithy comment: ''The picture tells the story.''[43]

In fact, it was not the story at all; it was at most an interesting footnote to the real election story. This bitter and enervating competition for the hearts and votes of the Canadian working class was a pathetic farce. The people paid it no attention. The two labour congresses remained firmly neutral during the campaign.[44] The UFO executive endorsed Harry Stevens, and Agnes Macphail ran as an independent "UFO-Labour" candidate above "petty partisan politics."[45]

The CCF at least was entirely on its own. Its campaign "war chest" was pitiful – about $10,000 centrally and $500 for a central Toronto riding[46] – and its national campaign consisted of little more than speaking tours for members of parliament. In Ontario, the newly-appointed organizer, E. B. Jolliffe, assisted ridings in putting together a viable canvass organization, while the provincial election committee made available to ridings at nominal cost ten crude and vulgar canvass flyers. The party also paid for a series of fifty province-wide radio broadcasts in which D. M. LeBourdais presented the CCF viewpoint.[47] Ironically, his message may have been counter-productive, for the party constantly reminded the voters that the old parties were now offering unprecedented reforms. Such reforms, needless to say, were "puny" and "half-hearted," and could appeal only to those who sought "easy and painless solutions." No, there was only one fundamental issue at stake: "It is a fight between those who stand for capitalism and those who are opposed to it. . . . Upon this the election must be fought."[48]

The results, in that case, were unchallengeably clear. Mackenzie King romped home with 171 seats, giving him the greatest majority in Canadian history up to that time. He took fifty-six of Ontario's eighty seats, a feat unequalled by the Liberals since 1874. King could not in conscience accept the credit for the magnitude of his victory, however, for the Liberals' popular vote was 46.8 per cent, only three-fifths of a per cent more than they received in their 1930 defeat. Thus their "landslide" clearly resulted from split opposition votes. In Ontario and the West, the Liberal percentage of the vote actually decreased. Moreover, the hope of many that the 1935 election could complete the restoration begun in 1930 of two-party government received a severe blow. To be sure, both the CCF and Stevens did far worse than either had expected. Reconstruction's nearly four hundred thousand supporters could elect only Stevens himself. The CCF, with fifty-five fewer candidates, polled just 3250 votes fewer than Stevens' party, but succeeded in electing only seven members. Still, the total vote of all minor parties – these two plus Social

Credit and Communists – was almost one-quarter of all ballots cast.

In Ontario, the Liberals polled 690,000, and the CCF 129,457 or eight per cent; but the CCF ran only fifty candidates. It was unfortunate – if not disastrous – for the CCF that no less than half those candidates faced Reconstructionists. Stevens' party proved to be eastern based; ninety per cent of its support came from east of Manitoba, and most of it, like that of the CCF, lay in the larger cities. Stevens polled fourteen per cent of the vote in Toronto, the CCF fifteen per cent. Outside of Toronto, Hamilton, and London, however, the CCF received only 4.6 per cent of the total vote.[49] It was perhaps not unfitting that Agnes Macphail, whose platform was a nice combination of both CCF and Reconstructionism with an added mixture of Social Credit, was the sole successful candidate in Ontario not running on an old party ticket.

How was the CCF's terribly disappointing showing accounted for? It was a socialist party, a depression was raging, and many still cherished the myth that radicalism finds fertile soil during an economic crisis. Many reasons were suggested, and all contain some element of truth. *Maclean's* political reporter believed it was partly Woodsworth's inability to present himself as a plausible alternative to the major parties.[50] It was also true that shortly after the CCF's formation, economic conditions, if they did not improve, at least ceased to deteriorate; hence there was reason to believe that the capitalist structure had not totally crumbled, which made Woodsworth a prophet of doom.

There was general agreement as well that the entry into the political field of the Social Credit and Reconstruction parties badly damaged the CCF both directly and indirectly. In Ontario cities, wherever the CCF appeared to have a fair chance, the Reconstructionists took votes that might otherwise have gone socialist. Moreover, the existence of numerous minor parties re-inforced the prevalent belief that a vote for the CCF was a vote "thrown-away" or "wasted," and rather than do that, many progressives undoubtedly supported King.[51]

Finally, CCF'ers pointed to the perennial handicap of a weak organization and lack of financial resources. All the pre-election self-congratulation in the *New Commonwealth* for the party's improved organization proved to be mere verbiage, inapplicable outside of a few ridings in Toronto, Hamilton, and London. Moreover, the Ontario party as a whole gave the impression of an organization beset by confusion. No one appeared to be in control. Except for the week Woodsworth made his tour, the

CCF presented no leaders familiar in all parts of the province. It did not, and could not, convey to the public an image of something it simply was not – a smooth-running and well-directed political party which was prepared to assume the reins of power in Canada. The public, in a word, had no reason to feel confidence in the CCF.

The CCF was unable to fulfil a widespread public need for renewed stability. Many people, perhaps most, appear in a crisis to need above all the assurance of personal future security by means not entirely disruptive of their former way of life. In Canada during the Depression, this need was met best not by radicals but by Mackenzie King. Around him, as Arthur Lower has said, he built a great centre party which had room for the many who were insecure and dissatisfied but who were not prepared to go as far as socialism. "The victory [in 1935] was not a tribute to King, it was not a proclamation in defense of liberty, it was not even a pronouncement on the issues of the day. . . . It represented the huddling together of frightened people, uncertain of their way in a chaotic world."[52] As Bruce Hutchison has written, Canada had "dismissed its own superman and pugilist, and had recalled the drab little family physician to prescribe his soothing remedies."[53]

As for the CCF, many of its members were properly disillusioned by their party's shattering defeat. Convinced by their leaders that the party would win forty to fifty seats and likely hold the parliamentary balance of power, the CCF ended up with fewer than half the members of the almost unknown Social Credit movement. The electorate had been offered a new, a utopian society, and they had irrationally, incomprehensibly, repudiated it. It was almost enough to make one doubt the perfectibility of man.

There was a different perspective on the situation to consider, however. As the *New Commonwealth* rationalized it, despite the disappointing results the CCF had irrevocably established itself in the Canadian mind; it would not disintegrate as all previous third parties had done. Was it not true that, given all the overwhelming obstacles in its path, the young movement had made satisfactory progress? Before 1931, after all,

> it would have seemed an idle boast to suggest that a social-ist movement could organize 120 ridings and support as many candidates. The tasks then seemed insuperable – no money, no press support, no organization. But those obsta-cles have been overcome and socialism is now a permanent and growing force in Canadian politics.[54]

Such rhetoric, of course, helped bolster the sagging morale of the troops. But it is unjustified simply on that account to discount its validity. For this indeed had been the first challenge to the entire nation by a movement which explicitly repudiated the historic, commonplace shibboleths of Canadian public life. Seen in that context, the CCF's nearly four hundred thousand supporters had in point of fact made history; and with just the slightest amount of forced optimism, one could look forward to steady, continued progress in the years to come.

And whatever might happen in the future, what of the great contribution to Canadian life which the party had already made? Had it not, as the *New Commonwealth* boasted, "forced all other parties to make some appeal to the public opinion the CCF created"?[55] The Toronto *Star*, in its insufferably patronizing way, agreed:

> The Cooperative Commonwealth Federation has come out of the election with a slim following. . . . Yet the CCF has, we think, accomplished much good. It has set men thinking as seldom before, and if it has been in advance of most of them, it has at any rate been a beacon lighting the way toward reform. Its work is not done. The cause of reform needs just such spade work as the CCF speakers and writers have given it.[56]

It was a fitting beginning; the party's first general election began a great tradition which ended only with its dissolution. In each general election, the CCF would be badly defeated, invariably doing worse than its leaders would compulsively promise. And in each election, another small section of the CCF platform would be taken up and advocated by one or both of the two major parties. While the Canadian socialist party called itself the CCF, it was doomed to lose every national and almost every provincial election it contested, and destined to see an inordinate number of its "utopian" welfare schemes implemented by parties which had once passionately denounced them one and all.

References

1. *Saturday Night*, June 16, 1934.
2. Loeb Papers, Bert Robinson to CCF affiliates, May 30, 1933; *Weekly Sun*, June 15, July 13, 1933; Toronto *Globe*, June 17, 1933.
3. McKenty, *Mitch Hepburn*, p. 40. The CCF would have "removed the liquor question from politics" by having all decisions made by public referenda. Toronto *Star*, May 22, 1934.
4. D. W. Buchanan, *Saturday Night*, August 25, 1934; G. V. Ferguson, Winnipeg *Free Press*, June 9, 1934; Toronto *Star*, June 5, 1934.
5. D. M. LeBourdais Papers, Organization of Ontario for the 1934 Election; Suggestions for Sub-Organizers or Constituency Organizers; Suggestions for each Constituency Council.

6. Loeb Papers, Report of the Annual Provincial Convention, April 20, 1934.

7. Loeb Papers, 1935, Provincial Convention Report; *New 'Commonwealth*, July 21, 1934.

8. G. V. Ferguson, Winnipeg *Free Press*, June 9, 1934.

9. R. E. Knowles, Jr., *Saturday Night*, June 9, 1934.

10. D. W. Buchanan, *ibid.*, August 25, 1934.

11. Ferguson, Winnipeg *Free Press*, June 9, 1934.

12. Toronto *Star*, June 16, 1934.

13. *C.A.R.*, 1934, p. 177.

14. The *Canadian Forum* pointed out, however, that a strictly proportional result would have given the Liberals forty-two seats, the Conservatives thirty-six, the CCF seven, and Independents five (July 1934).

15. According to Roderick Lewis' *Statistical History of all the Electoral Districts of the Province of Ontario*, the final totals were Liberals 778,137; Conservatives 619,384; and CCF 108,961. It should be noted that the *C.A.R.*, 1934, p. 178; the *Canadian Parliamentary Guide*, 1935; and D. A. Bristow, *Agrarian Interest in Ontario Politics*, p. 254, all give totals different from Lewis and different from each other. Lewis's is the latest volume.

16. D. H. Wrong, "Ontario Provincial Elections," *C.J.E.P.S.*, August 1957, p. 398; Bristow, *op. cit.*, p. 254; Oakley Dalgleish, Winnipeg *Free Press*, July 13, 1934; *Canadian Parliamentary Guide*, 1935.

17. D. W. Buchanan, *Saturday Night*, August 25, 1934, claimed the CCF was offered seats by the Liberals, money by the Conservatives, in exchange for not running candidates in certain specific ridings. The Ontario Provincial Executive affirmed that such offers were made, and, without exception, rejected. (Report of the Annual Provincial Convention, April 20, 1935, Loeb Papers.) At the Hamilton nominating convention, a large minority of the delegates favoured contesting only Hamilton East and Wentworth. Since the Liberals had already nominated in Hamilton Centre and Hamilton-Wentworth, it was rumoured that the minority, composed of Hamilton's more experienced Labour men, had reason to expect that if the CCF ignored these two ridings, the Liberals would not oppose Sam Lawrence and John Mitchell. The majority decided, however, against any "understanding" with the Liberals and nominated in all four seats. Toronto *Mail and Empire*, April 23, 1934. The Liberals still did not run against Lawrence, apparently realizing his personal popularity would assure a Conservative victory if the Liberals opposed him. Rather than give the Conservatives a seat, Hepburn conceded it to the CCF.

18. *New Commonwealth*, July 21, 1934.

19. *C.A.R.*, 1934, pp. 175-177.

20. Stewart Smith, *The United Church and Social Action in the 1930's*, unpublished undergraduate research paper (University of Toronto, 1961), pp. 30-34; Lipsett, *Agrarian Socialism*, p. 173; Zakuta, *A Protest Movement Becalmed*, pp. 31, 35-36.

21. Toronto *Globe*, June 21, 1934; Toronto *Mail and Empire*, June 21, 1934.

22. Toronto *Mail and Empire*, June 20, 1934.

23. *C.A.R.*, 1934, pp. 183-4; Toronto *Star*, August 1, 1934; Toronto *Globe*, August 2, 1934.

24. Toronto *Mail and Empire*, August 1, 1934.

25. Toronto *Globe*, September 12, 1934; Toronto *Star*, September 22, 1934.

26. Stuart Legge, *Saturday Night,* September 22, 1934.

27. For CCF activities, see any issue of the *New Commonwealth.* Murray Cotterill, Fred Dowling, and Eamon Park were but three of the CCYM leaders who later became influential union officials in Canada.

28. Toronto *Star*, September 21, 1934.

29. *New Commonwealth*, September 29, 1934.

30. *Canadian Forum*, December 1934.

31. Cited in *New Commonwealth*, January 5, 1935.

32. *C.A.R.*, 1935-6, pp. 2-4, 11, 13.

33. *New Commonwealth* January 12, 1935.

34. *Saturday Night*, June 1, 1935.

35. *New Commonwealth*, March 2 and June 15, 1935.

36. *Saturday Night*, August 10, 1935; *New Commonwealth*, August 10, 1935.

37. Toronto *Globe*, October 2, 1935.

38. Toronto *Star*, September 27, 1935.

39. *Ibid.*, October 7, 1935.

40. Report of the Seventh Session of the Communist Party of Canada, December 7 and 8, 1934, pp. 33-5, quoted in *New Commonwealth*, October 12, 1935.

41. *Resolutions of the Seventh Congress of the Communist International* (New York, 1935), pp. 25-31.

42. Tim Buck, *Thirty Years*, p. 110.

43. Toronto *Mail and Empire*, October 5, 1935.

44. *Canadian Congress Journal*, July 1935; *Canadian Unionist*, August and September 1935.

45. Macphail Private Papers, Grey-Bruce UFO-Labour Riding Association Newspaper, undated.

46. *New Commonwealth,* January 4, 1936.

47. Toronto *Star*, September 24 and September 20, 1935; *New Commonwealth*, August 17 and October 19, 1935.

48. *New Commonwealth*, September 28, 1935.

49. Escott Reid, "The Canadian Election of 1935," *American Political Science Review*, volume XXX, February 1936, pp. 111-13, 117.

50. Politician With a Notebook, *Maclean's*, August 15, 1935.

51. *Saturday Night*, editorial, October 19, 1935; Robert Caygeon, *ibid*, November 9, 1935; *New Commonwealth,* October 12 and October 19, 1935.

52. Arthur R. M. Lower, *Colony to Nation* (Toronto, 1964), p. 519.

53. Bruce Hutchison, *Incredible Canadian* (Toronto, 1952), p. 201.

54. *New Commonwealth*, October 12 and October 26, 1935.

55. *Ibid.*, October 12, 1935.

56. Toronto *Star*, October 17, 1935.

6 THE CCF IN LIMBO

For almost seven years after the 1935 election, the Ontario CCF simply did not count as a political factor in the province. Its almost total neglect by the press was no plot to keep the public in ignorance; the CCF was just not news. There was even a conspicuous lack of conviction in its leaders' hyperbolic rhetoric. Between 1935 and early 1942, the CCF assumed almost all the characteristics of an isolated sect, whose activities were conducted in a strangely unreal world entirely of its own making. Little the party said or did was of any significance outside its own small, faithful band of followers. It is not a period which calls for detailed attention.

This long, lugubrious interval began, fittingly, with James Simpson's defeat in his bid for re-election as mayor of Toronto. His fanatical anti-Catholicism cost him the essential support of the Toronto *Star*, which in turn virtually assured his defeat. From that point on, the party marched steadily downhill. It carried on busily in its private world of make-believe, with its euchres and bingoes, whist drives and dances, study groups and fund-raisings, amateur shows and concert nights, debates and street-corner meetings. On the streets, one participant later recalled, usually only a few kids would bother listening.[1] Conventions were held, solemn resolutions passed, and no one outside the party listened or was influenced. The need for improved organizational effort was incessantly harped upon, yet somehow no new inroads could be made. As the international situation steadily deteriorated, CCF declarations against war and fascism began to assume increasing prominence. By the middle of 1936, party members were vicariously fighting the battles of the Spanish Civil War.

And they also continued their more real, if infinitely more irrelevant, battle with the Communist Party for the putative leadership of the working class. The C.P.'s continuing call for a united front in general, and for a May Day "peace parade" in particular, seemed eminently sensible to many CCF'ers. Although the provincial council in April 1936 overwhelmingly re-affirmed the traditional policy against popular fronts, several leaders of the Toronto Regional Council became officers of the United May Day Conference in Toronto. The Provincial Council unanimously demanded the expulsion of those members, and of the four riding associations which had participated in the May Day celebrations.[2]

The dissidents reacted vigorously. They managed to bring 400 supporters to a meeting to protest the Council's actions. When the Council remained unmoved, a second large meeting in June unanimously endorsed a resolution to appeal directly to the National Council.[3] The appeal was successful. The Ontario Council was forced to back down and reinstate all the expelled units. At the same time, the national convention clarified the general position: complete political independence, of course, must be maintained, but the CCF declared itself ready to "cooperate and participate in immediate struggles."[4] This was, in a very real sense, a victory for the Communist Party. The convention's decision clearly contradicted the Ontario policy banning any cooperation with the C.P., but the Ontario Council announced its reluctant agreement to support the new national policy.[5] There was not much left of the Ontario party, but at least what there was would remain intact.

This kind of make-work crisis helped party members keep busy and feel useful. It also illuminates the basic attitude of the CCF towards Communism and the Communist Party of Canada in the thirties. It is clear that, except on the important question of violence, most socialists did not believe the difference between themselves and Communists to be irreconcilable. Both rank and file members and party leaders considered the Communists to be representatives of the working class, ultimately interested in the attainment of the perfect socialist utopia. This classless society was thought to be only quantitatively different from the one being built in Russia, and, with only minor changes, a society acceptable to most Canadian social democrats.

It was precisely this fear of the Communist Party as a competitor that accounts for the ambivalence of the CCF's attitude towards it. Both sides believed they were locked in mortal combat to determine the leadership of the Canadian working class; never mind the workers' support for the old parties: that was dismissed as a temporary aberration. But CCF'ers were not entirely confident that they could win this struggle, despite the electoral evidence to the contrary. They always retained a kind of terrified awe of Communist Party members for their utter dedication and cool amorality.[6] Yet since they were of the "left," there was deemed to be some crucial, natural affinity. Social democrats are always easy prey for self-styled radicals, however dangerous or irrational. It is a mushy, unjustified, and sometimes suicidal vulnerability. It helps account for the embarrassingly long time before the CCF acknowledged the true nature of Soviet Communism and of its sycophantic Canadian apologists.

The measure of the sham battle which the CCF and C.P. were waging was that neither organization was integrally involved in the truly significant Canadian labour drama that was beginning to unfold. Early in 1937, the Congress of Industrial Organization was imported into Ontario. The C.I.O. stimulated Ontario workers more in a matter of months than the T.L.C. and A.C.C.L. had done in a decade. Not surprisingly, it also provoked those who liked their workers docile. In the spring, Mitch Hepburn transformed a minor labour dispute at the General Motors plant in Oshawa into the most notorious strike in Ontario's history.[7]

It was a masterful political stroke. At one and the same time, Hepburn won the gratitude of the province's panicky industrialists and mine owners; of the large number of rural people and the significant Catholic and Protestant groups who, in their paranoia, were uninterested in Jesuitical distinctions between communists and labour militants; of all those who had once relied mainly on the Tories as the bulwark against godless radicalism; and, most shockingly, of organized labour. The All-Canadian Congress of Labour violently denounced the C.I.O. as "lawless Yankee invaders," while the T.L.C. tamely followed the ultra-conservative line of the American Federation of Labour.[8] Neither could tolerate a successful competitor.

For all those very compelling reasons, Hepburn called a completely unexpected election for October 6. It was no contest. Earl Rowe, the new Conservative leader, was not in the same league; even regular Tory contributors deserted to Hepburn.[9] The CCF was not a serious factor. It ran only thirty-nine candidates, fifteen of them in Toronto alone, and emerged with the smallest vote it ever polled in a provincial election – 83,000 or 5.4 per cent. Sam Lawrence's decisive defeat by a Liberal in Hamilton East ended CCF representation in Queen's Park for the next six years. In no riding did the CCF come second. The *Canadian Annual Review* said it all: "the results brought virtual elimination of the last struggling relics of third parties in Ontario."[10]

Indeed, almost everyone but the poor deluded CCF knew its demise was now inevitable. Since the party believed Hepburn's re-election meant nothing less than control of Ontario by "a group of capitalists based upon the northern mines," it followed that a socialist movement was as indispensable in 1937 as ever before.[11] Moreover, socialism was still pre-ordained. The party insisted its defeat had been caused by temporary, mutable factors which, when overcome, would remove all real obstacles in the CCF's path. This path led inexorably towards a new social order. "We cannot," declared the provincial Council,

> be beaten ultimately. The world is slowly but surely turning to socialism as the solution of its economic ills .... The results [of the election] do not discourage us .... With ideals such as we stand for, it would take more than a single defeat to discourage us .... [The CCF will grow] until it achieves its goal of socialism.[12]

With this unshakeable belief, the CCF was able to survive during the remainder of the decade – but only barely. The number of True Believers steadily declined, and those that remained were, though faithful, disillusioned and unenthusiastic. Looking at the condition of his party in Ontario and at the generally dismal Canadian and international scenes, M. J. Coldwell sadly concluded that the year 1937 had been one of "opportunities missed," and of "keen disappointments." The nation, Coldwell wrote, was drifting along hoping "something will turn up,"[13] and the CCF drifted along, listlessly, with it.

Nothing did turn up. Abroad, the war clouds spread and darkened. At home, the five hundred thousand unemployed and the one million on relief had become a public bore and nuisance.[14] As for the CCF, it was virtually comatose. Its leaders, well-meaning but uninspired and mediocre, watched helplessly as Ontario socialism sank ever deeper into the sea of obscurity. Both the public and party supporters alike realized that the CCF had lapsed into a state of lassitude; and unless something quickly changed, its ultimate extinction seemed virtually assured. The CCF, observed the Provincial Council in 1939 with unprecedented candour, "hit bottom last year."[15]

This was was somewhat exaggerated. Somehow, the worst was still to come. Hitler's march into Poland on September 1, 1939, forced Mackenzie King finally to reveal his foreign policy. And King's decision forced the CCF to face the realities of international politics. At the cost of losing its beloved national leader, a grim national council voted to support King's declaration of war, but with so many qualifications as to make that support all but meaningless.[16] As the Nazis pressed forward ominously in the following three years, the CCF policy would move forward realistically with it. In the meantime, even with the compromise, a large number of party supporters left the movement in protest against its equivocal stand – some supporting Woodsworth's pacificism, others wishing firmer action by Canada than mere economic aid to its allies. In Ontario, the problem of the war caused the creaky CCF machine to grind to a virtual halt. As the Depression decade came to an end, socialism in Ontario appeared to be a spent force. It had come to resemble, in Leo Zakuta's words, "the classic image of the radical sect. It was small, poor, ineffectively organized, and isolated from the larger society."[17]

The final proof of its demise appeared to come in the federal election on March 26, 1940. Although there was some general dissatisfaction with the government's early war effort, the results were never really in doubt. If the election was, as the *Canadian Forum* claimed, "by general agreement . . . the dullest within memory,"[18] it was also among the most decisive. King won a majority of votes across the country, including Ontario. The Ontario CCF polled a miserable 61,000 votes, 3.8 per cent of the province's total. This was half its 1935 vote, fifteen thousand less even than its piddling 1937 total. It had been virtually obliterated.

The reasons for King's great success were clear. There was a real reluctance among the voters to change the government in wartime. Prosperity was returning, income was climbing, unemployment was obviously declining. The efficient and wholehearted administration of the war was the overriding concern of a large majority of the electorate. The social issues raised by struggling third parties were at this point viewed with little or no interest. The Canadian people may not have been completely satisfied with the government's management of the war, but were not quite convinced by the Tory charges of gross inefficiency and maladministration. In general, there seemed a great reluctance about placing the nation's affairs in the hands of any but an established, familiar, more or less trustworthy institution.

This partly explains the CCF's dismal showing. Another reason, particularly relevant to Ontario, was suggested in a *Saturday Night* editorial. It was an unfair presentation of the party's war policy, but it probably reflected what most people believed. For the present, it stated,

The socialists have taken an almost isolationist position, favouring the minimum of Canadian participation short of absolute neutrality, and generally discrediting the entire war aims of Britain and France as having no significance for Canadians. We do not, therefore, see how any Canadian to whom the victory of the Allies seems the most important objective of the moment can do otherwise than vote for one of the two older parties.[19]

The CCF had become irrelevant. The public knew it. Even the party knew it. It had aimed at running only fifty candidates in the election. After "every effort in our power" was made, only twenty-four True Believers were found to make the gesture. The sense of defeatism was pervasive; all over Ontario CCF'ers decided, as the Election Committee acknowledged, that "there is no point running in *this* riding."[20] As King proceeded to weave his way through the war, Ontario socialism appeared to be a lost cause.

References

1. F. A. Brewin, *CCF 25th Anniversary Album* (1957), p. 35.

2. *New Commonwealth*, May 16, 1936; Toronto *Mail and Empire*, May 11, 1936.

3. Provincial Council Statement, undated, in Loeb Papers; Toronto *Globe*, June 30, 1936; Toronto *Star*, June 30, 1936.

4. *New Commonwealth*, August 8 and August 15, 1936.

5. *Ibid.*, October 10, 1936.

6. My authorities here are Frank Underhill, who believed he was speaking for many party leaders, especially those in the L.S.R.; Mr. I. J. Weinrot, active in the large group of Toronto Jewish socialists; Kenneth McNaught, a member of the CCYM in the second half of the decade; and J. B. Salsberg, a leading C.P. spokesman until 1956.

7. See, *inter alia*, Richard M. Alway, *Mitchell F. Hepburn and the Liberal Party in the Province of Ontario, 1937-1943*, M.A. thesis (University of Toronto), 1965.

8. See any issue of the *Canadian Unionist* (A.C.C.L.) and *Canadian Congress Journal* (T.L.C.) between January and May 1937.

9. *Saturday Night*, September 25, 1937.

10. *C.A.R.*, 1937-38, pp. 177-78.

11. *New Commonwealth*, October 9, 1937.

12. *Ibid.*, October 16, 1937.

13. *Ibid.*, January 1, 1938.

14. *Saturday Night*, March 26 and October 27, 1938; Woodsworth in *Debates, House of Commons*, May 2, 1938, p. 2637; *New Commonwealth*, April 16 and May 14, 1938.

15. Provincial Council Report to the 1939 Convention, in Provincial Convention Reports and Documents, 1937-45.

16. See the pamphlet, *Canada and the War – the CCF Position* (Ottawa, 1937).

17. Leo Zakuta, "Membership in a Becalmed Protest Movement," *C.J.E.P.S.*, May 1958, p. 191.

18. *Canadian Forum*, April 1940.

19. *Saturday Night*, March 23, 1940.

20. Report of the 1940 Election Committee, *op. cit.*

7 THE GOLDEN AGE

I

> The innumerable episodes of the war period, the dozens of interesting phenomena to which it gave rise, must be omitted.[1]

One of the more interesting Canadian war-time phenomena which historians have largely ignored was the astonishing public resurgence of the CCF. In 1940, the CCF received 8.5 per cent of the total national vote; in September 1943, it headed the Gallup Poll. Party membership as late as 1942 was 20,000 nationally, 2700 in Ontario; two years later, it had one hundred thousand members in Canada, almost one-fifth of them in Ontario. In 1943, the Ontario CCF entered a provincial election with no sitting members and emerged within four seats of forming the provincial government. Between 1943 and 1945, many thoughtful pundits predicted that, if the CCF did not form the next federal government, it would at least hold the balance of power in Ottawa. In the same period, this phenomenon had the direct and salutary effect of converting Canada's two major parties from cautious and orthodox disciples of nineteenth century liberal theorists into pious advocates of an elementary welfare statism.

How can one explain the remarkable rise in public esteem of a party generally considered to be discredited and defeated? It is possible to isolate a number of variables – all a function of the war – which intervened to translate discontent and anxiety into temporary support for the CCF. These included the demand for a better post-war world in which the causes leading to wars would be removed, the realization that national planning was practical and efficient, the new role of the Soviet Union, and the rapid growth of urbanization and trade unionism as a by-product of a booming war economy.

Following hard on the heels of the Depression, the pressures of wartime reinforced in Canadians a skepticism about existing values and conventions, and helped to shake people's minds out of their traditional grooves. It was not long before the thoughts of many were turning to what war's end might bring. It was "generally assumed," according to *Saturday Night*, that business activity would decline sharply and prosperity collapse when war spending ceased.[2] At the same time, Canadians learned, British service men were rapidly "going socialistic," proclaiming their refusal to return to "the dog-eat-dog atmosphere of pre-war civilian life" having "striven shoulder to shoulder, as brother with brother, in this struggle for survival."[3]

The belief was spreading that post-war Canada would have to be a country fit for heroes to return to, and part of that new order of things which would make impossible the recurrence of another disastrous war. There was "endless discussion," *Saturday Night's* cautious financial editor could write by mid-1941, about the post-war society, and "almost everyone agrees" that health and unemployment insurance schemes, regulation of business, and a sharp limitation of profits were all necessary to provide the individual with real security.[4] There was, he sensed, "a very wide and general feeling of insecurity [among investors] regarding the future of . . . private enterprise." For "the man on the street" had become aware during the Depression of the shortcomings of the existing system, and believed that "salvation lies only in a wide and permanent extension of the powers of government." Why, he asked, should young Canadians "be expected to want to save Democracy if that means preserving the kind of society which existed before the war?"[5] Mackenzie King, listening closely, appointed McGill president Cyril James to chair the important new Advisory Committee on Reconstruction.

It was also becoming clear that the methods advocated by the left during the Depression to end unemployment and poverty were, when finally introduced during the war, working very satisfactorily indeed. Economic planning by the federal government had begun in 1939; by late 1941, King had introduced almost his entire price-wage control measures. Canada, one observer later wrote, was as socialistic a regime "as that for which the CCF had been campaigning" for a decade, "with nearly all sharing in the general prosperity and standard of living, attaining levels which peace would not produce."[6]

This fact was widely appreciated. B. K. Sandwell, the influential editor of *Saturday Night*, reported in 1941 that "the most widespread source of bewilderment and puzzlement among ordinary Canadians today" was Canada's wartime capacity to employ several hundred thousand hitherto unemployable persons.[7] As these new stirrings began to take shape – vaguely and rarely articulated, no doubt, but yet real and profound – the politicians and businessmen who had dominated Canada during the Depression fell increasingly into public disrepute.

Ironically, as the capitalists became the nation's favourite scapegoats, Canadians, in common with all the Allies, were finding in the land of Communism their new heroes. In June 1941, an overconfident Hitler made the fatal blunder of attacking the Soviet Union, thus opening a vital second front for the Allies. The Russians' magnificent resistance, at a time when the western powers were cringing under Nazi might, magically transformed the Communist regime from a despicable pseudo-neutral into a great bulwark of freedom and democracy. As the Allies became dependent upon the Soviet Union, so they became sympathetic to her. The manifestations of this emotion were quite remarkable.

The Toronto *Globe and Mail*, hitherto fanatically anti-Communist, announced publicly it would no longer refer to Communists as "Reds," since the term "has come to be used in a contemptuous and derogatory sense" and Canada's gallant new ally "might resent the use of an epithet which has an opprobrious flavour."[8] The *Globe's* response was no more than typical. At one time or another during the war, the Lieutenant-Governor of Ontario, the Canadian Jewish Congress, Mackenzie King, George Drew, and Mitchell Hepburn, among other renowned anti-Communists, all paid glowing public tributes to the Soviet resistance to fascism. Thus the Russians became popular heroes, which made it somewhat more awkward to discredit a left-wing group simply by stigmatizing it as "communistic" or "communist-inspired." The importance of this basic attitudinal change to the CCF's growth can hardly be overestimated.

Nor can the importance of organized labour to the rise of the CCF be exaggerated. Particularly in Ontario, the war's demographic impact was dramatic. Its urban population rose from 61 per cent in 1931 to 68 per cent a decade later. Almost half the urban population was settled in the south-west between Windsor and Oshawa, and most of the ongoing urbanization during the 1940's occurred in that area. The demand for increased productivity for the war effort restored full employment to Canada. Ontario above all saw a phenomenal expansion in manufacturing. In 1939, it employed some 318,000 employees; in 1943, the number was 570,000, many of them migrants from the rural hinterland.[9] With this expansion went a concomitant strengthening of labour's bargaining power. Union membership climbed from a Depression low of 280,000 to 460,000 by 1941, and to a record high of 700,000 by the war's end.[10]

Moreover, the potential influence of this class was activated by the addition of a new and aggressive element in Canadian organized labour. In 1940, the Trades and Labour Congress obediently followed the dictates of the A.F. of L. and expelled all C.I.O. unions from its organization. The latter, which included such incipiently powerful bodies as the Steel Workers, Auto Workers, Mine Workers, and Packinghouse Workers, immediately began negotiations with the All-Canadian Congress of Labour, and in September 1940, the two congresses pooled their constituent unions in a new central labour organization, the Canadian Congress of Labour. The C.C.L. began life with 100,000 members; by 1943, it had 250,000.[11]

The merger was enthusiastically welcomed by those who believed in direct political action by labour. The Congress executive included Aaron Mosher, Silby Barrett, Sol Spivak, and Charles Millard, all socialists convinced that labour had a positive role to play in politics. Further, their positions enabled them to influence hiring practices in other unions. In a short time, the majority of the organizing staff of such unions as the Packing, Rubber and Textile Workers were active CCF members. Under Millard, the head office of the Steelworkers in the early 1940's consisted of ten persons, every one of whom was an active, participating member of the CCF.[12]

Most of these individuals were socialists and political activists by conviction.[13] But many trade unionists who were not were being driven into the CCF's open arms. Hepburn and Drew, the new Ontario Conservative leader, were self-evidently anathema to labour. It was on the national level that there was a perceptible movement away from traditional loyalties. Big labour was anxious for official recognition of its new status in the community. But Mr. King's priorities were elsewhere. Labour's demand for equal representation on administrative bodies was ignored. Labour also saw convincing evidence that the federal government's policies were designed to discourage effective organization and to remove capable and energetic leadership by interning union leaders "upon representation that they were a danger to the state, based upon some alleged action or utterance . . . which took place years ago. . . ."[14]

What was happening in the country was fascinating: by a kind of dialectical process, the Canadian political mainstream and the

CCF were moving perceptibly closer to each other. On the one side was the increasing legitimation of the CCF's traditional policies of economic planning and welfare statism; in a real sense, Canada was "turning left." At the same time, on the key index of attitude towards the war, the CCF was moving to a position of realism and respectability. After 1939 the threshold of tolerable involvement steadily escalated: from near-pacifism to conscription of wealth only to no conscription of men without conscription of wealth and finally, after Pearl Harbour, to conscription of both men and wealth. By the end of 1941, CCF policy had matured into a tough-minded demand that rich and poor alike must sacrifice to the fullest.

This approach perfectly caught the mood of the country. When Mackenzie King called three by-elections for February 9, 1942, however, there was no reason to foresee significant electoral movement. The January Gallup Poll showed 45 per cent Liberal, 30 per cent Conservative, 5 per cent CCF. King properly anticipated no problem in adding Humphrey Mitchell and Louis St. Laurent to his cabinet; the question was whether Arthur Meighen, who had again been foisted on the Conservative Party as its national leader by the mining and railway interests,[15] would emerge as Leader of the Opposition.

King's hatred of Meighen bordered on the pathological.[16] But Meighen was running in a pretty safe Tory seat. York South was a predominantly Anglo-Saxon working class riding on the northern fringes of Toronto which had returned Conservative candidates consistently since 1904. In 1940, the Conservative majority was a comfortable 2482; Joseph Noseworthy of the CCF ran a miserable third. Meighen seemed unbeatable. The Liberals chose to respect the dubious convention whereby party leaders were acclaimed in by-elections. The CCF chose to disregard it; Joe Noseworthy was nominated again with the thankless task of taking on Meighen.

Yet to its surprised delight, the party soon found that its policies, for the first time, were evoking remarkable public responsiveness; the CCF had really become the spokesman of the people. Its campaign slogan "Conscript wealth as well as men" was heard "everywhere today," *Saturday Night's* correspondent wrote, and observed that it "obviously implies that wealth is not conscripted now."[17] Meighen, sensitive and astute to the end, responded with the assertion that government was already taking most from those who had the most.[18] On the whole his personal campaign ignored the CCF, though his supporters busily spread the word that Noseworthy was a Communist whose plans would "ruin the country" and that he "ought to be in a concentration camp."[19]

York South was the first of the CCF's classical saturation by-election campaigns. Never before had the party mobilized its resources more effectively. A record $4000 was raised. Nearly every member in the Toronto area participated, as did literally hundreds of individuals who had never before been involved in left politics; almost a hundred of Noseworthy's high school students canvassed for him. Most of these new recruits loathed Meighen; they were the people responsible for the rise of reform to near the top of Canada's political agenda; and precious few of them were committed socialists. Many of them sympathized with the voters who told Mrs. F. H. Underhill they were voting CCF, then added quickly, "But don't tell our neighbours. We all read the *Telegram* up here."[20]

The Liberal Establishment was badly split. Mitch Hepburn thought it would be a good joke to support Meighen; when George Drew joined their ranks, this offensive and bizarre triumvirate launched an orgy of anti-King venom which successfully won for the Prime Minister widespread public sympathy. Meighen also received the public endorsement of the York South Liberal Association.[21]

In fact, however, Hepburn's support of Meighen was counter-productive; he provoked more Liberal support for the CCF than he brought to the Tories. King himself, much as he wished to intervene, seems to have played a negligible role. He himself claimed he did nothing more than to encourage Robert Laurier, Ontario's Minister of Mines, in his desire to resign in protest at Hepburn's apostasy.[22] Through Norman Lambert, former president of the National Liberal Federation and the controller of Liberal Party finances, Andrew Brewin received $1000 for the CCF's York South campaign; Lambert's motives were clear, but there is no evidence of King's involvement in this transaction.[23] Robert Laurier resigned from Hepburn's cabinet three days before the election. In that same last week of the campaign, but not until then, both Arthur Roebuck and Harry Nixon – once Hepburn's closest colleague – publicly and unequivocally threw themselves into the battle against Meighen.[24]

The CCF, then, which had entered the campaign only for symbolic purposes, saw almost every variable intervene in its favour, sweeping it to an unexpected triumph. Noseworthy beat the former Prime Minister of Canada by 16,408 votes to 11,952.

The Liberals reacted to Meighen's defeat as ecstatically as the CCF did to Noseworthy's victory. In a real sense the Liberals won all three by-elections that day. Meighen and Hepburn both had been decisively repudiated, and there was general agreement that the results reflected anti-Tory, not pro-CCF, sentiment.[25] It was indisputable from the results that large numbers of Liberals voted CCF while many Conservatives simply stayed at home. Nevertheless, CCF'ers were understandably beside themselves with excitement. As far as they were concerned the entire future was open and inviting once again. As Arthur Meighen reluctantly acknowledged, "I think the CCF are starting to make inroads in the working vote of both parties."[26]

II

Every society and every social movement has its "golden age" – its period of muscularity and vigour – where the sense of growth is sure, the surge to power seemingly irresistible, and the crest of victory the only point in the line of vision.[27]

The CCF's spectacular success in York South ushered in the golden age of Canadian socialism. Noseworthy's victory had the immediate effect of reinvigorating the party and reawakening its enemies.

The CCF began the new age by recognizing its two major internal weaknesses; negligible grass-roots organization and no recognized public leadership. Membership in Ontario was a laughable 2000 and revenues were all but non-existent.[28] No provincial leader had ever been chosen, a function largely of the party's ambivalence towards the provincial arena. York South put paid to that attitude; after February 9, all levels of government were to be taken seriously. Accordingly, the provincial convention in April 1942 chose Edward Bigelow Jolliffe as the CCF's first Ontario leader. Jolliffe was 33 years old, a Rhodes scholar, former newspaperman and lawyer who had been in the party hierarchy since 1935. He came from an established and respected old Ontario family, a fact which shone through his radical rhetoric. This was considered to be politically desirable although it predictably created certain internal tensions. Some felt he was too young, others that he was excessively cerebral and aloof. But he was experienced and devoted, eloquent and confident, and projected an image of a dedicated yet reasonable crusader. He had no serious competition for the leadership and the party quickly and happily moved in behind him.

The convention then adopted a programme for Ontario,

stressing above all policies consistent with those of organized labour and organized agriculture.[29] Finally, with a new programme, a full-time leader, and an evangelistic flavour that had been absent for many years, a buoyant party launched a good, old-fashioned organizing drive across Ontario; you sometimes felt as if you had joined the Salvation Army in those years, one member later recalled.[30] Literally thousands of meetings were held in the following year. The leaders of the party – Jolliffe, Noseworthy, Bert Leavens, Agnes Macphail again, George Grube, Andrew Brewin – stumped the province, addressing rallies, selling memberships, and assisting local units to improve their organization. Between January and December 1942, Ontario membership quadrupled.[31]

Not even money-raising seemed an insurmountable obstacle in those exhilarating days. At a CCF dinner rally in Toronto in March 1943, for example, Jolliffe received pledges totalling 3500 dollars, only a little less than had been raised two years earlier for a full year's expenditure. More significantly, the greatest new source from which the CCF was deriving members and revenue was Ontario's mushrooming trade union movement. Neither major labour congress officially endorsed the CCF until after the 1943 Ontario election. But only eight month's after Noseworthy's victory, the Canadian Congress of Labour convention, theoretically representing 160,000 trade unionists, passed with only one dissenting vote a resolution specifically recognizing the CCF as labour's champion in parliament and recommending to its affiliated unions "that they study the program of the CCF."[32]

Even Trades and Labour Congress affiliates were manifesting a new determination to increase labour's political power. In July 1942, the CCF Trade Union Committee organized a conference of trade unionists in Toronto. Sixty-nine Ontario locals of thirty-four unions, from both the T.L.C. and the C.C.L., sent delegates to hear Coldwell and Jolliffe attack the Liberals' labour policy. The delegates were evidently impressed. They unanimously adopted a resolution affirming the need for labour political action through the CCF and calling on unions to affiliate and contribute generously to the CCF. Coldwell hailed the move as one of the most significant in Canadian political history. For the first time the CCF would receive the support not of insignificant radical labour sects, but of "big labour." And for the first time, a breach had been created in the T.L.C.'s cherished "no politics" stand. To be sure, Gomperites, Communists, and Liberals still had great influence within the T.L.C., but the ranks of the CCF's friends were rapidly increasing.

In September 1942, Clarence Gillis was brought from Cape Breton to Ontario as director of the CCF Trade Union Conference, his activities financed by a special fund raised by the unions at the July meeting. For the next four months, Gillis, a popular labour man, ceaselessly toured the province, speaking to union locals, emphasizing the importance of direct union affiliation to the CCF. In that time, nineteen locals with about 12,000 members affiliated to the CCF. Part of the dues of affiliated locals of the Steel and Mineworkers from Nova Scotia went to Ontario, so it could claim 35,000 trade unionists as affiliated members. This was clearly a major and unprecedented breakthrough for the CCF. But the nature of the resulting contribution should not be exaggerated. Each member of an affiliated local paid the CCF two cents a month, which was divided equally between the national and provincial offices. The entire business, then, meant precisely $350 more each month in the Ontario treasury.[33] Few outside the party understood this, however, and preferred to believe that labour's money bought it overwhelming influence in the CCF.

In fact labour support was in every respect very much a mixed blessing. It created serious and far from creative tensions within the party. The attitude of CCF members who were not labour leaders was always ambivalent to the trade union relationship. On the one hand, the party needed labour's money, manpower, and potential mass base; on the other, the movement felt threatened by the pragmatism and realism of many trade unionists. The Ontario Provincial Council in September 1942 approved easier terms for affiliating locals by a one-vote margin. This attitude inevitably made many labour people feel unwanted and unappreciated in a party which they in any event felt was overrun with "academics" and "intellectuals" who knew little of the real world.[34]

Moreover, many Canadians undoubtedly agreed with *Saturday Night's* judgement that labour's new demands for greater power "do not appear reasonable to any but the strongly unionist element of the electorate, who, though more numerous than three years ago, are still far from being able to swing more than a very few constituencies."[35] Equally foreboding were the predictions that labour's growing influence in the CCF would result in the party's stressing policies such as higher wage levels which would assure the continued hostility of rural Ontario.[36]

This was a real problem. The war was having a disruptive

effect upon rural Ontario. There was a large exodus of farm labour to the cities (which proved to be a bulwark for the old parties), while the extreme cost-price squeeze had aroused considerable discontent in agricultural communities. The CCF believed it had the capacity to exploit rural dissatisfaction. In May 1942, Agnes Macphail, who had recently returned to the CCF, was persuaded to undertake the job of full-time rural organizer. After conferring with most of the province's farm leaders, she concluded that, although "almost all" were personally friendly to the CCF, they were determined that they themselves and the organizations they represented would remain scrupulously non-political.[37] When, at the end of the year, Macphail was forced to give up her organizing work, no permanent replacement was hired. A committee of farmers was assigned further organizational tasks, but with very modest results.[38] The CCF also announced a policy officially to recognize the Federation of Agriculture as the authoritative voice of the farm community. This approach, it was hoped, would indicate that no conflict existed between the policies of the CCF and those of the Federation, and that the two movements should be considered complementary.[39]

It was actually not utopian to hope Ontario farmers might join the fold; everyone else seemed to be. Late in 1942, reporting on a cross-country journey he had just completed, that old weathercock, Elmore Philpott, declared himself impressed by one fact above all others:

> the steadily increasing importance of the CCF in the national scheme of things. . . . In a country now sadly lacking in a positive faith in any institution, the CCF represents to an ever increasing mass of the ordinary people the hope of a better after-the-war world.[40]

The Gallup Poll confirmed Philpott's impressions. At year's end, the Liberals nationally registered 36 per cent, the Conservatives 24, and the CCF 23; in Ontario, it was respectively 32, 32, 27.[41] The "new social order" that was once again on the lips of all socialists appeared imminent. In the meantime, the party won two federal and three provincial by-elections in Canada in the eighteen months after January 1942. No wonder that by the provincial convention in April 1943, the Ontario CCF could talk of itself as a party "prepared to assume the responsibilities of office at the earliest occasion" – and be taken seriously.

The party's internal momentum responded to the mood of the

public. It had already nominated twenty-eight candidates for a provincial election that had not yet been announced. The convention welcomed 298 delegates and a hundred alternates, far more than ever in the past. And, for the first time in the CCF's history, a large number of delegates from affiliated unions of both Congresses were in active attendance.[42]

The convention officially set in motion the party's pre-election machinery. Whenever the election would be called, the CCF was determined to be ready. Nominations continued apace. Hundreds of thousands of copies of the provincial program were printed. Riding associations were confidently and energetically organizing: holding public meetings, finding new members, canvassing, and building up local election funds. In the province-wide drive for a central campaign fund, six thousand dollars had been raised, and thousands more were being sought to ensure a serious centrally-sponsored media campaign. Additional organizing staff was taken on. Northern Ontario was driving ahead on its own momentum, without central assistance. By June, nominations there were almost complete, and CCF support was palpably growing. Travelling through this area in June, Jolliffe addressed twenty-eight meetings. One, near Port Arthur, coincided with a Liberal rally; the Liberals had ten people while Jolliffe packed the hall. A CCF club was formed in Kenora on April 8 and when Jolliffe spoke there on June 3, over 150 members had been signed up.[43]

This phenomenon went neither unobserved nor unheeded. As early as August 1942, *Saturday Night* was warning that "at almost any time [the CCF may] have to assume, if not entire charge, at least a partial responsibility along with some other parliamentary group for the conduct of public business."[44] In March of the following year, a political reporter noted that the Ontario CCF "is no longer a lurking political shadow. It has become a party with resources and a deep-rooted influence. It has a real chance of becoming the opposition or even the Government in Ontario." Nor, he added, was the CCF's growing strength, particularly among trade unionists,

> being taken lying down by the major parties. The Progressive-Conservative emphasis on labour is an obvious counter-move. The much mooted Heenan [Ontario Labour Minister] collective bargaining bill is an obvious Ontario Liberal sop. The Communists are opposing the CCF within the unions, doing their best to build up Heenan as an alternative labour saviour."[45]

Arthur Meighen had another alternative. He was able, according to one historian, "to persuade major Conservative interests their salvation from socialism" lay in choosing as their new national leader the Progressive Premier of Manitoba, John Bracken.[46] Bracken finally indicated his willingness to accept the leadership if the party adopted the title "Progressive-Conservative" and a generally progressive platform. It did both. *Saturday Night* wrote that the new Conservative program was drafted "with no idea except to make sure that the CCF do not climb into power when the Liberals go out."[47]

At almost the identical moment, Meighen's old ally in Ontario was also completing his life's work. On October 21, 1942, with absolutely no advance warning and for no rational reason, Mitch Hepburn resigned as Premier. He selected as his successor his Attorney-General Gordon Conant. Conant had no merit for the job and no support from his party. In May, but for much better reasons, he followed Hepburn into the back benches. Now it was the party's turn to choose, and they turned to a man whose image was in every respect antithetical to Hepburn's, Harry Nixon. A *Maclean's* writer described Nixon as a leader "in a good, serviceable grey . . . grey-haired, grey-suited, grey-personalitied." Mackenzie King was delighted that the long, acrimonious feud between Queen's Park and Ottawa was at an end. But so was the Liberal party of Ontario as a viable political force. The process of disintegration which Hepburn had begun had gone too far for a Harry Nixon to reverse.[48]

But at least Hepburn's departure allowed Mackenzie King to deal with other tensions more carefully. Towards the end of 1942, according to Jack Pickersgill, the marked rise in CCF support and its developing alliance with the labour movement gave the Prime Minister "some concern," although "his main interest was not yet with the CCF."[49] By early 1943, however,

> Mackenzie King believed the conscription issue had been settled; he was convinced the war would ultimately be won; and he began to look ahead to the future with some confidence. The newly named Progressive-Conservative party under John Bracken's leadership he did not consider a serious threat; he was much more disturbed by the rising strength of the CCF which, he felt, must be countered by increased emphasis on the post-war policy of the Liberal Government.[50]

Accordingly, he soon set up a parliamentary committee to produce a programme of social security legislation for the future.

There was, however, another, more negative, way to undermine the socialists than by selectively adopting their policies. One could demonstrate how miserable life would be under socialism. This approach could be clearly seen as early as April 1942. The program adopted at the CCF's Ontario convention was greeted by its enemies as the sure way to eliminate individual initiative.[51] The financial page of *Saturday Night* soon featured a lengthy weekly article describing the dangers that increasing "collectivism" meant to individual liberty if it were not curtailed after the war. The Toronto *Globe and Mail* allowed that, though it had changed its attitude towards Russia and "Reds," it still loathed the CCF and its program of "national regimentation," since, under socialism, "some bossy civil servant would tell every Canadian what he must do, where he must go, what doctor he must call, and what kind of soap he must use."[52] *Saturday Night's* life insurance expert, George Gilbert, pointing to the CCF's policy to nationalize both banks and life insurance companies, advised his readers that "It would be the height of folly to wait until after its advent to power before taking measures to counteract such a radical and uneconomic move.... "[53] Thus was begun the destruction of the CCF's golden age.

III

Harry Nixon had been chosen by the Ontario Liberals because of the way he juxtaposed against Mitch Hepburn. He did not let them down. In the summer of 1943 he called the first provincial election in six years.

The Liberal campaign largely revolved around Nixon, first as a man of the soil, then increasingly as Ontario's only hope of salvation from the socialist menace. One large Liberal ad warned that

If the CCF wins on August 4, the light of democracy goes out in Ontario.... You give up the title of your farm, your business, your insurance, and you vote away your freedom for the regimentation of your life and that of your children.[54]

The Liberals were also reduced to peddling a document on the Labour government of New Zealand which one non-CCF'er described as "not only shameful to the political party that printed it, but a disgrace to Canada."[55] Its argument was that compared to democratic socialists, "There is more virtue in Naziism. There is more honesty in Sovietism."[56] Ontario Liberalism had been psychopathic under Hepburn; under Nixon it was merely pathetic and desperate. Even Mackenzie King was aware that "People have lost confidence in a Liberal administration at Queen's Park."[57] At Nixon's final rally in Toronto, Massey Hall was only one-third full.[58]

Nixon as anti-socialist demagogue made little sense. But it was that kind of campaign. George Drew emerged as an anti-socialist reformer. He introduced a Twenty-Two Point Platform which his adoring friends on the *Globe and Mail* described as "the finest social document in Ontario's history."[59] As it happens it was a remarkable document when compared to the tired Tory programmes of the 1930's. A Drew government would provide "economic and social security from the cradle to the grave." "Advanced and fair labour laws" would include "comprehensive collective bargaining legislation." The Platform promised to "wipe out slums, improve housing conditions, and so provide large scale employment"; to increase educational opportunities, and to augment mothers' allowances and old age pensions.[60]

Drew's other stratagem was to indulge himself in occasional, though venomous, anti-CCF diatribes. He warned that dictatorship, "which our young men are fighting and dying to destroy," lay in the doctrines preached by "the evil geniuses" of socialism. Mussolini, he felt obliged to recall, began as a socialist, and the very word "Nazi" was an abbreviation of National Socialism.[61] Drew also spoke strongly against those who were calling for "the liquidation of the British Empire." As the *Globe and Mail* reported it,

> He said he believed in personal freedom, but did not go to the point where he would allow any school teacher to create doubts in the minds of the children of the importance of the great fellowship that was the British Empire.[62]

It is true that the Conservatives were sufficiently complacent of victory to use anti-socialism only as a secondary campaign theme. It is also true that Drew could afford to take a relatively high-minded approach and leave the hard-core demagogy to others. The daily press, for example, was, with the exception only of the Toronto *Star*, consistently and hysterically anti-CCF.[63] The publishers of the *Canadian Veteran*, an "independent" paper for veterans, sponsored a large ad in the *Globe and Mail* to reveal that "THE CCF WOULD GET RID OF WINSTON CHURCHILL. . . . they'd get rid of Drew, they'd get rid of freedom itself and make everybody a serf of the socialized state."[64] Two phony labour organizations, the Canadian Labour

Press and the Industrial Worker, suddenly materialized as sponsors of crude ads challenging the CCF's claim to be a workers' party.[65]

For sheer breath-taking hysterical propaganda, however, the indisputable champion was Montague A. Sanderson. Popularly, and rather scornfully, known as "Buggsy," Sanderson was the manger of a firm called Reliable Exterminators and, as each of his legendary political advertisements boldly proclaimed, "one of Canada's leading pest control operators." Sanderson was also, from 1942 until his timely death in 1947, one of the busiest political propagandists in Canada. His first political advertisement appeared in December 1941, denouncing Mackenzie King's plebiscite. By 1943, however, he had discovered the CCF, and proceeded to spend the entire profits of Reliable Exterminators – profits which actually increased as a result of his public notoriety – attempting to destroy it. According to his son, Sanderson received no outside financial support, apparently believing he was carrying on some kind of crusade. His son estimates that his father spent about 75,000 dollars in his five politically active years, mostly against the CCF.[66] Sanderson's attorney once described his client's motives in publishing his propaganda as "partly patriotic, partly for the glory and publicity, and partly the advertising [it] obtained for his business."[67]

During the 1943 campaign, Sanderson placed four large anti-CCF advertisements in the Toronto *Globe and Mail* alone between July 13 and July 29. The format was constant. The top left corner bore a small picture of Sanderson over the caption "You Bet I'm a 'Vet'." At the bottom of each was his name, firm, credentials, and the phrase "VOTE TO KEEP YOUR RIGHT TO VOTE." Sanderson's repetitive and melodramatic copy was also frighteningly effective, simply because it was catchy and easily remembered. His favourite line, drilled into the public consciousness by incessant repetition, concerned the "Communists-CIO-CCF dictatorship" which "would exterminate democratic government by violence."[68]

To meet this challenge – and the unique opportunity which had triggered it – the CCF was better equipped than ever before in its history. Its aroused rank and file, now numbering eight thousand as compared to two thousand one year earlier, had been preparing an election organization for months past. Its provincial office had collected from party and union sources the unprecedented total of twenty thousand dollars for a central election fund; the sum was a joke in itself, but for the CCF it represented comparative opulence. Clarie Gillis, Grace Mac-

Innis, M. J. Coldwell, and J. H. Brockelbank, leader of the opposition in Saskatchewan, had all agreed to stump the province for the party. The CCF contested eighty-six of the ninety seats and spent just under 250 dollars on each from the central fund. This included newspaper advertising, radio broadcasts, billboards, and several leaflets. Each riding of course tried to raise additional funds, though few did as well as Bill Dennison's $547 and many did much worse. This hardly allowed for lavish campaigns, though the two inexpensive central leaflets and another contributed by the Trade Union Committee made things easier.[69]

The CCF's primary message to the voters was negative: it evoked the fears and anxieties which had developed during the Depression – a Depression, it was constantly pointed out, that was inevitable under a capitalist system. "When our armed forces come back," asked one large advertisement, "will it be to this?" – picture of a dilapidated slum area, "Or to this?" – picture of a bright and friendly suburbia.[70]

> We all remember the utter failure of the old parties during the Depression – the bread lines – the despair and suffering from unemployment and want.
> Full employment in PEACE as in war – to win freedom and security for all.

VOTE CCF

When the party was not prophesying utter doom under capitalism, it devoted its energies to refuting, explicitly or by implication, old party charges. The CCF was pronounced the only hope of freedom for war veterans and workers in war industries. Monopolies would be curbed by social ownership, since huge corporations controlled all important business and were regimenting and crushing the individual initiative of their employees; which specific corporations would be "socially owned" was never made clear.[71] Some advertisements were designed to counter charges that the CCF would confiscate savings, life insurance, other property, farms, and generally would own everything and control everyone. The truth, in fact, was that a CCF government would create the conditions whereby everyone would have more freedom – and more property. It would plan for post-war employment, introduce an "effective" collective bargaining act, guarantee adequate health service for all, increase opportunities for education, undertake a large scale public housing development, increase mothers' allowances and old age pensions, and, above all, develop Ontario's natural resources "as a public trust, with revenue thus gained going to pay for health services, education, and other benefits to the people of the province."[72] It was a programme just perceptibly to the left of George Drew's.

The final aspect of the CCF's campaign was the increased attention it paid to that special interest group known as organized labour, now 211,000 strong in Ontario. It was a natural tactic. As union membership climbed almost daily during 1943, so did the number of locals affiliated to the CCF. By election day, 25,000 unionists were paying their two cents a month to the party. Now was the moment to consummate the relationship. The CCF distributed special trade union leaflets and inserted several advertisements in the *Canadian Unionist* describing the terms of the collective bargaining agreement a socialist government in Ontario would implement. In return, the C.C.L. opened the pages of the *Unionist* to well-known CCF members who took the opportunity to explain various aspects of their party's programme. Other than that, the trade unionist was to be reached in his riding by the door-to-door canvass.

On election day, a final Gallup Poll was published. To the CCF's profound and everlasting anguish, it appeared too late to affect the election results. That poll stands unique in Ontario's history: it showed CCF 36 per cent, P.C. 33, Liberals 31.[73]

If the actual results reversed the poll's findings, they were still, as the *New Commonwealth* jubilantly trumpeted, a "SMASHING CCF VICTORY." While the Conservatives won and doubled their representation from 19 to 38 seats, and the Liberals plummeted from 59 to a mere 15, the CCF had skyrocketed from no seats at all to the status of official opposition with 34 members. Though seven CCF'ers won by fewer than a thousand votes, four lost by fewer than 750, nine were defeated with a 30 per cent vote, and nine lost who polled between 25 and 30 per cent. Nine CCF M.P.P.'s, all in the north and northwest, had won by clear majorities, and seven had majorities of four thousand votes or more. The final results gave the Conservatives 469,672 votes, or 36.7 per cent, the CCF 418,307 votes or 32.4 per cent, and the Liberals 409,307 votes or 30.9 per cent. The CCF had thus increased its 1937 vote by about 350,000 while the Liberals dropped almost 300,000 and the Conservatives 150,000 despite their increase in seats.

The majority of CCF votes were garnered in predominantly industrial constituencies, as were all its seats. Fifty of Ontario's ridings were more or less non-agricultural, forty were rural. The CCF polled only 17 per cent or about 82,000 of the rural votes.

Still, in a dozen rural constituencies in central Ontario the CCF received a quite respectable vote even though its organization had been feeble. In eastern Ontario, however, it was a negligible factor; the golden age of socialism did not penetrate east of Oshawa.

In non-agricultural ridings, it was very nearly a CCF sweep. It took 34 of the 50 urban seats, with an amazing 40 per cent of the votes; the Conservatives polled 32 per cent, the Liberals 26. No fewer than 19 of the CCF's winning candidates were trade union members, ten belonging to T.L.C. affiliates, nine to the C.C.L; two of them, Charles Millard of the Steelworkers and Bob Carlin of Mine, Mill and Smelter, were heads of their union. The CCF took all but one of the seats in Hamilton and the Niagara Peninsula, all but one in Windsor, eleven of twelve in the north, and all four Yorks. Thanks to these last four victories, the party won a majority of the Toronto area's seats, though not a plurality of the popular vote; it was Conservatives forty per cent, CCF thirty-seven per cent. The CCF's Toronto total was hurt by devastating defeats in Bellwoods and St. Andrew's; these two heavily ethnic working-class ridings were won by Communists Albert MacLeod and J. B. Salsberg, and the CCF could poll only nineteen and thirteen per cent respectively.[74]

There were some unanticipated breakthroughs. Serious inroads were made in ridings generally regarded as safely Liberal because of their French-speaking Catholic population. This was particularly true in constituencies in northern Ontario, most notably Sudbury and Cochrane North and South. And the CCF swept the service vote. Since the Liberals' scheme of proxy voting was, as expected, a failure, most of the armed forces overseas never got the opportunity to vote. Of those still in Ontario military camps who voted, 6,755 voted Liberal, 9,443 Conservative, and 11,736 CCF. In Toronto High Park, George Drew received sixty-six service votes, the Liberal twenty, and CCF candidate William Temple 160; Drew's margin of victory was only 460 votes.[75]

How can one explain the CCF's phenomenal success which exceeded, one leading member privately admitted, all party expectations?[76] No one saw in the results a positive endorsement of socialism. Mackenzie King attributed the CCF gains to labour's resentment of the government's wage stabilization policy, and even more to the fact that "some of my colleagues have become surrounded by interests that are at least not sympathetic to labour." He felt "much work will have to be done" to regain labour's support and that its loss "was the greatest threat to the chances of the Liberal party winning the next election."[77] One commentator reported that Ottawa really saw the CCF's tremendous success "as a sign of popular impatience with both old parties and a desire for more progressive administration closer to the realities of everyday life of the ordinary man and woman. This development," he predicted, "will doubtless affect the party platforms of both parties at the next federal election."[78]

Maclean's believed Drew's victory indicated that "many electors were impressed by his efforts to make the Conservative party truly progressive."[79] *Saturday Night* concluded that had the national Conservative party not adopted a progressive platform and elected a progressive leader in 1942, "there would have been no Conservative government at Queen's Park. There might have been a socialist one."[80] The Toronto *Star* thought the results showed

> the determination of the great masses of the people that a better day shall dawn for the common man . . . a declaration of lost faith in the old way of doing things. . . . Conditions which obtained before the war must not obtain after it. Whatever else the electors may have felt or known about CCF policies, many did feel that this party was facing forward and going somewhere, and that its older rivals, while moving somewhat, were still looking back wistfully over their shoulders to a social order which is no longer acceptable.[81]

The Star's analysis seems sound. Certainly the results did not prove that an enlightened electorate had reasoned that socialism was the only alternative to a doomed and decaying capitalist system. What they did reveal, rather, was the strong desire for a reformed post-war society characterized by increased personal security from want. Some no doubt believed that the new Drew could satisfy these vague, inarticulate yearnings. But a great many of those who looked forward hopefully to a better post-war world – labourers, white collar workers, farmers, service men, young people, many of whom had never been able to find a job when the old parties were in power – believed that only through the CCF could they realize their hopes and dreams. They would gamble on this young movement, though most could say only that "it helps the working man";[82] but which other party could they say that about?

The 1943 election has been called "probably the most important in Ontario's history" since it introduced to the province "the serious three-party system which has now become the hallmark of the province's politics."[83] Something of its importance was immediately perceived. After all, as the *Globe and Mail* pointed out, "Ontario is the key province in the Dominion. What is done [here] will not only affect every man and woman in Ontario but will be of vital importance to every Canadian."[84] To succeed in Canada, the CCF must win Ontario. To save Canada from socialism, the CCF must be stopped in Ontario. That struggle now began in earnest.

References

1. Lower, *Colony to Nation*, pp. 530-1
2. P. M. Richards, *Saturday Night*, January 10, 1942.
3. *Ibid.*, October 12, 1940.
4. *Ibid.*, May 10, 1941.
5. *Ibid.*, August 9, 1941.
6. Lower, *Colony to Nation*, pp. 529-30.
7. *Saturday Night*, March 22, 1941.
8. Toronto *Globe and Mail*, July 23, 1941.
9. Jacob Spelt, *The Urban Development in South-Central Ontario* (Assen, The Netherlands, 1955), pp. 171, 184.
10. Logan, *Trade Unions in Canada*, pp. 77-8.
11. *Canadian Forum*, October, 1940; Logan, *op. cit.*, p. 387.
12. M. M. Armstrong, *The Development of Trade Union Activity in the CCF*, p. 40. Mrs. Armstrong, secretary of the Steelworkers in these years, points out that the Auto Workers alone refused to support the CCF. They were led by George Burt, a "political opportunist" whose opposition to political action won him the support of the large Communist element in the U.A.W. The Communists, of course, were prepared to back anyone who would impede the growth of the CCF (pp. 36-7).
13. See *Canadian Unionist*, January, 1942, *et seq.* The magazine continued as the C.C.L.'s official organ.
14. Editorial, *Saturday Night*, September 13, 1941.
15. *Canadian Forum*, January, 1942; Pickersgill, *King Record*, p. 277; *Saturday Night*, November 22, 1941.
16. Pickersgill, *op. cit.*, pp. 278, 344, 347.
17. P. M. Richards, *Saturday Night*, March 7, 1942.
18. Toronto *Star*, January 29, 1942.
19. *Canadian Forum*, January, 1942.
20. Underhill interview.
21. Toronto *Globe and Mail*, January 29, 1942.
22. Pickersgill, *op. cit.*, pp. 344-5.
23. Norman Lambert's personal diary, January 29, January 30, 1942, cited by J. L. Granatstein, "The York South By-Election of February 9, 1942,"

C.H.R., Vol. XLVIII, No. 2, June 1967, p. 155. In an interview in June 1972, Brewin acknowledged receipt of the contribution, but believed it was $500.

24. Toronto *Star*, February 3 and February 6, 1942.

25. Toronto *Star*, February 5, 1942; *Maclean's*, March 1, 1942.

26. Toronto *Star*, February 10, 1942.

27. Daniel Bell, "Marxian Socialism in the United States," In Egert and Persons, *Socialism and American Life*, p. 267.

28. Auditor's Report to the 1941 Provincial Convention.

29. Toronto *Globe and Mail*, April, 4, 1942.

30. Interview with Mrs. Margaret Stewart, 1961.

31. Report to 1943 Provincial Convention.

32. *Canadian Forum*, October 1942.

33. CCF Trade Union Committee Report to the Provincial Conventions of 1943 and 1944; CCF National Office Files; Toronto *Star*, July 17, 1942; Conroy Cunliffe, *Saturday Night*, March 13, 1943.

34. Gad Horowitz, *Canadian Labour in Politics*, pp. 83, 150.

35. *Saturday Night*, March 13, 1943.

36. *Ibid.*, July 3, 1943.

37. Macphail's Report to Provincial Council Meeting, September 27, 1942, in Provincial Council and Executive Minutes.

38. Macphail's Report to Provincial Executive, November 6, 1942.

39. *New Commonwealth*, February 1943.

40. *News*, November 14, 1942.

41. *New Commonwealth*, January 1943.

42. *Ibid.*, May 13, 1943.

43. *Ibid.*, May 27, June 24, 1943.

44. *Saturday Night*, August 1, 1942.

45. Conroy Cunliffe, *ibid*, March 13, 1943.

46. J. R. Williams, *The Conservative Party in Canada*, pp. 67, 70.

47. *Saturday Night*, December 19, 1942.

48. *Maclean's*, June 15, 1943; McKenty, *Mitch Hepburn*, pp. 258-9; Pickersgill, *op. cit.*, pp. 491-3.

49. *Ibid.*, p. 453.

50. *Ibid.*, p. 467.

51. According to a Toronto *Star* editorial, April 7, 1942.

52. Toronto *Globe and Mail*, February 4 and April 26, 1943.

53. *Saturday Night*, March 13, 1943.

54. Toronto *Globe and Mail*, July 28, 1943.

55. L. L. Golden, *News*, August 7, 1943.

56. Cited in *ibid.*

57. Pickersgill, *op. cit.*, pp. 568-9

58. *News*, July 31, 1943. Hepburn played no role in the Liberal campaign. He ran and won easily in Elgin as an Independent Liberal. He claimed to support Nixon though he praised Drew as a gallant soldier and cooperative opposition leader. Toronto *Globe and Mail*, July 13, 1943.

59. Toronto *Globe and Mail*, July 10, 1943.

60. *Maclean's*, August 1, 1943.

61. Toronto *Globe and Mail*, July 12, 1943.

62. *Ibid.*

63. The headline over a Toronto *Telegram* editorial, July 30, 1943, was typical: "CCF Stands for Socialism – Socialism Would End Freedom For the People of Ontario."

64. Toronto *Globe and Mail*, July 30, 1943.

65. *Ibid.*, July 26 and July 28, 1943; *Ottawa Citizen*, July 28, 1943.

66. Interview with Donald Sanderson, 1961.

67. Cited in E. C. Guillet, *Famous Canadian Trials, Volume 50, Political Gestapo*, unpublished typewritten manuscript (Toronto, 1949), unpaginated.

68. See, for example, Toronto *Globe and Mail*, July 13, July 19, and July 29, 1943.

69. *New Commonwealth*, December 9, 1943; CCF Trade Union Committee Report to 1944 Ontario Convention.

70. Toronto *Globe and Mail*, August 2, 1943.

71. *Ibid.*, July 10 and July 22, 1943.

72. *Ibid.*, July 27, 1943.

73. Toronto *Globe and Mail*, August 4, 1943.

74. *Canadian Parliamentary Guide*, 1944; D. A. Bristow, *Agrarian Interest in the Politics of Ontario*, p. 256; Dennis Wrong, "Ontario Provincial Elections," *C.J.E.P.S.*, August 1957. p. 398.

75. *News*, October 30, 1943; *New Commonwealth*, August 12, 1943.

76. CCF National Office Files, Lloyd Shaw to F. C. Jennings, August 14, 1943.

77. Pickersgill, *King Record*, 571-2.

78. H. R. Armstrong, Toronto *Star*, August 5, 1943.

79. *Maclean's* September 1, 1943.

80. *Saturday Night*, August 7, 1943.

81. Toronto *Star*, August 5, 1943.

82. Gallup Poll survey, in *Canadian Forum*, September, 1943.

83. John Wilson and David Hoffman, "Ontario: A Three-Party System in Transition," in M. Robin (ed.), *Canadian Provincial Politics* (Toronto, 1972), p. 215.

84. Toronto *Globe and Mail*, July 24, 1943.

8 THE BATTLE

I

After the August 1943 election, the CCF set out to consolidate its electoral strength, much of which was superficial and devoid of conviction and commitment. Those who believed themselves threatened by the CCF, both in the political and the real world, set out to exploit that superficiality and bring the voters back to their senses.

For one tantalizing instant, it appeared that the first task would be superfluous, the second futile; the socialist tide appeared to be rushing forward furiously with a seemingly irresistible momentum. A wild fever appeared to be consuming the staid Canadian nation. On August 9, two more parliamentary members had been easily added to the CCF contingent in Ottawa, through by-elections in Selkirk, Manitoba and Humboldt, Saskatchewan. Just one week later, in a provincial by-election in Manitoba, the party swept The Pas, John Bracken's seat for the past twenty years, with three-fifths of the votes.

The climax of the great Canadian political orgy erupted in September 1943 with the issuing of a Gallup Poll. If a federal election had been held at that moment, the CCF would have received 29 per cent, the Liberals and P.C.'s 28 each. There were, to be sure, regional variations. East of Ontario the CCF remained a joke. In western Canada, it was CCF 41 per cent, Liberals and P.C.'s 23 each, New Democracy (Social Credit) 11. In Ontario, the Tories were ahead with 40, the CCF followed with 32, and the Liberals trailed with 26 per cent. Even more encouraging was the class breakdown. Representatives of four broad occupational categories were asked which party they believed would treat their own group best. The response was beyond the wildest socialist phantasy:

	Farmer	Labour	White Collar	Business
CCF	25%	42	19	5
Liberal	25	17	26	21
P.C.	23	11	22	44

As the *New Commonwealth* ejaculated ecstatically, "CCF SWING SWEEPS CANADA."

The party was on the peak of the wave and seemed destined to ride it to victory. Historical inevitability, though, needed some mortal reinforcement. As the most formidable and devastating propaganda campaign in Canadian history began to unfold, the CCF began, both privately and publicly, preparing confidently and innocently for power.

For the first time in a serious way, substantial thought was being given to a concrete program of action once elected. The Ontario Research Committee recommended in 1944 that the National Council be approached

> with a view to determining and announcing a Four Year Plan of Socialization and Social Development to be carried into effect . . . in the first four years of office of CCF governments in both Ontario and the Dominion . . . .
>
> The main stages provided in the plan should be made public as far as possible to allay public fears that the CCF plans a chaotic overnight transformation on the one hand, or that the CCF has no specific plans on the other.[2]

At the same time, organizational consolidation was stepped up significantly. Meetings, rallies, speaking tours, leadership schools, summer schools, fund-raising gimmicks, card parties, banquets, moonlight cruises, radio broadcasts – these were the kind of activities which occupied the time of buoyant CCF members after the 1943 election. Five of the party's new M.P.P.'s were hired to assist in organizing priority ridings. A pamphlet outlining the CCF's post-war rehabilitation program was sent to numerous service men overseas. The Education Committee was interviewing editors of the foreign language press with a view to having them publish articles on the CCF.[3]

This frenetic activity and excitement was reflected in party growth. By mid-1944, the *New Commonwealth* had tripled its circulation from a year earlier to almost 30,000 readers. David Lewis and Frank Scott published *Make This Your Canada* and saw it sell an astounding 25,000 copies. It outlined, with implacable confidence, a simple and apparently irrefutable thesis which many other Canadians had already begun to consider: if national planning brought such unprecedented wartime prosperity, why should it not do the same in time of peace?[4]

Yet the successes were not unqualified. It is true, for example, that Ontario membership almost doubled through 1943 from 8044 to 15,823. On the other hand, the *New Commonwealth* admitted, this was considerably below the expectations of provincial office.[5] Similarly, though the 1943 finance drive increased the central treasury from $20,000 to $34,000, this too was significantly below quota. This fact was more than merely discouraging to party leaders; it could also, they well knew, spell ultimate disaster. For as the unprecedented anti-CCF progaganda campaign continued in unwavering intensity, the need for increased CCF resources grew increasingly crucial. As a solution, the *New Commonwealth*, on February 24, 1944, announced a massive "Victory Fund Drive."

> For several months [it explained], the CCF has experienced the most bitter attacks, the most vitriolic outpourings of lies and distortions about its aims and policies that any political party in Canada has ever known. Financed to the tune of hundreds of thousands of dollars by representatives of the wealthiest corporations in Canada, and engineered by unscrupulous propagandists who have not hesitated to spread the most barefaced defamations, the campaign has made use of every vehicle of publicity. A daily flow of anti-CCF editorials have appeared in the press throughout Canada. Radio broadcasts . . . and leaflets "explaining" the CCF . . . newspaper ads published by banks, insurance firms and trust companies warning against the menace of socialism . . . speakers denouncing the CCF before service clubs, church groups and similar organizations . . . .
>
> The CCF now has plans for a campaign that will carry the TRUTH about the CCF into every house in Ontario. It will include a weekly radio broadcast . . . ads . . . [organizers]. . . .
>
> But such a campaign needs money – large quantities of money . . . . IT MUST HAVE YOUR SUPPORT FOR VICTORY IN 1944.

The amount the party in Ontario sought was $300,000, a tidy sum for a movement whose national office was then receiving only $30,000 annually.[6] This objective was as unrealistic as it was vital. The Provincial Council was soon forced to postpone such important projects as a weekly *New Commonwealth*, an extensive radio campaign, and a larger organizational staff. In the end, given the need and the goal, the campaign was a dismal failure: only $50,000 was ultimately collected. This woefully inadequate result was particularly shameful when contrasted with achievements in other provinces. The Ontario CCF did not receive or spend as much money as the Saskatchewan CCF, and only about 50 per cent more than the British Columbia party. In mid-1944, the Ontario CCF's entire administrative and organizing staff numbered ten persons; so did that of the British Columbia CCF. This was so obviously insufficient that the Ontario staff was doubled in the next six months, salaries coming from Victory Fund receipts.[7]

Another ten thousand dollars collected through the drive was used for a series of newspaper advertisements designed to counter the anti-CCF campaign. To combat a never-ceasing barrage of anti-CCF propaganda, party leaders decided to insert three small ads to appear in thirty daily newspapers across the Dominion during April 1944.[8] These advertisements were prepared by a friendly professional advertising concern, the William Orr Advertising Company, in consultation with Lewis, Douglas, Scott, Jolliffe, Coldwell, MacInnis, and Knowles, all of whom approved the final product.[9]

The grotesque aberration in judgement, then, was their responsibility. In the first place, as Charles Millard observed, the advertisements "might well have been just a little more in contrast to the technique and style being used by Gladstone Murray [a leading anti-CCF propagandist], or in other words, a wee bit more dignified. . . . "[10] The ads were crude and offensive. Their basis was a raw devil theory of history. One portrayed a vile octopus, its tentacles choking a farmer, a soldier and a housewife. Another showed two fat cat capitalists, bedecked in top hats and tails, slinging mud at an advancing army of socialist realism-created workers, farmers, and soldiers. Fortunately, and predictably, the ads were hardly noticed. The secretary of the British Columbia party wrote David Lewis that "there has been little reaction to the advertisements published. I have not received a single letter commenting on them one way or another and I have asked several of our members whether they had seen the ads and not one of them had seen them."[11] David Lewis admitted that this was the general verdict.[12] For the CCF, in fact, the only bright spot in this p.r. debacle was the refusal of eleven newspapers to accept one or more of the ads, thereby saving the party precious financial resources.[13]

The party had one other invaluable resource: organized labour. For though it was true that no less than half the leadership and a quarter of the membership of the Ontario CCF were middle class radicals,[14] the large majority of the rank and file was plainly working class. This was only to be expected. These were dynamic, expanding years for Canada's labour movement. Its membership grew to more than double, from 300,000 in 1939 to 664,000 in 1943. There were over 200,000 trade unionists in Ontario, a third of them in Toronto. Small wonder that after the 1943 Ontario election there began "a terrific amount of manoeuvring . . . for the control of the political influence of organized labour."[15]

Labour would not be bought cheaply, however. Its leaders vociferously voiced labour's many grievances and threatened to take positive action to remedy those grievances. Unless Canadian workers were assured of jobs after the war, warned Pat Conroy, C.C.L. secretary-treasurer, the old parties would find ever more of them changing their political allegiance.[16] Even the T.L.C. informed Mackenzie King he must either "fulfil his promise to organized labour" by giving it full representation on war boards and Crown companies, or "submit its record to the people of Canada so that democracy may prevail."[17] Now it may have been true, as one biassed observer argued, that most labour men were not fully convinced socialists and that if the capitalist parties could develop a program reasonably geared to meet labour's demands, many unionists would gladly accept it.[18] But the fact was that by 1944, Canadian capitalism had not yet made itself attractive to labour, although it was beginning to make the attempt.

In fact the opposite was true. The faith of the labour movement in the utility of direct political action had been powerfully stimulated by the Ontario election results. In September 1943, the C.C.L. convention took a momentous and historical decision. An overwhelming majority of the delegates agreed that

> Whereas . . . the policy and programme of the CCF more adequately express the view of organized labour than any other party:
> Be it therefore resolved that . . . the C.C.L. endorse the CCF as the political arm of Labour in Canada, and recommend to all affiliated and chartered unions that they affiliate with the CCF.

It was made clear that the Congress itself was not in politics; it was a labour, not a political body. Political action would be left to the CCF, hopefully with strong support from C.C.L. affiliates.[19] Nevertheless, it was a singular breakthrough for the CCF.

Party leaders were determined to exploit this unprecedented opportunity. After intensive consultation with senior trade unionists, Brewin and Jolliffe drafted a new Trade Union Act to replace the existing Ontario Collective Bargaining Act. The draft was circulated to all Ontario locals for comment, and during the subsequent months the party received "many letters all expressing approval of the Act."[20]

This was good politics, but good organization was necessary as well. Consequently, in October 1943, Charles Strange, M.P.P. for Brantford and a U.A.W. member, was appointed director of the Trade Union Committee to carry on the work originally begun by Clarence Gillis. In the next six months, Strange travelled across Ontario, attempting to convince local unions of the benefits to be derived from affiliating with the CCF. He helped set up CCF union committees in half a dozen industrial towns to "carry on local CCF-union work." In the year after the Ontario election, eight additional locals had affiliated, including the large steelworkers' local in Hamilton. By mid-1944, forty thousand unionists, including the thirteen thousand members of District 26 of the Mineworkers in Nova Scotia, were affiliated with or had endorsed the Ontario CCF.[21]

To some extent, Strange's task was facilitated by the C.C.L's endorsement of the CCF. For several months after its convention, no move had been made actively to implement that decision. Finally, in April 1944, the C.C.L. announced the appointment of a Political Action Committee (P.A.C.). Its primary functions were to institute a program of political education for affiliated locals and to act as a liaison between the Congress and the CCF.

One of the P.A.C.'s first measures was the adoption of a political program to submit to the October 1944 C.C.L. convention. The document emphasized the need to conquer unemployment, poverty, fear, and insecurity in peacetime, and stressed labour's political role in achieving such a goal.[22] At the convention, a deliberate attempt was made to defeat this program, which in effect would have reversed the earlier endorsement of the CCF. The opposition took the quaint form of an alliance between right-wingers from Quebec, old line Gomperites, and the Communist minority within the Congress. Finally, despite such formidable opposition, CCF supporters triumphed and the P.A.C.'s program was accepted by a vote of 272 to 185.

Subsequently, when that program was submitted to the various political parties, the CCF ·alone gave it wholehearted support. King replied "in his conventional, non-commital style," while the Conservatives, Communists, and Social Credit made no reply whatever.[23] The C.C.L. thereupon reaffirmed its preference among Canada's political parties, and formal CCF-C.C.L. cooperation, through the P.A.C., was once more resumed.

In truth, however, the P.A.C.'s contribution to the CCF between 1943 and 1945 was meagre and ineffectual. To be sure, some educational work was done, some leaflets were published, and a few local labour councils were persuaded to establish political action committees in their district. But all this was, at best, a grave disappointment to CCF leaders who expected the P.A.C. to raise large sums of money for the party and to place many organizers in the field, as the C.I.O.-P.A.C. did for Roosevelt in the United States.[24] Moreover, the mass union support for the CCF expected after the Congress' 1943 resolution never materialized. It was soon apparent that the resolution was too radical a departure from traditional attitudes towards political action. Local unions misrepresented it, believing they were being forced to affiliate with the CCF to retain membership in the Congress. Gomperites, Communists, Liberals, and Conservatives all attempted to sabotage the C.C.L.'s decision. Hence many union leaders refused to advise their locals to follow the convention's directive and, according to one active participant, the majority of trade unions refused to support the CCF morally or financially.[25] And even trade union leaders who did support the CCF were giving it only sporadic assistance, relying largely on their personal prestige to bring the rank and file into the party with them. But as the CCF learned to its dismay, conversion by example was an utter failure in the labour movement.[26] Then, as since, the reality was that most union leaders, many out of conviction, some as a function of their position, supported the party more or less actively. The preponderance of their rank and file, however, consistently followed more traditional voting patterns. This reality never tempered the hostility of many middle class CCF'ers to "labour bosses" or their devotion to the mass of workers who persistently repudiated their overtures.

While the C.C.L. thus supported the CCF with no great energy, the other half of organized labour in Canada did not even make a pretense of its political sympathies. The refusal by the Trades and Labour Congress officially to endorse the CCF was a great blow to the party. Although the T.L.C.'s 1943 convention was highly-charged with a general anti-government sentiment,[27] delegates would not go further than a guarded resolution calling upon affiliated unions to create political action committees,

> so as to enable the trade unions to play a more direct and more appropriate role in influencing and shaping the great movement for independent political action . . . ; we further recommend the labour unions support candidates who favour the policies of this Congress.[28]

During the following year, little or nothing was done to translate the resolution into concrete action, and the 1944 convention witnessed many demands for immediate steps towards fulfilment. This was, however, a distinctly minority sentiment. There was instead a general emphasis on non-partisanship, reflecting in part a reaction to the C.C.L.'s decision, in part the craft union basis of the Congress, and partly the tactic of a Liberal-Communist coalition, represented by Percy Bengough, T.L.C. president and a Liberal, and secretary-treasurer Pat Sullivan, a Communist. The majority agreed that union members should receive political information from the "centre," but that the T.L.C. should support no political party; it should be free to oppose any "reactionary" government. The political action resolution was even less resolute than the one of 1943.[29]

Like that of the industrial worker, the attitude of the rural community to the revived CCF was initially ambiguous. And like labour leaders, the spokesmen of rural Ontario were growing increasingly wary about free enterprise without advocating or accepting socialism. The influential *Rural Co-operator*, circulation 25,000, called for a postwar extension of public ownership as well as "a considerable extension of profit-sharing and control-sharing with employees in so-called private business."[30] It echoed the CCF cry that "our society has broken down. . . . Reconstruction of our society is what we have to do to avoid war and depression."[31]

The *Co-operator*, however, had powerful competition from two well-established, popular and absolutely fanatic anti-CCF rural papers, the *Farmers' Advocate* and the *Countryman*. They viewed the CCF as a simple crypto-Communist conspiracy, and more importantly, as a labour-dominated organization hostile to rural interests. The politicians soon followed this lead. The magnitude and effectiveness of this attack, as early as January 1944, was indicated in a letter to David Lewis from a United Church minister in rural Ontario "re the barage [*sic*] of poison gas against the CCF. Some more of it in my mail tonight. . . . The suggestion that socialism would mean that farmer-owners would cease to own their farms is old stuff, but effective in certain quarters."[32]

The CCF appointed a rural organizer who operated with a certain amount of apparent success.[33] It also attempted, according to David Lewis, to create a "psychological environment in the party" in which the farmer "feels himself at home." "At every step," he claimed, "the farmer is given as prominent a place in the party's literature, programme and deliberations as the industrial worker."[34] In Ontario, however, unlike Saskatchewan, the disjunction between what the CCF said and what it was could not be disguised. This was as true in 1944 as it had been in 1934. Intellectually, the party spoke a language at best irrelevant, at worst abhorrent, to rural Ontario. Politically, its primary focus was palpably on industrial areas. The unmistakeable truth was that farmers were viewed almost in the abstract, simply another peripheral group whose problems, as Agnes Macphail's biographers observed, "were only part of a general struggle for betterment."[35] But rural Ontario's collective ego needed far greater attention than that. The CCF was intrinsically incapable of responding to that need. In consequence, the anti-socialist propagandists spoke to an audience to which their cant was almost self-evident truths.

In fact it is clear that a large part of the CCF's support in 1943 was, at best, tenuous. This fact received its first public confirmation in a remarkable civic election in Toronto on January 1, 1944. That election saw the Ontario CCF make the most determined bid in its history for recognition on the municipal level. It also saw the party's opponents make their most desperate effort ever to defeat CCF candidates. Since municipal politics in Ontario had always been dominated in fact if not openly by the old parties, all CCF'ers ran under the party label. This immediately evoked the accusation that socialist "bosses" were trying to control city hall, and, according to *Maclean's* Magazine, that absolute "domination in every administrative and educational division is essential to the CCF program."[36]

Toronto newspapers conducted a determined anti-CCF campaign, in which they fully developed the line that the CCF was akin to fascism and "national socialism." A typical cartoon in the Toronto *Telegram* pictured a Torontonian and a German reading local newspapers with the respective headlines: "CCF To Contest Toronto Civic Elections" and "Nazi Party To Make

Bid For Local Government."[37] There was also a significant "Get Out The Vote" movement. Insofar as it supported no specific candidates, it was a non-partisan organization. But since it was openly sponsored by the Toronto Board of Trade, it was known to be a thinly-veiled attempt to assure that anti-CCF voters turned out at the polls. Its advertisements called upon "Men of Influence" to "Use your influence with your employees and associates to get them to vote – and set the example by voting yourself."[38]

The incredible culmination of this campaign came on its last day when a large and nauseatingly crude advertisement appeared in both the Toronto *Telegram* and *Globe and Mail*. It was headed: "THIS IS THE SLATE TO RUB OUT NEW YEAR'S DAY!" Toronto's voters were told they "should ask questions about ... these candidates who seek their votes. Here they are, hold your nose, and read them over." There followed a list of all the CCF municipal candidates including George Grube, William Dennison, Herbert Orliffe, and Murray Cotterill, with the flat, unequivocal assertion that every one of them was a Communist.[39] This document was the work, as might be expected, of Mr. M. A. Sanderson, which he prepared, it was later proved, with the assistance and in the office of Constable W. J. Osborne-Dempster, a secret agent in the employ of the Ontario Provincial Police.[40]

Sanderson, the Board of Trade, and the daily press successfully accomplished their mission. On January 1, Toronto's property holders stormed the polls in a panic of hysteria brought on by the warnings of "regimentation," "dictatorship," and "the end of freedom of opinion and voting" unless every CCF candidate was defeated.[41] The city's solid burghers made no mistake, for the entire CCF slate – twenty-three persons – was rejected. At least this part of "the CCF plot to get control of Canada"[42] was thwarted. It was a job well done: in many sections of Rosedale and North Toronto, between seventy and eighty per cent of those eligible voted; in working class districts, exactly the same number did not bother voting. Due to the CCF's failure to rouse its supporters as its opponents had done, the average vote in industrial areas was about one-quarter of those eligible, only slightly higher than the 1943 percentage.

The Toronto election provided a great stimulus to old party supporters across Canada who hailed it as the first substantial setback for the CCF since the Ontario election. *Saturday Night*, for example, felt vindicated in its oft-repeated theory that the

CCF gains since 1942 were due not to any desire of the electorate for a socialist government, but rather for an effective opposition

> to provide a more efficient chetk upon the more predatory elements in our economic life than either of the old parties. The function they were desired to perform was purely negative. When ... they made themselves the second largest party in the Ontario legislature and began to look like a possible government, the reaction of the electors was exactly what one would expect in these circumstances. . . . The situation is simple. The CCF desires to ditch the system of private enterprise. The electors do not want this system ditched. They will not vote to put the CCF in a position to ditch it.[43]

This was an acute and precisely accurate analysis. The September 1943 Gallup Poll was the first and last of its kind in Canadian history. Early in 1944, a new poll was released; it read Liberal 30 per cent, P.C. 29, CCF 24. The socialist tide was beginning to recede; the anti-socialist campaign was gathering momentum. Canada was on its way back to normality.

II

In 1920, Canadian business raised one million dollars to wage a propaganda campaign against rising free trade sentiment and its main proponent, the Progressive Party.[44] Then the threat was no more than the possibility of somewhat smaller profits. A socialist party, on the other hand, could legitimately be perceived as a challenge to the very existence of the profit system. It became evident soon after the Ontario election to what lengths business would go to meet such a challenge.

Between August and December 1943, the following events occurred. A meeting of insurance salesmen was told by a national officer of the Canadian Underwriters' Association of the "supreme necessity of combating the menace of the CCF"; he suggested that his audience inform their clients across the nation that, under the CCF, life insurance policies and individual savings would be confiscated. A meeting of the Executive Board of the Canadian Chamber of Commerce scrapped its regular agenda and discussed instead propaganda schemes designed to "combat the menace of socialism"; it was decided that no consideration of cost be allowed to stand in the way of this task. In Toronto, a meeting of the Property Owners' League of Ontario discussed as its main topic the need to defend "free enterprise" from the CCF's attacks.[45]

Finally, and most importantly, a special public relations office for business was established in Toronto. Its head, William Ewart Gladstone Murray, was a Rhodes Scholar who had joined the Canadian Broadcasting Corporation as General-Manager in 1936, but had resigned in 1943 at the request of a Special Committee of the House of Commons for failing to account for moneys he received and spent.[46] When he left the C.B.C., Murray went to see J. P. Bickell, the mining magnate, and offered himself as an "adviser" to business.[47] Bickell accepted, and helped set Murray up as the head of "Responsible Enterprise." Shortly thereafter, on June 21, 1943, Frank B. Common, a Montreal lawyer, invited a group of businessmen to a private luncheon in Montreal to be addressed by Murray. A "confidential memorandum" was prepared by Common for his guests, which included a copy of Murray's speech; but one of those in attendance was an apostate who sent a copy of the document to the *New Commonwealth*.[48] The meeting had been arranged so that Murray could "sell" himself as "a point of reference" for business. More "imaginative planning" and "psychological initiative" were needed to promote free enterprise; Murray stated that "the step was taken upon the advice of leaders in finance and industry to fill the gap that clearly existed. Public education through existing channels" – which he later listed as "all agencies of idea-distribution and propaganda: the press, private radio stations, service clubs, schools, and all other accessible organizations"[49]

> should be strengthened and inspired. . . . Something of the old pride in individual achievement was to be recaptured in the public imagination. . . . The problem of primary importance [to business] is to see that free enterprise is interpreted correctly and attractively outside the realm of practical politics. . . . New opportunities for venture capital, given the conditions of confidence, are incalculable. . . .

The organization plan drawn up for Murray by "the head of an industrial concern in consultation with the head of one of the chartered banks," covered a period of three years, beginning April 1, 1943, with an expenditure "limited" to $100,000 a year. "The participating concerns so far represent the oil industry, mining, newsprint and radio," from which sixty thousand dollars had already been raised. The purpose of the luncheon was to raise the remaining forty thousand dollars for 1943. However, despite Murray's assurance that "there is reason to believe . . . that the amounts are admissible as a business expense for income tax purpose," the entire sum may not have been pledged, for Common sent out copies of Murray's address to a further list of prospects the same day.[50]

On the day of the Ontario election, Murray himself wrote to a group of potential business supporters, emphasizing the "sweep forward" of the CCF "to power at Ottawa." His report continued: " . . . for Private Enterprise, there is as yet only a faint realization of the danger of the trend. *Numerous* organizations and agencies are operating in an isolated patchwork, often overlapping, and sometimes, conflicting." Two days later, when the Ontario results were known, Murray added the plea that it was time "to recover lost ground – the 40% of Ontario voters who supported the CCF – and to re-establish the case for free enterprise through continuous and concentrated education for which this project was created."

The Ontario results, Murray knew, would shock businessmen into the need for an anti-socialist counterattack. To convince them that he was the man to take charge of this campaign, he noted that his supporters "now include leading corporations in industry, finance, mining and public utilities." The group of companies, both Canadian and American, represented by the "sponsors" he then listed was certainly impressive. They included six banks, eight trust companies, seven insurance companies, seven investment companies, twelve steel companies, eight oil companies, thirty mining companies, four railways, six pulp and paper companies, three power companies, nine milling and grain companies, and almost forty miscellaneous concerns including Massey-Harris, Dominion Glass, Wabasso Cotton, Imperial Tobacco, Consumers' Gas, and Bell Telephone.

The twenty-one business leaders to whom Murray was referring "prospects" in soliciting their support comprised a veritable "Who's Who" of Canadian industry. Included were a former prime minister; a former federal Liberal cabinet minister; the presidents of Continental Oil, Imperial Oil, International Nickel, McIntyre Porcupine Mines, Noranda Mines, Imperial Tobacco, National Breweries, Consumers' Gas, the Ontario Paper Company, and Massey-Harris, and the Canadian representative of Colonel Bertie McCormick of the Chicago *Tribune*. Together, these men held at least 52 company presidencies, 17 vice-presidencies, and 106 additional directorships. Directors and officials of American business concerns supported Murray as well, representing such enterprises as United States Steel, Chase National Bank, the American Bank Note Company, and General Electric.

The individuals involved were no less prestigious. There was the Rt. Hon. Arthur Meighen, then president of two trust companies; King's former finance minister, Charles A. Dunning, president or director of nine companies; Charles McCrea, a Conservative cabinet minister in Ontario from 1923-1932, with interests in mining and trust companies; James S. Duncan of Massey-Harris; Murray's mining friend J. P. Bickell, who held interests as well in Maple Leaf Gardens, the Bank of Commerce, Inco, and the National Trust Company; Burnham Mitchell, assistant general-manager of the Royal Bank of Canada; and R. C. Stanley, president of Inco.[51] A further letter added the names of eight "additional supporters," all prominent industrialists with the notable exception of one Stephen Leacock of Orillia and McGill.[52]

Murray's venture embodies several characteristics which were common to the entire subsequent anti-socialist campaign. Despite the support of Charles Dunning, Conservatives were more active supporters than were Liberals, and Tory politicians more freely borrowed his style and content than did Liberals. That style can be described as paranoid. This did not necessarily mean that those employing it suffered from paranoia. It was a deliberate strategy, in the words of Richard Hofstadter, to portray the CCF as part of a "vast, insidious, preternaturally effective, conspiratorical network designed to perpetrate acts of the most fiendish character."[53]

This strategy was demonstrated in the content of the propaganda, which can be broken down into four overriding themes. First, because of the reality of the Russian contribution to the Allied war effort, it was necessary to downplay the equation of the CCF with Soviet Communism and instead to identify it with German Naziism. It followed, in the second place, that a CCF government would mean absolute regimentation, totalitarianism, and an end to individual freedom and choice. In short – this was the third theme – the CCF would undermine the Canadian Way of Life because it was a foreign conspiracy led by non-Canadians; xenophobia and anti-Semitism were particularly popular in connection with David Lewis. Finally, a puritanical anti-intellectualism was exploited to describe the CCF's leaders:

they were a group of "academic snobs" with no practical business experience, amateurs and irresponsible idealists who had never met a payroll.

These accusations may not have been true, but they were at least profitable. Attacking the CCF soon developed into a flourishing little commercial empire. According to *Maclean's* Ottawa correspondent, there were in April 1944 no fewer than twelve private anti-socialist organizations operating across Canada. One was in British Columbia, one or more in Ottawa, and three each in Montreal and Toronto; the others he did not specify. He claimed that with the exception of Murray's "Responsible Enterprise," these outfits were small and had only modest funds "put up by little groups of corporations or individuals."[54]

This was inaccurate; there existed a second propaganda concern of more than "modest" scope and resources. Indeed, Murray's endeavours were beginning to shrink into insignificance in the face of a new body which burst into prominence in May 1944, under the stirring name, "The Society For Individual Freedom (Opposing State Socialism)." "Only by vigorous, combined and immediate action can this threat to our system of Democracy [i.e. State Socialism] be completely destroyed," declared its introductory announcement. The sentiments are Murray's, but the voice was that of Burdrick A. Trestrail, Canada's newest saviour of free enterprise. "Can it be possible," mused the *Canadian Forum*, "that here is a rival contender for Murray's profits?"[55]

Trestrail had come to Canada from Missouri during the first war and had held a variety of jobs, the latest of which was personnel manager at the John Inglis Company. Late in 1943, he left Inglis to manage the Board of Trade's successful anti-CCF campaign in the Toronto municipal election. In February 1944, Trestrail organized General Relations Services Limited, a firm created "to carry on business as industrial and merchandising counsel and as campaign organizers." It was this company, controlled by Trestrail, which was "appointed" to handle all finances for the Society of Individual Freedom, of which B. A. Trestrail was national secretary.

The Society, or Trestrail, immediately unleashed a torrent of newspaper advertisements, daily radio broadcasts and direct-mail propaganda against what was invariably called "State Socialism." Its material declared that the Society was sponsored by no particular group or class, but the CCF was again put in possession of a private letter sent to an executive of a firm which Trestrail was soliciting for funds. The letter, and the "Plan of Organization" accompanying it, suggested that this boast would be difficult to substantiate.[56]

The information revealed that the Society was sponsored by some thirty-five men, who, between them, were directors of at least ninety-eight corporations, including six chartered banks, six insurance companies, four trust companies, plus such firms as British-American Oil, Algoma Steel, Canadian Breweries, John Inglis, Robert Simpson, Canadian General Electric, Loblaw's, Kresge's, Woolworth's, and several others. All of them, according to Trestrail, had "indicated their willingness to support [his] movement." The list of individual sponsors included Edgar Burton of Simpson's, Clifford Sifton of the Winnipeg *Free Press*, the general manager of the Bank of Nova Scotia (on both Murray's and Trestrail's lists), the general manager and the director of the Imperial Bank of Canada, the president of the Bank of Toronto, the director of Algoma Steel (on both lists), the assistant general manager of the Royal Bank of Canada (on both lists), the general manager of the Dominion Bank, and the director of the Canadian Bank of Commerce (also on both lists).

The letter disclosed that, to raise the funds "for launching and conducting the campaign to combat State Socialism . . . a full time field representative will start soliciting from large and small firms in Toronto." Each letter included a "temporary monthly fee suggested for your organization," with the hope that a cheque would shortly be submitted. The enclosed "Plan of Organization" informed recipients that

> Mr. Stewart Wallace, Librarian of the University of Toronto, has accepted the position of [national] president [of the Society] and B. A. Trestrail has been appointed national secretary. . . . A National Management Committee, composed of prominent business executives, has been appointed to approve all the preliminary plans and expenditures. . . . The executive services and staff of General Relations Service Limited have been retained for the purpose of organizing and conducting the campaign [against State Socialism]. All . . . revenues and all disbursements will be handled by this company. . . . Fees received from clients will be used to provide such clients with the Company's Industrial Relations and Labour Service, and to finance all costs of the Society's campaign.

The "Plan" further outlined a minimum Toronto budget of

$14,000 per month, or $168,000 each year, to be divided as follows:

Fees to General Relations Services Limited	$3000 per month
Toronto Branch Operating Expenses	3000 per month
Toronto advertising and literature	7500 per month
Miscellaneous	500 per month

In addition, it indicated that the cost of expanding the campaign to other parts of Ontario would be an additional five thousand dollars per month, plus "operating expenses."

It is not possible to determine with any accuracy the cost of the anti-socialist campaign waged by Murray, Trestrail, and their several small-time competitors between 1943 and 1945. But we know enough about the magnitude of the campaign to conclude with some confidence that it was the most massive propaganda drive in Canadian political history.

The nature of corporate public relations during the war facilitated the task. As early as 1940, many businesses began adopting "institutional advertising," a gambit wherein their particular contribution to the war effort was stressed more than the superiority of their product. By 1943, such advertising had become commonplace. After the Ontario election, however, the message began subtly to change. Slowly at first, but with increasing frequency through 1944 and 1945, corporate advertisements began shifting the emphasis from one's contribution to the war effort to the virtues of the free enterprise system. The Canadian Pacific Railway, of all things, was declared with a straight face to be a "product of free enterprise" which "exemplifies the initiative and resource of free Canadian enterprise."[57] "But Four Freedoms are not enough!" the E. B. Eddy Company pictured a typical man telling his typical wife:

> The greatest democratic freedom of all [is] – freedom of individual enterprise .... The right of free choice ... [of] our opinions, our words, our religion, our homes .... It takes in every man's right to ... bet on his own ability to get ahead as far and as fast as his own talent and initiative will carry him. .... [58]

The shift in emphasis from selling Victory Bonds to selling free enterprise was, without question, most apparent in the voluminous outpouring of Canada's chartered banks and insurance companies. Since in those days the CCF constantly re-affirmed its pledge that the nationalization of banks and financial institutions would be the first action of a federal socialist administration, it was logical that the nation's private bankers should have been most concerned by the Ontario election.

From the very next day, the banks, through such agencies as Gladstone Murray's, began industriously and lavishly advertising the merits of democracy, arguing that democracy was indissolubly wedded to free enterprise and personal profit. "The opportunity to make a fair profit," announced the Bank of Toronto, "is one of the essential freedoms in any freedom loving country."[59]

> Only the business that fills a public want at prices the public is willing to pay can remain profitable. Thus the profit motive in business is actually a lever in the hands of the people controlling industrial activity, keeping it in line with public demand. (Bank of Toronto.)[60]

> What is private enterprise? It is the natural desire to make your own way as far as your ability will take you; an instinct that has brought to this continent the highest standard of life enjoyed by any people on earth. It is democracy on the march. (Royal Bank of Canada.)[61]

In December, 1943, three separate full-page advertisements appeared in *Saturday Night*, reporting in full the speeches given at the annual meetings of three chartered banks (Dominion, Montreal, Commerce) by their respective presidents; each denounced socialist "dictatorship" and "regimentaion" and saw "greater opportunities under [the] system of free enterprise." Pointing to such advertisements, the magazine's financial editor noted that, "though the CCF's attitude toward banking has existed for many years, it is only comparatively recently that the banks themselves have begun to do something about it, using press and radio advertisements. Now the banks' big guns are being brought into action."[62]

Hardly less ammunition was being expended by the frightened life insurance companies. In December 1943, Lloyd Shaw, CCF National Research Director, announced that a CCF government would consider nationalizing life insurance companies, since they charged "unfair" prices and since interlocking directorates between insurance companies and major industries had created "monopolistic control and economic dictatorship" in Canada.[63] As a result of this statement, as M. J. Coldwell stated, "Vast sums of money have been spent in newspaper ads to place the records of life insurance companies in a satisfactory light before the Canadian people, and to meet – at least implicitly – CCF criticism." Moreover, he noted, "The political servants of capitalism are busy too, trying to make the electors believe that the CCF is out to destroy your life insurance policies and to confiscate your savings."[64] Coldwell's reference was to the type of newspaper headline which read: "Every Insurance Policy in Peril If CCF Elected, Drew Warning to Voters."[65]

The campaign took other forms besides advertisements and radio broadcasts sponsored by industry. *Maclean's* mass-circulation publication, for example, reversed its traditional non-partisan political policy in order to combat the CCF menace. This was done not only editorially. For the greater edification of its readers, the program of the American Federation of Labour and statements by its anachronistic president William Green were quoted often and with pleasure. "Free enterprise and free labour are interdependent," declared the A.F. of L. "Neither can last without the other."[66] Bruce Hutchison became *Maclean's* favourite professional anti-socialist, his frequent articles tirelessly re-iterating the proposition that "we know by experience that personal freedom can only survive on the principle of competing powers. We cannot," he cautioned, "give up our liberty and freedom for a promise of security handed down from the top."[67]

The attack raged on all sides. The CCF national office accumulated about forty books and twice as many pamphlets in those years attacking the party. William S. Gibson, president of National Cellulose, for example, wrote a long answer to Lewis and Scott's *Make This Your Canada*. Called *You Knew What You Were Voting For*, Gibson's easily digested work was circulated by at least one federal Conservative candidate in the 1945 election.[68] Stanley F. Pearson's anti-socialist tract, *It's A Good Life*, sold in any local cigar store for twenty-five cents.[69] The president of the Canadian Construction Association told his colleagues that the "first step" in combatting the "dangerous movement" of socialism was to "enable our employees to be properly informed as to the significance of what is going on. . . . "[70] Frederick Gardiner, reeve of Forest Hill Village and an upwardly mobile Tory, told a businessmen's meeting that

> Socialistic rule in Canada would mean "muscle-men and gangsters," who understand mob organization and the handling of machine guns, and they are already fomenting discontent in the belief that they will be commissars should the Karl Marx philosophy come to this country . . . .[71]

Radio Station CFRB in Toronto refused to sell the CCF time to answer charges made by the Society For Individual Freedom over that station; its official policy was to have no political broadcasts between elections, and "we do not consider the Society's broadcasts political. They are not for or against any particular party."[72] The press distorted reports of speeches made by CCF leaders, particularly one by Harold Winch, leader of the British Columbia party; as the Canadian Press filed it, Winch stated that "the power of the police and military would be used by a CCF government to force obedience on those opposed to the law," and that "those who defied the government's will would be treated as criminals; if capitalism says no, then we know the answer – so did Russia."[73] At the same time, literally each day brought forth new editorials warning against the grave menace of "state socialism."

The Conservative Party adopted the strategy of referring to the CCF on every possible occasion as the "national socialist" party. Bracken liked to couple references to the CCF with references to the Nazis in Germany,[74] while Drew labelled the CCF "an anti-British, revolutionary, National Socialist party."[75] Arthur Meighen declared there could

> be only two systems, the totalitarian and our own. . . . Force has to come if the higher incentives [i.e. "the incentive of reward, bigger earnings . . . "] go. In every socialist country today, the Gestapo, the O.G.P.U . . . stands behind the whole population. . . . Freedom of enterprise and political freedom live together and can never live apart. . . . "[76]

The Society For Individual Freedom unleashed door-to-door canvassers, ostensibly taking a public opinion poll, asking Toronto residents whether they supported or opposed "State Socialism." This term they defined as "the sort of system they have in Germany and Russia, where the government takes everything away from you and tells everybody what to do."[77] Indeed, no medium of communication, from personal contact to press, radio, public speeches, and letters to the editor,[78] failed to be exploited against the CCF. As three clergymen complained, in separate letters to the United Church *Observer*, "The barrage is on . . . with the mails filled with propaganda from those who fear the growing influence of socialism."[79] The battle had been joined, and neither side was yet confident of the final outcome.

130   *The Dilemma of Canadian Socialism*

References

1. *New Commonwealth,* October 14 and October 28, 1943.

2. Memorandum, 1944, in Provincial Convention Reports.

3. CCF National Office Files, Isabel Thomas, Education Committee Chairman, to Lloyd Shaw, November 18, 1943.

4. David Lewis and Frank Scott, *Make This Your Canada* (Toronto, 1943).

5. Organization Committee Report to 1944 Provincial Convention; Secretary's Report to *ibid.; New Commonwealth,* January 27, 1944.

6. *New Commonwealth,* February 24, 1944.

7. Minutes, Provincial Council Meeting, October 8, 1944; *New Commonwealth,* November 8, December 14, and December 28, 1944.

8. CCF National Office Files, letter from National Secretary to all CCF Provincial Secretaries, February 1, 1944.

9. National Office Files, Orr to Lewis, February 5, 1944; Lewis to Scott, March 8, 1944.

10. *Ibid.,* Millard to Lewis, March 15, 1944.

11. *Ibid.,* Frank Mackenzie to Lewis, May 2, 1944.

12. *Ibid.,* Lewis to Harry Wilks, April 25, 1944.

13. The Montreal *Star,* St. John *Telegraph Journal,* Montreal *La Presse,* Moncton *L'Evangeline,* and five small Saskatchewan weeklies rejected all three advertisements. The Toronto *Star* and Sudbury *Star* rejected the advertisements using the octopus, which referred to Hitler as "Public Enemy Number One" and monopoly capitalism as "Public Enemy Number Two." The latter's publisher sanctimoniously wrote that this advertisement "struck a new low in advertising ethics and patriotism.... You try ... to link up many of the most stable, substantial and patriotic institutions we have in Canada with the most hated name in the world.... I do not feel that I have been 35 years building up a newspaper to subscribe to any such tactics. The authors of this calumny have a helluva gall and impudence to ask any decent paper to publish it." CCF National Office File, W. E. Mason to Tandy Advertising Agency, April 17, 1944.

14. Leo Zakuta, "Membership in a Becalmed Protest Movement," *C.J.E.P.S.,* May 1958, p. 199, footnote 6.

15. *Saturday Night,* September 11, 1943.

16. *Canadian Unionist,* January 1944.

17. Cited in *New Commonwealth,* September 9, 1943.

18. Hugh Mackenzie, general-manager of John Labatt, Ltd., in *Canadian Unionist,* November 1943. Mackenzie based his conclusions on a series of interviews conducted by himself with "a representative cross-section" of labour leaders.

19. Cited in Logan, *Trade Unions in Canada,* p. 555.

20. CCF Trade Union Committee Report to 1944 Convention.

21. *Ibid.;* National Office Files.

22. *Canadian Unionist.*

23. Logan, *op. cit.*, p. 560.

24. McHenry, *Third Force In Canada,* pp. 105-6.

25. M. M. Armstrong, *The Development of Trade Union Political Activity in the CCF,* pp. 44-5. Mrs. Armstrong was then secretary of the United Steelworkers and an active CCF member.

26. George Burt, U.A.W. president, provides a fair example of this situation. CCF-M.P.P. William Riggs wrote David Lewis that "Our big weakness [in Windsor] is that we do not have enough active members in the U.A.W. I saw Burt, and he stated that he was disappointed that after his joining our movement so few followed him." National Office Files, Riggs to Lewis, June 5, 1944.

27. *Report of the Proceedings of the 59th Annual Convention of the T.L.C. of Canada,* August 30-September 3, 1943.

28. Logan, *op. cit.*, p. 434.

29. *Ibid.,* pp. 435-7.

30. *Rural Co-operator,* October 24, 1944.

31. *Ibid.,* November 9, 1943.

32. National Office Files, Rev. R. E. Fairburn to Lewis, January 20, 1944.

33. Provincial Executive Meetings, December 3, 1943; February 18, 1944.

34. David Lewis, "Farmer-Labour Unity: The Experience of the CCF," *Antioch Review,* Summer 1944, pp. 167-8.

35. Stewart and French, *Ask No Quarter,* p. 272.

36. *Maclean's,* February 1, 1944.

37. Toronto *Telegram,* December 31, 1943.

38. *Saturday Night,* January 1, 1944.

39. Toronto *Telegram,* December 31, 1943; Toronto *Globe and Mail,* January 1, 1944.

40. See *Report of Royal Commission Appointed May 28, 1945, To Investigate Charges Made by Mr. E. B. Jolliffe, Justice A. M. LeBel, Commissioner,* pp. 24-25. The sheer mendacity of this particular advertisement angered the CCF more than most of the propaganda current at the time. In January, two series of writs were issued against Sanderson and the two publishers, claiming damage for libel on behalf of six plaintiffs, members of the CCF mentioned in the advertisement.

    One year later, a "special" jury of businessmen found the advertisement was a malicious libel of these plaintiffs. They were awarded damages of one dollar each. The *Telegram* paid the plaintiffs' cost of three thousand dollars. All of them presented evidence proving the advertisement contained numerous falsehoods. *News,* January 22, 1945.

41. Front page editorial, Toronto *Telegram,* December 31, 1943.

42. *Ibid.*

43. *Saturday Night,* January 15, 1944.

44. S. D. Clark, "The Canadian Manufacturers' Association," *C.J.E.P.S.,* November 1938, p. 513.

45. *New Commonwealth,* December 9, 1943.

46. Edwin Guillet, *Famous Canadian Trials, volume 50, Political Gestapo*, chapter IV, section 4.

47. Interview with Gladstone Murray, 1961.

48. Jolliffe was reluctant to divulge the identity of this contact. At the 1945 "Gestapo" hearing, Murray admitted that a document shown him by Andrew Brewin was an accurate copy of his Montreal speech. Guillet, *op. cit.*, chapter IV, section 4.

49. Circular from Murray, September 29, 1943, in Guillet, *op. cit.*, Appendix G, Selections From Gladstone Murray's Circulars. Guillet's appendices consist of documents produced in evidence before the LeBel Commission investigating Jolliffe's charge of 1945 that the Drew government was maintaining a secret political police.

50. Cited in *New Commonwealth*, January 27, 1944.

51. Murray's Circular of August 4, 1943, in Guillet, *op. cit.*, Appendix G; also *Canadian Who's Who*, 1944.

52. Cited by Guillet, *op. cit.*, Appendix G, without quoting the entire letter.

53. Richard Hofstadter, *The Paronoid Style in American Politics and Other Essays* (New York, 1956), p. 14.

54. *Maclean's*, April 15, 1944.

55. *Canadian Forum*, March 1944.

56. *New Commonwealth*, June 22, 1944. Unfortunately, I have been unable to locate the original of this important document. There is, however, little reason to believe that, because the CCF paper is the only source for its contents, it is a fabrication. The organizational plan is quite consistent with later Trestrail plans for which original documentation is available. Moreover, although these facts appeared in every CCF provincial organ across Canada and in the *Canadian Forum*, there was, as far as I know, no attempt by any of those claimed to be Trestrail backers to deny it.

57. Advertisement in *Saturday Night*, May 12, 1944.

58. *Ibid.*, October 28, 1944.

59. *Canadian Forum*, January 1944.

60. *Saturday Night*, September 25, 1943.

61. *Ibid.*, September 18, 1943; *New Commonwealth*, January 13, 1944.

62. *Saturday Night*, December 18, 1943.

63. *Time*, January 3, 1944.

64. P.A.C., Macphail Papers, vol. 3, copy of Coldwell's speech, undated.

65. Toronto *Star*, May 31, 1945.

66. *Maclean's*, November 1, 1943; also January 1 and September 1, 1944.

67. *Ibid.*, November 15, 1943.

68. There is a copy of Gibson's book, with an inserted picture of a message from Allan Cockeram in the CCF Ontario Archives. Cockeram defeated Noseworthy in York South in 1945.

69. *New Commonwealth*, May 25, 1944. Socialists, if elected, wrote Pearson, "would form a class by themselves – a governing class like the Nazis in Germany."

70. Cited in *Canadian Unionist*, January 1944.

71. Toronto *Telegram*, November 30, 1943.

72. Cited in *New Commonwealth*, June 22, 1944.

73. *Ibid.*, November 25 and December 9, 1943. Even undistorted it was hardly a tasteful speech.

74. As cited, for example, in *ibid.*, December 23, 1943.

75. Cited in *Canadian Forum*, December 1943.

76. `"Socialism," in Meighen, *Unrevised and Unrepented*, pp. 433-52.

77. *New Commonwealth*, July 13, 1944. This incident was reported by a CCF'er who was visited by one of these canvassers.

78. My own favourite attack on the CCF was in a letter to the editor of the Toronto *Globe and Mail*:

     "If he gets to work at sixteen, a boy will learn his trade and get married when he should. Many others without very much education have become tremendously famous (example, John A. MacDonald, Lincoln, Shakespeare). ... Now take the other side of the picture. We have something over 232 Rhodes scholars, the most educated men alive. Most of them became CCF'ers or school teachers or ministers. Not a single solitary one of them made a fortune or made a nation-wide name for himself about anything." Cited in *Canadian Forum*, June 1944.

79. Cited in *New Commonwealth*, February 10, 1944.

9 POLITICIANS AT WORK

I

In a real sense, the CCF could feel proud and vindicated by the capitalist campaign against it. The intervention of the Communists, however, had few redeeming features. In June 1943, the Communist Party, outlawed by the King government early in the war, was transmuted into the legal Labour-Progressive Party. Its new catchword was democracy, its aim respectability: hence Tim Buck's gracious announcement that his party intended to work in closest cooperation with the CCF as a farmer-labour party "whether the leaders of the CCF liked it, or the members of the CCF. . . . "[1] In September, however, the CCF National Council bluntly refused the Communist application for affiliation to the party on the grounds that the L.P.P. was still a Communist organization and therefore was "anti-democratic, disruptive, opportunist, and irresponsible."[2]

On December 1, 1943, Stalin, Churchill, and Roosevelt signed the historic Teheran Declaration, promising to "work together in the war and in the peace that will follow."[3] With Teheran came a dramatic reversal in the Communist Party line. "After this," Tim Buck wrote with unusual realism,

> CCF leaders made matters easy for reactionary forces by . . . their speeches on "Socialism Now." . . . their "Socialism Now" contradicted the objective conditions prevailing in Canada and misrepresented the limited political aims of most Canadian workers. So the L.P.P. though still believing in socialism, appealed to the CCF to recognize that . . . in the conditions then prevailing in Canada, baseless declarations that the only alternative to the post-war policies of capitalist reaction would be "socialist planning by a CCF government" could only divide the forces that should be united in the struggle for democratic progress.[4]

Accordingly, the L.P.P. renounced its "socialist" ideology and pledged itself instead to elect a "government of national unity."

The problem was, unity with whom? The Conservatives were *a priori* "reactionaries," so automatically eliminated. The CCF was the obvious choice, but it refused to work either with capitalist or Communist parties. This left only the palpably absurd alternative of the Liberals, for it was, after all, the King government which had outlawed the Communist Party and St. Laurent who had refused to consider lifting the ban. That, apparently, was historically determined and therefore forgiveable. On May 29, 1944, the L.P.P. declared that a "Liberal-Labour" coalition government in Canada was the party's objective in the next general election, although the CCF would be welcome in the "Labour" section of the proposed alliance. This remarkable policy prompted several grotesque declarations from L.P.P. spokesmen. In August 1944, Tim Buck was quoted as saying that of all current political philosophies, that of King's Liberal Party most closely approached what "used to be known as Communism."[5] And Albert MacLeod, L.P.P. member of the Ontario legislature, asserted that "the CCF would virtually make the province and the nation an isolated island of depression in a sea of world prosperity. They would establish a medieval system of Communism in which the people would share their poverty."[6]

These inanities could not cloud one important fact: the Communists' attitude toward the CCF had not changed since they attempted to split the labour vote in the 1930's and urged unionists to support Drew in 1943. The CCF, no matter how desperate the means, had to be prevented from winning power. And, for the first time since 1935, they were prepared to admit this fact. The main objective of the Communist Party, said a leading spokesman in 1944, must be "a resounding defeat of the CCF at the polls."[7] During 1944 and 1945, the L.P.P.'s new policy led it to support the Liberals and harm the CCF wherever possible, while the Liberals reciprocated by choosing to ignore the question of the L.P.P.'s legality, although the Communist Party as such was still officially outlawed.[8]

The intricacies of the consequent party manoeuvring were reflected in the machinations taking place in Queen's Park, with the additional complication, of course, of the Conservatives' own strategy. By the time Drew called the first session of the twenty-first legislature on February 23, 1944, it was clear he planned no coalition with the Liberals as many observers had expected. Indeed, one reporter believed his standing with the electorate had so improved since the election that he would attempt to force an election at the earliest possible opportunity. Drew's problem was arranging this to his party's best advantage; it was in his interest to be defeated on a vote of non-confidence. But it was obvious that neither the Liberals nor the CCF had any intention of satisfying his needs. The Liberals wanted no part of an election. They had "undoubtedly sunk even lower in estate than ever since last August" and "word is that King most definitely would not want another Ontario contest before he calls the federal contest, for his party's fate in a provincial contest in Ontario would undoubtedly deliver another stunning blow to Liberal prestige in general. Bracken and Drew both appreciate this."[9] As for the CCF, its protestations to the contrary notwithstanding, it was in no hurry to begin again the difficult hunt for campaign funds. The deluge of anti-socialist propaganda was beginning to worry party leaders, who wanted all the time possible to strengthen the CCF's relatively weak organization. And no party wished to bear the onus of forcing an election at a time when most people believed one unnecessary.[10]

Accordingly, in reply to Drew's first throne speech, Jolliffe openly acknowledged that

> in recognition of the electors demand for a change [as proved by the 1943 election], the Throne Speech contains the promise of considerable progressive legislation. We will give the government credit for whatever progressive measures it brings in, though taking some credit for ourselves. For many of the Throne Speech reform measures appeared in the CCF's 1937 program. [Then they were ignored by the old parties.] At long last, when we became a powerful political force in this province, some of them suddenly appeared in the Progressive Conservative election platform. That was no coincidence!

The CCF, Jolliffe stated, was "prepared to consider all legislation on its merits and give the government the fullest opportunity to implement its program." And, if the government lost a division during the session, the CCF would not consider such a defeat a non-confidence vote "unless it is stated on our behalf prior to such division that, so far as we are concerned, the question is one of confidence or no confidence."[11]

The CCF's decision not to force an election was vindicated by Drew's first by-election victory in Haldimand-Norfolk late in March. Because the government candidate received 2800 votes more than the late Conservative who had won the seat in 1943, some saw the results as indicating a decline in CCF strength and "a pretty general satisfaction with Drew as premier."[12] But since the CCF had increased its vote from 2500 to 4500 in a largely rural area while the Liberals' vote declined from 7000 to 3900, socialists read the outcome as yet another step in their supplanting of the Liberals as the second major party in Ontario.[13] Yet even were this true, the by-election indicated that the CCF was some distance from becoming the first party in the province. Consequently, it would now be even more difficult for Drew to get himself defeated in the House; his opposition would not be carelessly drawn into voting non-confidence in the administration.

During the budget debate, for instance, Jolliffe declared that, though the CCF desired to get on with the business of the House, it felt its duty was to protest the government's "inadequate" policy as represented by the budget. He therefore moved an amendment, "regretting" that the administration had not undertaken "measures on a fully democratic basic toward the planned development of the natural resources of the province, and the social ownership of monopoly enterprises. . . . "[14] It was a patent political ploy; the Liberals could never support an amendment so worded and it predictably lost.[15]

Such gamesmanship was no doubt necessary. But the arcane intrigues of the Legislature were quite lost on the public consciousness, while they imposed real constraints on Jolliffe's leadership. Drew's personal abuse of Jolliffe became less restrained, a stratagem which at least one correspondent understood. "From the gallery it has been obvious that while the CCF leader has undoubted ability, his lack of practical political experience and popular appeal were a handicap and that he would make a vulnerable target." Jolliffe's major blunders came in the first few days of the session, when the novelty and centrality of his new role made him unnecessarily militant, aggressive, and unreasonable. His initial bow in the House had been made "not too gracefully, in a manner which lacked assurance and left the impression that he had a chip on his shoulder. . . . He took exception to the traditional procedure in appointing the speaker [and] both Nixon and McLeod [the L.P.P. House Leader] . . . dissociated themselves from this objection.

Indeed, there actually seemed to have been talk of replacing Jolliffe.[16] It is clear he had certain unfortunate personal characteristics which detracted from his leadership: a lack of capacity to be intimate with people; an inability to move easily with ordinary workers or to unbend with strangers; an impression of being a snob, a "returned Rhodes Scholar," and excessively solemn and unsmiling. He made more average people feel uncomfortable and even inadequate in his presence.[17]

But that Jolliffe was never replaced was attributable to more than the absence of a logical substitute. It was true that since a trade union leader might evoke a negative public reaction, Charles Millard, "the ablest CCF'er in the House," was eliminated. Aside from Millard, "there is no one in the Opposition who gives evidence of being able to take on the leadership. Garfield Anderson (Fort William) is the most mature of the few eligibles and might carry on ably in the House, but politically he is even more lacking in colour than Jolliffe and would not have the advantage of the latter's youth."[18] Agnes Macphail, one of the most widely known CCF members, was past her prime; she assumed too often "the *grande dame* manner in the House. . . . " She and Millard as well were inclined to form a puritanical partnership of their own on such moralistic questions as the liquor issue and make priggish statements quite different from the general feeling of the party.[19] With Jolliffe, these were the CCF's three best members in the House; to a lesser extent William Dennison, William Grummett, and Bert Leavens may be included among the other effective CCF parliamentarians. Of the remainder, they either had disqualifying personal idiosyncrasies or else were simply not natural leaders; two turned out to be fellow travellers while Mrs. Rae Lucock was "too inclined to stay home and do the family wash on Monday morning instead of attending caucus meetings."[20] Still, one must keep the situation in its proper perspective. After all, of thirty-four members, only Agnes Macphail had ever sat in parliament before. To have emerged with seven more or less able parliamentarians in a group of *arriviste* public figures was in fact a tribute to the inner strength of the CCF. Had the party won in 1943, its cabinet would have been substantially superior to the mediocrities represented in the average old party provincial administration.

But it was more than a mere process of elimination that kept Jolliffe in his post. The CCF's fear of prodding Drew into calling an election did nothing to increase the effectiveness of its members in the legislature; they were too intimidated by such a prospect to provide the most vigourous opposition possible. This feeling, it was understood, inhibited Jolliffe as much if not more than the rest of his following.[21] Moreover, as one observer pointed out, Jolliffe had not fared quite as badly as some unfriendly reports attempted to make it appear. After the early days of the session, with time to accustom himself to his position, he proceeded more constructively and impresssively. "In the debate and conduct of the House, he has been forceful and has held up his end well, and if he has not scored it must be remembered that in Drew he is opposed by an extremely able and experienced parliamentarian."[22] One writer, all adverse criticism notwithstanding, could still describe Jolliffe as the "radical who knows how to make left-wing doctrines seem ordinary to the orthodox."[23]

During the summer recess, the several parties kept busy mending their respective political fences. By far the most controversial political event during that period was Drew's vicious attack on the federal government for its announced intention of introducing "baby bonus" legislation. To paraphrase more gently what he told Harry Nixon, Drew did not intend to have Ontario pay for Quebec's prolific procreation,[24] the real function, as he saw it, of the family allowance scheme. This attack, B. K. Sandwell pointed out, would appeal to that large element in Ontario which was traditionally antipathetic to French-Canada. As Drew stated, he was not opposed to Ontario assisting poorer provinces to family allowances, or even to large families; but he did not favour and would not assist "large families of people that will not fight for Canada."[25]

The CCF feared Drew's devout bigotry would force an election. Jolliffe believed Drew's hope was to take advantage of the anti-King, anti-Quebec, anti-"Zombie" feeling prevalent in large sections of Ontario. Like the CCF, Nixon would certainly oppose Drew's baby bonus stand in the House, so the government's defeat was virtually assured. The CCF, consequently, had "no alternative but to take the lead and oppose the government forthwith. The caucus has agreed that the issue is both a false and dangerous one. The Tories would like to run wild in the campaign, arousing violent racial feelings which they will try to cash in on. We must do all we can to prevent the racial question from becoming the issue of the campaign."[26]

These calculations – indeed, everyone's calculations – received a sudden jolt when, early in October, Mitchell Hepburn bounced back as a self-proclaimed "reformer" to the Liberal fold he had left with equal abruptness two years earlier. Everything in the past was forgotten, not to say reversed. His new battle-cry was "national unity"; his new *bête noire*, to replace the c.i.o. and

Mackenzie King, was George Drew. By December 1944, "with the silent blessing of Ottawa Liberals,"[27] Hepburn was able to resume the leadership of the sixteen Liberals in Queen's Park from Harry Nixon. The reason he was welcomed back with such alacrity was obvious even then: if anyone could revive the hapless Ontario Liberal Party, it was the dynamic Hepburn, not the "likeable but colourless" Nixon.[28]

In the Ontario legislature it was felt that Hepburn would help crystallize the anti-Drew sentiment which had been increasing since the Premier's baby bonus speech. The L.P.P. in particular had intensified its campaign against the premier into an all-out demand for a coalition government to oust "the forces of Toryism." And Hepburn was listening to the L.P.P. "with an open mind." What he would ultimately decide to do was of more than mere academic interest. For the Ontario situation was in many ways a microcosm of the federal picture. Many observers believed that the next national government would be a minority one. The groups that would coalesce to form such an administration – whether a combination of the old parties against the CCF, or of all "left wing" groups against the Conservatives – might be foreshadowed by what transpired in Ontario.[29] In the new year, it seemed certain, all these complicated stratagems and machinations would, in some yet unpredictable manner, be resolved at last.

Indeed, in at least one province, the culmination of a similar series of events had already taken place. On June 15, 1944, the province of Saskatchewan had become what its new premier, T. C. Douglas, called "a beachhead of socialism on a continent of capitalism."[30] Not only had a socialist party actually conquered a provincial jurisdiction, it had won a most overwhelming and decisive victory.[31] Delirium raged among CCF'ers once more. Coldwell, with justifiable hyperbole, described the results as a "prelude to victory in the federal field."[32]

Less strongly emphasized was the crucial distinction between the nature of the Saskatchewan party and of all the other provincial units, not least the one in Ontario. One of Seymour Lipset's academic successors described the phenomenon in this way: "The voters of Saskatchewan elected the socialists after all other attempts at achieving a solution to unbearable economic problems failed. In electing the CCF, they chose the 'natural opposition' to the Liberals.... [The Party] meshed grass roots sentiment with locally respectable..., culturally acceptable..., aggressive provincial political leadership that represented the farmers."[33] Lipset himself had made clear that the Saskatchewan CCF was not seen as a movement for unnatural social and political change; rather, it was considered the logical new spokesman for the majority of the province's citizens. "It is the political voice of the rural community and is led by the 'normal' community leaders."[34]

Partly as a result, the prototypical North American attitude of passivity and quiescence towards political participation was reversed in Saskatchewan. The CCF there had "succeeded in involving more people in direct political activity" than probably any other party in Canadian or American history. Eight per cent of the 1944 Saskatchewan electorate were CCF members. In Toronto, the figure was three per cent. Based on the Saskatchewan ratio, Ontario should have had 150,000 members in 1944; in fact it had 15,000. As a result, the Ontario CCF "resembles the traditional North American parties, with little direct contact between the organization and the major part of the electorate."[35] Moreover, unlike their Saskatchewan counterparts, the Ontario party's leadership, membership and programme – those elements, in short, which created its public image – were all more or less "unnatural" and outside the mainstream of the province's political culture.

While the Ontario leadership was not unaware of such distinctions, it naturally chose to play them down. The Saskatchewan results, it was pointed out, changed the entire complexion of the national political scene. After the 1943 Ontario election, many anti-socialists had declared that the significant fact was not the CCF's "near win," but the reason it came only second: the farmers "saved Ontario" and could be counted upon to "save" the nation. Douglas's victory crushed such hopes; the defenders of free enterprise would have to resort to a new strategy. During the 1943 campaign, they had reminded rural Ontario that labour's demands for higher wages were forcing up the prices on commodities the farmer had to buy; and they took the August results as a vindication of this approach. June 15, 1944 suggested that more convincing propaganda would have to be devised.[36]

As anticipated, the national significance of the Saskatchewan results was being minimized by the old parties. They pointedly attributed the CCF victory to purely local conditions. This, suggested *Saturday Night's* Ottawa correspondent, was to ignore the fact that the socialists' triumph in part at least reflected

widespread sentiment elsewhere in Canada. He advised supporters of private enterprise to be less sanguine in their attitude, for

> There are signs that Canadians at large are increasingly
> distrustful of the old parties, if not towards the old order
> itself, that many of them . . . are looking towards the end of
> the war for pie in the sky . . . . The Saskatchewan results has
> [*sic*] piled up more good publicity for Coldwell's party than
> either the orthodox parties are likely to get between now and
> federal voting day. The psychological effect of Saskatchewan
> is bound to be considerable.[37]

Saskatchewan, then, seemed a forecast of things to come; and
there were other portents of the future that one could find, all
combining to form a vague but fairly consistent pattern. In
March 1944, the Gallup Poll asked Canadians whether the government should "own all industries that handle and distribute
certain necessities of life like milk, meat, bread and fuel, and sell
them to the public without profit." A remarkable 44 per cent
favoured such a proposal, 45 per cent opposed it, and only 11
per cent had no opinion.[38] Two months later, the poll revealed
that the prospect of post-war unemployment troubled Canadians
more than any other single problem.[39] Earlier, a business
reporter had noted that "everyone is discussing the prospects of
post-war business and employment, and the more discussion
there is, the more pessimistic nearly everyone seems to be . . . .
Most of the public appears to be convinced that there won't be
nearly enough to go around, that we're bound to have another
tremendous depression sooner or later, and that . . . private enterprise can't meet the requirements . . . ."[40]

In June, the survey asked people in various nations whether
they wanted to see many changes and reforms after the war or a
return to pre-war conditions. In America, 32 per cent favoured
change; in Canada 71 per cent replied that they hoped for a
better post-war world. Equally interesting, when asked to make
the invidious choice between "Big Business" or trade unions
controlling the government, 63 per cent of Americans preferred
business, 65 per cent of Canadians chose labour.[41]

Such sentiments seemed to augur well for the CCF. Early in
1944, *Time* magazine's Canadian stringer predicted a division of
political power among three parties instead of two in the next
election, with the old parties' vote split in such a way that the
CCF could form a minority government.[42] In August, a writer in
the *Financial Post* gave the CCF 100 to 110 seats, the Liberals 80

or 90, the rest divided among "others."[43] A *Maclean's* editorial in November was entitled "Split Vote May Bring Socialism," and it called upon all believers in free enterprise to unite to defeat the CCF.[44]

Such opinions were also based, naturally enough, upon election results since Noseworthy's celebrated 1942 victory in Toronto. Since that time, there had been fifteen provincial and eleven federal by-elections. The CCF and Liberals had each won nine of them, the Conservative, L.P.P., Social Credit and Bloc Populaire parties one apiece. Of twelve by-elections west of Ontario, the CCF had won eight, the old parties none. There had also been six provincial elections during 1943 and 1944; the CCF was the only party in Canada to increase its popular vote in every case.

Almost every sign pointed to an all but irresistible victory by the socialists. In fact, however, the tide had already been stemmed. In September 1944, the Gallup Poll revealed that while the CCF, with 24 per cent, was maintaining its popular support, and the Conservatives had dropped two points since January to 27 per cent, the Liberals had climbed significantly from 30 to 36 per cent in six months. Why could the party of government ownership, of "pie in the sky" and change and reform, of trade unions, of planning to prevent depressions, not broaden the base of its support in a nation which explicitly favoured just these things?

There seem to be several major reasons. The powerful anti-socialist campaign had successfully increased the anti-CCF ranks and had deflected the widespread demand for radical reconstruction, though not for reform through welfare legislation. The CCF was unable to convince a majority of the electorate that the attractive reforms it offered were worth gambling for against the unspeakable horrors which would allegedly result from a socialist victory. Finally, it was increasingly believed that the desire for reform could be realized by supporting the older parties, which were industriously competing to prove that they offered the most advanced possible social and political thinking without the evils that might accompany a CCF government. By 1944, to vote for either of the old parties was by no means the equivalent of voting for a return to the *status quo ante bellum*. As one anti-socialist wrote, "were Liberal and Tory plans for the post-war the same as their pre-war ideas, popular acceptance of the CCF would be very much greater than it is."[45]

In the race between the old parties to prove to the public their great devotion to reform, the Liberal Party, as the September Gallup Poll very clearly indicated, was emerging a strong favourite. Indeed, it can be argued that once again in the early 1940's, as was the case exactly two decades earlier, Prime Minister Mackenzie King, more than any other single individual in Canada, was responsible for thwarting a left-wing challenge to the traditional major parties.

From August 4, 1943, the strength of the CCF was a consistent, major factor in King's political deliberations and decisions. The Ontario election and the four federal by-elections which the Liberals lost on August 9 reminded King that there were other than military wars to be won. He knew even before these contests that it was not the Conservatives he had to fear but, as he told John Bracken, "there was no doubt that the CCF was a common enemy."[46] The loss of the four by-elections he hoped would teach his followers that "labour has to be dealt with in a considerate way . . . . What I [now] fear is we will begin to have defections from our own ranks in the House to the CCF."[47] Later in the month he told Churchill "how great the necessity was for me to begin the mending of my fences, getting my party properly organized and seeing to it that I did not lose any members through the CCF . . . . I did not want to get my party undermined by the CCF"[48]

In September, King began to move. He asked Brooke Claxton, his parliamentary assistant, to prepare proposals for a post-war programme, based on the idea of giving the nation "clear hope of a better future after all its sacrifices had produced victory." When Claxton presented the Prime Minister with a detailed programme for his next election, "King liked it all except for the item of family allowances." He thought such prodigality was "ridiculous." But political considerations obviously must take precedence, and the Prime Minister finally capitulated.[49]

On September 27, the Advisory Council of the National Liberal Federation met and endorsed proposals which would mean, according to Bruce Hutchison, that "The state . . . [would] guarantee a job to anyone who wished to work, at least subsistence to those who could not work, a richer life for the nation as a whole. . . . He [King] had given it [his party] a new program so comprehensive and radical as to cut the ground from under any other party."[50]

King knew, however, that these new policies would not make their impact upon the public for some time, and that the CCF remained a serious threat. During October, he stressed more than once the necessity of reducing taxation in the budget "at the session immediately before the election," then expected in 1944. "Further taxation would mean we might as well hand over the Government in its entirety to the CCF," since such a tax increase "would raise such a feeling throughout the country that the Government would certainly meet defeat and [make it] equally certain that the CCF would come in its place. . . . "[51]

At the same time, post-war reform became more and more the keynote of the "new Liberalism" upon which King knew his party's very survival depended. In December 1943, the Prime Minister announced that his proposed policies for peace-time would include a floor under farm prices, a better deal for labour, and a social security programme. He was particularly concerned about the labour vote. According to Pickersgill, he "continued to deplore the extent to which the Liberals appeared to be losing the support of organized labour to the CCF and sought to recover some of the lost ground by consultation with the Labour Congresses in the final stages of the preparation of the Labour Relations Code which the federal government had been working out with the provincial governments since November 1943." The Code was finally announced on February 17 as P.C. 1003, promising compulsory collective bargaining and equal representation of labour and management on governmental boards dealing with problems with which labour was concerned. King was pleased that Bengough of the T.L.C. and Mosher of the C.C.L. "commented very favourably on the code. . . . It relieved a tremendous weight from my mind and I felt we had at last done the right thing." The day after the Code was announced, King talked with Percy Bengough who "told me he wanted to be helpful. Did not want to see the CCF make any headway."[52]

By May 1944, the government seemed to be emerging from the nadir of 1943; once its legislative programme passed the House, King "was satisfied he could win the next election not long hence without extending himself."[53] Of the several items in the "package of reform" accepted by the House, family allowance legislation was unquestionably the *coup de grâce*. It would involve "giving away," beginning in mid-1945, money each month to every child in Canada under sixteen years of age, ranging in amount from five to eight dollars monthly per child. With the average Canadian's income under 750 dollars, the allowance, wrote one magazine, was "prime political bait thrown out by a government whose election prospects have been steadily diminished by the rise of the socialists."[54]

The federal Conservatives had labelled the idea a "diaper

dole," Bracken had called the measure "political bribery," and the Tories unanimously supported it. "In the end, the Conservatives voted with the Liberals because, like them, they live in mortal fear of Canada's up-and-coming socialists. Said a Tory after the vote: 'Everyone in Canada is a reformer today.' "[55] According to one realistic neophyte in parliament, John George Diefenbaker, if the Conservatives had not supported family allowances, "when an election came along, we would be placed in the position of having opposed social change."[56]

Under direct pressure from the CCF, then, the political elite was obliged to humanize the capitalist system to which it was devoted. For the CCF it was, needless to say, an overwhelming moral victory. In the short run, it cost the party whatever real chance it had for an electoral breakthrough. In the longer run, the reforms which it forced helped shore up a tottering capitalism and made the system not only more efficient but more palatable. Messianic demands for radical social change soon lost public credibility. The CCF was left to tinker with the superficial excesses of a system whose legitimacy had been re-established. The average Canadian was left with a more tolerable human existence. Meaner contributions have been made to the welfare of a nation.

II

The federal and the Ontario elections of 1945 were possibly the most crucial to Canada in this century. This was largely understood at the time, and elections in both jurisdictions were widely anticipated. Accordingly, the year began with the sides still tightly drawn. On the one side, the Political Action Committee of the C.C.L. re-affirmed its endorsement of the CCF as well as its determination to do "everything possible to elect a CCF government at the next general election."[57] On the other, Gladstone Murray warned a meeting of the Ontario Retail Furniture Dealers Association that a socialist government would decide what furniture was to be manufactured and sold, and that "comforts such as sofas and chesterfields would not be favoured because it [*sic*] would be enervating and bad for the youth of the Socialist New Order."[58]

The January 1945 Gallup Poll showed a two point decline for the CCF to 22 per cent, yet observers continued to predict 70 to 100 federal seats for the party.[59] At least a few old party supporters believed the CCF could form a minority government, and demanded that King, Bracken, and Blackmore of Social Credit unite against the CCF since "The time has come for unity in fighting the common foe."[60]

The Communists too continued to press for a coalition, but one consisting of "progressive" forces. Not all CCF'ers could resist the L.P.P.'s blandishments. Early in 1945, two Ontario CCF M.P.P.'s, two in Manitoba, and a federal candidate in Alberta either withdrew or were suspended from the party because they wished to "cooperate with other left-wing parties." In Ontario, trouble arose over two fellow-travellers, Nelson Alles (Essex North) and Leslie Hancock (Wellington North). Difficulties with the former had begun as early as October 1943, when he accepted an invitation to welcome Albert MacLeod at a Windsor meeting, against the expressed wishes of his constituency club.[61] Alles was reprimanded and agreed to stay in line. By the following October, however, now joined by Hancock, he was again advocating tactics which, for both ideological and tactical reasons, the CCF found intolerable. In January 1945, Alles was expelled by his riding association and the executive of the Wellington North CCF recommended that the Provincial Council expel its member; before such action could be taken, however, Hancock resigned from the party.[62] Thereafter, Alles sat as an Independent Labour member, Hancock as Independent Farmer-Labour; neither ran for re-election in the 1945 election.

In the nature of the CCF and its members, it could hardly avoid such gratuitous disruptions and acrimonious internal conflicts. This was precious little consolation, however, in the face of the external battles which had to be waged. In February 1945, King held a by-election in the riding of Grey North, which included Owen Sound and the surrounding rural district. It was hardly the heartland of socialism, yet the CCF insisted upon placing great symbolic significance upon the results. A victory "may well prove to be, like York South, another historic milestone in the progress of the CCF in Canada." The party candidate, Air Vice-Marshal Earl Godfrey, was in fact a man of exceptional calibre. Moreover, the representatives of the riding's 1200 trade unionists endorsed Godfrey as "labour's candidate," while the C.C.L.-P.A.C. promised full support in the campaign.[63]

The Liberal nominee was National Defence Minister Andrew McNaughton, the man charged with making the government's conscription policy work, and a lifelong Conservative until he entered the federal cabinet. McNaughton was assisted in the campaign by Mackenzie King, who asked personally for his minister's election on three separate occasions, and by King's new ally, the L.P.P. On February 3, a large advertisement in the local newspaper announced that "Union Leaders Coast to Coast Support McNaughton." Pictured below this headline were such known Communists as Fred Collins, Pat Sullivan, Bruce Magnuson, C. S. Jackson, and Dewar Ferguson – some of whom, as it happened, had been interned by the King government earlier in the war; they now urged support for the Liberal candidate. The advertisement was "Published by the authority of the North Grey Liberal Association."[64]

The Conservative candidate, Garfield Case, was the only "home-town boy" of the three and, curiously, a lifelong Liberal until the by-election. Case denounced McNaughton as a Catholic (it was not true, his wife was), Godfrey as a "bloated, mean capitalist," and the CCF's National Secretary, David Lewis, as a "Russian-Jewish refugee" who spent his time concocting Communist plots.[65] Case described Quebec as "a community . . . lacking in courage, loyalty and resolve," and he based much of his campaign on the issue of "making Quebecers fight," or, as it was sometimes described with more dignity, assuring "equality of sacrifice."[66] It was your typical Tory campaign.

Grey North was a more crushing defeat for the CCF than for King. The final returns showed 7338 for Case, 6099 for McNaughton, and a disappointing 3116 for Godfrey. King's compromise conscription policy had not convinced a majority of the electorate; this, however, would not be an overwhelming obstacle in the future since the Prime Minister would not call an election until the war ended and conscription became but a memory. For the Conservatives, the result indicated that anti-Catholicism was still a heartfelt emotion in a preponderantly Protestant riding.[67]

The CCF was profoundly shaken by the results. Perhaps the most ominous portent was the failure of the P.A.C. to produce the results expected of it, to unite labour behind the CCF. In Owen Sound, Godfrey polled less than 30 per cent of the votes; in Meaford, the only other urban area in the riding, less than 20 per cent.[68] Or was the problem more general and more amorphous than this? Was the CCF in fact losing what one report called its "magic touch"?[69]

CCF leaders took the only steps possible after Grey North to save morale: they ignored their preposterously optimistic pre-election statements, pretended the defeat was an unfortunate but only temporary set-back, and continued their organizing and finance drives. For the CCF in particular, because it was not a party deeply rooted in the Canadian tradition, organization was required that was more efficient and more intensive than that of the old parties. The CCF failed dismally to meet this need. If in some constituencies it had a moderately good organization, perhaps equal to those of its rivals, in few was it superior. In its own way, the CCF attempted to remedy this glaring weakness. Speakers' tours, youth organizers, radio broadcasts emanating from a dozen local stations, leaflets, election manifestos, educational lectures and seminars, lengthy meetings beyond number – such was the stuff of CCF pre-election politics.[70]

These mundane activities were the lifeblood of the CCF. Without them, the party ceased to exist. Yet there was something distinctly incestuous about them. CCF'ers spent an inordinate amount of time and energy dealing with each other. This may have made sense in Saskatchewan, where the CCF constituted a significant element in the community. In Ontario, where party members were but a tiny fraction of the citizenry, this tendency functioned as often as not to keep the CCF out of the public eye.

Moreover, the party signally failed to get the organizational reinforcement it needed from its elected members. The responsibility of an M.P.P. between elections is to consolidate his personal position so well that only in an electoral landslide can he be dislodged. This is effected through rigorous service to his constituents and the tender cultivation of his riding association. A later era came to know this as the Martel-Stokes syndrome.[71] On the first count, the neophyte CCF members had an honourable record. On the second, they were an unmitigated disaster. With only a few exceptions, the CCF M.P.P.'s failed to realize the importance of such a task, perhaps because they were all too inexperienced to appreciate its significance, perhaps because they had almost all been elected with a minimum of organization and believed they could repeat this feat once again. Nor were the party leaders themselves – Jolliffe, Millard, Macphail – sufficiently interested in that aspect of politicking to prod their backbenchers into greater effort. As one CCF'er has said, "They may not have been great parliamentarians, but the CCF members were worse organizers."[72]

The party's finances in Ontario were just as inadequate. In the months before the election, the Ontario CCF trailed embarrassingly behind Saskatchewan and British Columbia in funds accumulated for the Victory Drive. By February 1945, Saskatchewan had sent the CCF National Office $30,000 for campaign purposes, British Columbia $9,000, Ontario but $7,000. By April,

Ontario's own Victory Fund totalled $37,000 (its objective had been set at $130,000), that of Saskatchewan $151,000, British Columbia's $98,000. In Ontario, for the year ending March 31, 1945, the Victory Fund provided slightly more than half of the CCF's total revenues of $69,000. It is significant that of the portion raised aside from the Victory Fund, sixty per cent was derived from membership fees, eighteen per cent from literature, twelve from club dues, and only a meagre five per cent from union dues.[73] Clearly the party's 18,624 members were a far more reliable source of assistance than were the CCF's trade union affiliates.

The CCF, then, was badly handicapped by considerably smaller revenues than it needed and dramatically fewer members than it expected, and by union affiliates whose commitment ranged from moderate to insouciant. And it was precisely at this inopportune moment that events at Queen's Park, and then Ottawa, were about to demand from all parties their greatest effort of the decade.

The Ontario legislature resumed its sittings on February 16, with the Throne Speech enumerating the "many important changes" the government had made in virtually all fields. Jolliffe, in reply, presented a detailed review of the government's legislation as it compared with the Conservative's 1943 platform, and pronounced a verdict of promises but no action. Jolliffe's amendment to the Throne Speech was a comprehensive indictment of the administration's failure to implement its program in such fields as education, health, labour, and agriculture. Unlike his amendment of the previous year, however, there was nothing so radical in this motion that could not be supported by the Liberals; the only phrase that could be considered remotely socialistic was one calling vaguely for "planning and organizing the resources of Ontario to guarantee productive employment in the post-war years . . . ."[74]

The amendment signalled a new political reality. What had happened simply was that Mitchell Hepburn's latest aberration precluded delaying a showdown much longer. Hepburn had developed a close, if unnatural, rapport with Albert MacLeod of the L.P.P. Macleod had convinced him that Drew's immediate defeat was imperative. When Salsberg and Macleod failed to convince the CCF of such urgency, Hepburn himself invited Jolliffe to join with the Liberals in voting the government out. Hepburn promised that in return he would support Jolliffe's demand to assume the premiership, and would accept any portfolio in a coalition cabinet. Jolliffe informed the former Premier that he was "dreaming": no Liberal but Hepburn would consider supporting Jolliffe's bid for the premiership, and no CCF'er would tolerate a coalition with the Liberals. Jolliffe would not work in collusion with Hepburn and his friends, the two Communist M.P.P.'s. But it was clear that Hepburn would then introduce some anti-Drew amendment which the CCF would be forced to support. The Liberals could not be allowed to take the initiative, to appear as the real opposition to Drew. Consequently, although prudence dictated otherwise, Jolliffe was forced to introduce an amendment which the Liberal members could easily support.[75]

On March 22, after Hepburn's sub-amendment deploring the government's introduction of a program of compulsory religious education was defeated (with almost half the CCF members opposing the sub-amendment, including such libertarians as Millard, Dennison, and Agnes Macphail), Jolliffe's amendment was put to a vote. Drew, with obvious satisfaction, declared the matter one of confidence, and a straight anti-Conservative vote of 51 to 36 carried the amendment. Jolliffe thereupon moved, "in view of what has just taken place in this house," and in order to give the members "time to consider what has taken place here tonight," that when the legislature adjourned that evening, March 22, it would stand adjourned until March 27 when it should meet again. The government agreed.[76] Two days later, however, on March 24, "in defiance of the expressed will of the House," as the CCF would later describe it,[77] Drew announced that the legislature had been dissolved and that an election would be held.

The prospect of a sudden election was greeted with pleasure by everyone concerned – everyone, that is, but the hapless CCF. Drew's followers were confident that if they could not win a majority in this election, they never would. They believed that while they would maintain their usual support, a strengthened Liberal Party would cause severe divisions in the opposition ranks. Commentators were predicting the Liberals could win twenty-five or thirty seats, twenty of which had a strong French or ethnic element, still considered Hepburn's greatest source of strength. On the other hand, the popularity of Tom Kennedy, Drew's Agriculture Minister, made it seem doubtful that the Liberals could regain the farm vote they lost in 1943.

But for the CCF this was far from a propitious moment. Although Jolliffe's personal reputation as a parliamentarian had increased considerably in the 1945 session,[78] internal dissension had damaged the party's image and the Grey North defeat had tarnished its prestige. There was a feeling that its "magic touch" had indeed disappeared, that the inevitability of a socialist victory had become at most a possibility, and that it need no longer be supported as the party of the future. The anti-socialist campaign had not decreased in intensity, while CCF replies to the charges hurled against it were at best ineffectual. The Communists were preparing to oppose the party in key labour seats, and "most observers," it was said, were predicting it would win only fifteen to twenty seats, fewer even than the Liberals.[79] For all these reasons, the CCF viewed another election with much dismay, a perception which soon proved entirely warranted.

References

1. *Saturday Night*, September 4, 1943.

2. *New Commonwealth*, September 23, 1943.

3. Cited in Tim Buck, *Thirty Years*, p. 194.

4. *Ibid.*, pp. 196-8.

5. *Ottawa Citizen*, quoted in *New Commonwealth*, August 31, 1944.

6. *Ibid*, June 22, 1944.

7. John Weir, *Canadian Tribune*, December 16, 1944, copy in CCF National Office.

8. A Liberal-Communist coalition was also maintained in the hierarchy of the Trades and Labour Congress, where Percy Bengough, a Liberal, and Pat Sullivan, a Communist, were consistently returned by acclamation as president and vice-president respectively. Together the two groups prevented the T.L.C. from endorsing the CCF.

9. D. P. O'Hearn, *Saturday Night*, February 19, 1944.

10. *News*, January 22, 1944; Brewin interview.

11. *Debates and Proceedings of the Ontario Legislature* (hereafter *Debates*), vol. 1, 1944, pp. 25-58.

12. Editorial, *Saturday Night*, March 25, 1944; L.L.L. Golden, *News*, April 1, 1944.

13. *New Commonwealth*, March 30, 1944.

14. *Debates*, vol. 2, 1944, p. 1594.

15. *Ibid.*, p. 1608. The vote was twenty-seven CCF'ers for the amendment, fifty Liberals and Tories opposed.

16. *Saturday Night*, March 25, 1944.

17. Interview with Frank Underhill and other leading CCF members who for obvious reasons prefer to remain anonymous.

18. D. P. O'Hearn, *Saturday Night*, March 25, 1944.

19. Stewart and French, *Ask No Quarter*, p. 230.

20. *Ibid.*

21. Interview with Andrew Brewin.

22. D. P. O'Hearn, *Saturday Night*, March 25, 1944.

23. *Time*, January 10, 1944.

24. Quoted by Nixon to Larry Zolf and repeated to the writer.

25. *Saturday Night*, August 19, 1944.

26. Provincial Council Meeting Minutes, September 10, 1944.

27. *Maclean's*, November 15, 1944.

28. *Time*, December 18, 1944; D. P. O'Hearn, *Saturday Night*, October 14, 1944.

29. Editorial, *Saturday Night*, October 14, 1944; O'Hearn, *ibid.*

30. Cited by Lipsett, *Agrarian Socialism*, p. 282.

31. The CCF won 47 of 52 seats with 200,000 votes, the Liberals 129,000, the Conservatives 41,000. Sixty per cent of the service vote went to the CCF. *New Commonwealth*, June 22, 1944.

32. *Time*, June 26, 1944.

33. Sanford Silverstein, "Occupational Class and Voting Behaviour: Electoral Support of a Left-Wing Protest Movement in a Period of Prosperity," in Lipset, *Agrarian Socialism* (1968 edition), p. 435.

34. Lipset, *op. cit.*, p. 229.

35. *Ibid.*, pp. 259-60.

36. *New Commonwealth*, July 13, 1944.

37. G. C. Whittaker, *Saturday Night*, June 24, 1944.

38. *New Commonwealth*, March 7, 1944.

39. *Ibid.*, May 11, 1944.

40. P. M. Richards, *Saturday Night*, February 12, 1944.

41. *Maclean's*, June 1, 1944.

42. *Time*, January 31, 1944. *Time* erred.

43. Cited in *New Commonwealth*, August 17, 1944.

44. *Maclean's*, November 15, 1944.

45. P. M. Richards, *Saturday Night*, April 8, 1944.

46. Pickersgill, *King Record*, p. 566.

47. *Ibid.*, pp. 570-1.

48. *Ibid.*, pp. 554-5.

49. Hutchison, *Incredible Canadian*, pp. 325-6.

50. *Ibid., pp. 329, 331.*

51. Pickersgill, *op. cit.*, p. 598.

52. *Ibid.*, p. 643.

53. Hutchison, *op. cit.*, p. 338.

54. *Time*, July 3, 1944.

55 *Ibid.*, August 7, 1944.

56. *Maclean's,* September 1, 1944.

57. *Canadian Unionist,* February 1945.

58. Toronto *Globe and Mail,* cited in *Canadian Forum,* February 1945.

59. See, for example, *Maclean's,* February 15, 1945.

60. R. C. Wood, *Saturday Night,* April 21, 1945. Wood was a prominent Conservative speech writer and speaker.

61. National Office Files, F. A. Burr, president, Windsor CCF, to David Lewis, October 3, 1943; Mrs. J. A. McKay, secretary, Windsor CCF, to Lewis, October 7, 1943.

62. Provincial Council Meeting Minutes, October 8, 1944; Provincial Executive Meeting Minutes, January 2 and January 16, 1945.

63. *New Commonwealth,* January 11 and February 8, 1945.

64. Owen Sound *Daily Sun-Times,* February 3, 1945.

65. *New Commonwealth,* February 8, 1945.

66. Cited in *Saturday Night,* January 13, 1945.

67. Wilfrid Eggleston, *Saturday Night,* February 17, 1945.

68. Provincial Executive Meeting Minutes, February 13, 1945; *Saturday Night,* February 10, 1945.

69. *Time,* February 12, 1945.

70. Report of Publicity Director to 1944 Convention.

71. After Eli Martel (Sudbury East) and Jack Stokes (Thunder Bay), whose superb constituency work from 1967 to 1971 won them landslide victories in the 1971 Ontario election.

72. Interview with Andrew Brewin.

73. McHenry, *Third Force in Canada,* pp. 90-2; *New Commonwealth,* February 8, 1945. Almost half Ontario's revenues were spent on the salaries of office staff and organizers. One-fifth went to National Office, twelve per cent was used to purchase literature.

74. *Debates of the Ontario Legislature,* vol. 1, 1945, pp. 1-22, 193-228, 402-450.

75. Interviews with Jolliffe, William Dennison, and J. B. Salsberg.

76. *Debates,* vol. 3, 1945, pp. 2228-32.

77. CCF election pamphlet, *Why An Election Now: A CCF Challenge to Tory Arrogance.*

78. See, for example, editorial, *Saturday Night,* March 24, 1945.

79. D. P. O'Hearn, *ibid.,* March 31, 1945.

10 THE SHOWDOWN

In the knowledge that King planned to call an election in the immediate future, Drew determined to hold the Ontario contest first; when the legislature gave him his opportunity, he declared June 11, 1945 the date of the provincial election. Believing with Drew that the expected defeat of the Ontario Liberals would damage the federal party, Prime Minister King thereupon announced June 11, 1945 as the date of the National election. Outraged, Drew re-scheduled the Ontario contest for June 4. King was finally outmanoeuvred and the arrangement remained final.

There was, inevitably, a certain consequent public confusion, but out of the campaign a number of themes emerged more or less clearly. When the Conservatives discovered that a campaign based on dissatisfaction with King's manpower policy, so successful in Grey North, could not arouse much interest with an allied victory imminent, Drew and Bracken both turned their efforts in other directions. While Drew could campaign on his record, Bracken was forced to present promises for the future. Most of these stressed the "progressive" aspects of the Progressive-Conservative Party, particularly in the field of labour relations. The CCF was pronounced a dire peril to "our" democratic way of life.[1]

For Drew, the lines in the election were starkly drawn. "The decision," he knew, "rests between freedom and fascism right here at home." He courageously chose freedom. After quoting from the Communist Manifesto to show its similarities to the CCF's ideas, he concluded that "It is time to stop talking about fascism having been destroyed. This is fascism."[2]

Conservatives spread this message, or variations thereon, in several ways. The Toronto-Riverdale provincial candidate mailed out literature stating that "German and Italian Socialism had lost the war and democracy emerged successful."[3] In Drew's riding of High Park, where a former Liberal, Lewis Duncan, was running as the CCF nominee, a Conservative campaign sheet widely circulated in the riding declared, according to a local minister who received one, that

> High Park electors have a duty to perform on June 4. It is to tell the ex-Hepburnite, now turned CCF, and ex-town mayor of Bonn, Germany, J. L. Duncan, that he is not wanted.

As the minister pointed out, "to the uninformed, this would subtly suggest that Mr. Duncan is really a German who has changed his name, instead of a man who fought for Canada bravely."[4]

Mackenzie King attempted to avoid such innuendo in his personal campaign. He knew full well that, the conscription issue aside, his problems had been created by the CCF's appeal to liberal supporters of his party,[5] and operated throughout the campaign "on the assumption that his real danger was from the left," not from the Conservatives or Social Credit. King realized too that the warm feelings, relative prosperity, and full employment which Canada enjoyed in the victorious days of mid-1945, would vitiate the appeal of radical socialist demands while leaving intact the desire for post-war security against depression and unemployment; he therefore attempted to destroy the CCF "by swerving far enough to the left to expropriate anything of use in its doctrines. . . . "[6] As one political scientist later wrote, the CCF was out-manoeuvred by the Liberals who had "moved cautiously as new champions of state social welfare. . . . "[7]

Indeed, to undermine the CCF's chance of national success, the Liberal Party offered not merely reform, but no less than a government which would "BUILD A NEW SOCIAL ORDER" in Canada. Liberal policies would create "JOBS," bring "the Dawn of A New Day," and guarantee "Security With Freedom." "Your Liberal government under King," the electorate was informed, "has taken practical steps to see that every Canadian after the war shall have a wide-open chance to make a real success of his life"; and if the Liberals were re-elected, there would be farm improvement loans, more homes, better labour conditions, reduced taxation, veterans' benefits, and, above all, family allowances.[8]

If some cynics wondered why such appealing ideas had not been implemented before the election, many saw in them sufficient reason for a *rapprochement* with the party they had temporarily deserted. The most outstanding example was Canada's largest labour organization, the Trades and Labour Congress. A letter from the P.A.C. to its 350,000 members urged them to work for the re-election of the Liberal government, warning against "inexperienced" parties winning power "at this time."[9] The beleaguered CCF had not anticipated this devastating blow.

King also received loyal support from such people as Charles Kelz, his candidate in Toronto-Greenwood, who warned voters through about a dozen advertisements in Toronto newspapers during the campaign "How easily democracy can slip unwittingly into a totalitarian way of life."[10]

Similarly, a leaflet issued by a federal Liberal candidate in Winnipeg consistently identified the CCF with German Naziism and Italian fascism. Those who believed that individual liberties and democratic government were unimportant were reminded that "that is what the German people thought in 1935 [sic] when they allowed the Nazi Party executive to gain control." The pamphlet also used a Jack Boothe cartoon taken from B. A. Trestrail's *Social Suicide*, showing a Canadian soldier struggling against the forces of "National Socialism."[11]

Mitchell Hepburn's campaign was pathetic. As his biographer summed it up, "his campaign staff was small, Hepburn's funds were hard to come by. and significant newspaper support almost non-existent. . . . Mitch Hepburn, enervated physically, drained emotionally, and relying as he had for a long time on alcohol to take up the slack, was at the end of his tether, a spent force."[12]

One of Hepburn's few assets was the support of the Communists, still in their "unity of all democratic forces" stage. He showed no compunctions about exploiting the alliance. Their close cooperation in Queen's Park continued on the hustings, reaching its remarkable climax in the city of Windsor. There, three candidates were put forward under the label "Liberal-Labour," officially nominated by the Liberals and endorsed by the L.P.P. One, Alex Parent, was a member of the L.P.P.; George Burt was the head of the U.A.W., and had been connected in the past both with the CCF and the Communists;[13] the third was Arthur Reaume, who had run as a Conservative in 1943, when he was defeated by his CCF opponent.[14] It is difficult to determine which was the most phantastical aspect of this mind-boggling arrangement – the Liberals nominating a known Communist, an important official of a C.I.O. union running for Mitchell Hepburn's party, or Liberals and Communists uniting to support a life-long Conservative.

All this manoeuvring, however, obscures one clear fact: the Communists, realizing Hepburn had little chance of victory, were attempting to help return Drew to office by defeating as many

CCF candidates as possible. Despite all their public protestations of hatred for "reactionary Toryism," this conclusion is inescapable. The L.P.P. contested thirty-seven seats in the Ontario election. No less than twenty-seven of these were ridings held by CCF'ers since 1943. Only five CCF M.P.P.'s did *not* face Communist opposition; only five of the thirty-eight Conservative incumbents *did* have an L.P.P. opponent. The intention, of course, was simply to split the CCF vote wherever possible.

Reinforcing the efforts of all the anti-socialist politicians were all the professional anti-socialist propagandists. No sooner had the elections been announced than the indignant Ontario *CCF News* could announce:

> They're at it again. Once again the paid propagandists of Big Business are flooding the country with lies about the CCF. . . . They're using every method of high pressure publicity to spread their slanderous falsehoods: three million pieces of scurrilous literature sent to every postal address in Canada, big ads in daily newspapers, coast to coast, a whole series of radio broadcasts, and propaganda "directives" to old party speakers to make sure they all sing the same tune of anti-CCF slander.[15]

Most of the editorials and advertisements had become familiar. Hiram Walker's and Sons stated that in Canada "any man's son may become premier" thanks to "The Canadian way – the spirit of friendly and open competition."[16] The Bank of Toronto continued to praise "man's progress under free enterprise during the last 200 years."[17] *Maclean's* warned editorially that "you can't 'try' socialism" because "it can work only when socialists are permanently in power. Which means that opposition couldn't be tolerated."[18] An outfit calling itself "*The Labour Leader*, Canada's National Labour Newspaper," bought space in other papers to denounce "the totalitarian state" planned by the CCF and to laud Drew's progressive legislation."[19]

Some novelties had by this time been added to this campaign. *The Road to Serfdom*, Professor F. A. Hayek's polemic against socialism and a planned economy, was being promoted by old party candidates and supporters. The *Reader's Digest* had thoughtfully condensed this effective work, which the Book-of-the-Month Club made available at the nominal price of eighteen dollars per thousand.[20] Unknown persons were mailing free copies of this book as well as Trestrail's *Social Suicide* and *Stand Up and Be Counted*, and William Gibson's *You Knew*

What You Were Voting For, to postal addresses across Canada.[21]

Two Montreal firms – and probably many others – placed special election notices in the pay envelopes of their employees. Hugh Millar, president of Lyman Tube and Supply Company, wrote that

> ... it is not my privilege to tell anyone for what party to vote, but I do want everyone to know that I regard the CCF program as a deadly danger to our future, not only in the matter of jobs, but the world we live in outside our jobs.
>
> So whichever OTHER way you want to vote is your business, but it is my firm belief that if the CCF should prevail, none of us will ever again have a chance to cast a ballot.
>
> The accompanying booklet [*Social Suicide*] will give you plenty of reasons why I think as I do, and I subscribe to them all.[22]

President J. H. Andrews of Lyman's Ltd., a wholesale drug firm, was less dramatic. He simply dismissed all CCF'ers as "college professors, school teachers, and idealists," and left the rest to Hayek's anti-socialist tract which accompanied his special letter to every employee.[23]

Trestrail's presence, it is evident, was central to the anti-socialist campaign. Having missed the 1943 election, he over-compensated in 1945. One cannot ascertain precisely the extent of Trestrail's resources in the latter year, whether he received seven hundred thousand dollars as Coldwell claimed, or one million dollars as other CCF'ers suggested; whatever the amount, his was the most powerful, the most intensive, and, it is arguable, the most effective attack upon any party ever undertaken in Canada. During the previous year, Trestrail had collected large sums of money from corporations throughout Canada for the announced purpose of "saving Canadian business from the CCF."[24] Just prior to the 1945 elections, he completed a nation-wide tour of the Dominion, adding to his funds through a personal appeal. Although the precise amount collected remains obscure, its approximate size, as well as his approach in soliciting contributions, can be indicated.

On May 1, 1945, after his trip, Trestrail sent a form letter to prospective supporters across the country. One such appeal was sent to the president of a Montreal firm who happened to be a CCF sympathizer. After crossing out his own and his company's name, he submitted this document from Trestrail to the CCF office:

> Starting early in May [Trestrail wrote] a mass educational campaign will be launched from coast to coast by the Public Informational Association to acquaint Canadians with the truth about State Socialism. It will be the only national attempt to post Canadians on the seriousness of the situation . . . .
>
> This campaign . . . will be based on the findings of surveys covering more than 2000 Canadians in all walks of life . . . .
>
> Meetings have been held with groups of citizens in 22 cities and sufficient support has already been secured to cover about one-half the cost of the complete campaign. This support comes from hundreds of individuals and companies who appreciate the necessity for some such effort, completely divorced from any political party.
>
> No remuneration is being paid to anyone in connection with the campaign except for operating expenses, nor is it sponsored or controlled by any group or class.
>
> This campaign merits the support of every individual who has a stake in Canada, and the purpose of this letter is to solicit your support as an individual or on behalf of your company . . . .

An outline of the "Proposed Educational Campaign" accompanied Trestrail's personal appeal. It revealed that "an experimental campaign" had been conducted in Toronto in 1944 "to ascertain to what extent public interest could be aroused over the issue of State Socialism and the degree to which such thinking could be influenced." The results of this and other surveys "provide fairly conclusive evidence that from 25% to 40% of the people can be diverted from the possibility of voting for any candidate committed to State Socialism – if they are provided with proper information in the proper manner." For this purpose,

> this Association plans to conduct a very comprehensive campaign including
> 1. Direct distribution of the tabloid "Social Suicide" to every postal address in Canada.
> 2. Newspaper advertising and radio broadcasting, carrying to citizens the true significance of State Socialism.
> 3. Supplying of material regarding State Socialism for speakers and candidates from coast to coast.

Finally, it was stated that the reaction from "groups of leading citizens" already canvassed for support had been "uniformly unanimous in endorsement and support of the Campaign." At this point the recipient would discover an enclosed retainer form, made out to General Relations Services Ltd., with the single statement: "We hereby engage the services of your Company as Industrial and Commercial Counsel and subscribe to your Industrial Service for __ months, for which we agree to pay you a fee of $__ . . . . "[25]

Besides radio broadcasts and material supplied to anti-socialist speakers throughout the country, Trestrail employed his considerable propagandist skills during the election campaign in two main areas. The first was through huge, attractive advertisements in the press, over the name "Public Informational Association, B. A. Trestrail, National Director." Eight such advertisements appeared in the Toronto *Telegram* alone, between May 15 and June 4, 1945. Although each was sufficiently different from the one preceding to maintain continued public interest, the message was always numbingly identical. Electing a CCF government would not merely mean a change in administration; it would change the entire system of government, substituting "a foreign-born scheme of State Socialism for our democratic way of life. The CCF politicians" wanted "complete control of our lives" in order to impose their "absolute dictatorship." Under "State Socialism," we would become "like animals in a zoo." "The people who are preaching State Socialism for Canada are largely theorists – visionaries with no practical experience. . . . It was the same type of 'thinkers' who started Italy on the road to dictatorship and destruction." "NEITHER YOU NOR YOUR CHILDREN WILL EVER FORGET IT – IF. YOU SHOULD VOTE FOR STATE SOCIALISM."[26]

The final attraction of these advertisements was based, appropriately enough, upon the spirit of competition and the profit incentive. "To encourage Canadians to post themselves on State Socialism," one read,

> we are conducting a "quiz" contest open to all Canadian voters. 235 separate cash prizes totalling $5,000.00, ranging from $1,000 to $5.00, will be awarded to readers of the booklet "Social Suicide" which carries full details of the contest.[27]

The quiz consisted of answering questions relating directly to statements made in *Social Suicide*, the twenty-four page tabloid which was Trestrail's second major weapon. The questions required only "yes" or "no" answers. "Under State Socialism, could the small businessman be sure he would *never* be taken over by the government?" "Under the system of state socialism now in force in Russia, can the people displace their government if they so desire?" "Has the population of New Zealand declined since they started their experiment in State Socialism?" Perhaps even more remarkable than the mindlessness of Trestrail's contest was his claim that no fewer than 27,000 people submitted entries;[28] it is not certain whether any money was ever disbursed to the winners.

Social Suicide had been condensed from Trestrail's longer tract, *Stand Up and Be Counted or Sit Still and Get Soaked* (McClelland and Stewart, Toronto, 1944). Both works were propaganda masterpieces. Trestrail's writing style commanded attention and made one want to continue reading; it was simple, sensational, and memorable. His book was masterful as well in its scope. In it, cleverly juxtaposed, were incorporated virtually every anti-socialist chestnut and every tribute to free enterprise that had been used since 1943. "Opportunity" and "regimentation," "individual achievement" and "bureaucracy," "Jack Canuck" and "Fanatic Russians," "study, ability, hard work, thrift" and "something for nothing," "grocers, butchers" and "professional social students"[29] – it was a genuine *tour de force*.

Pointed, artless caricatures were scattered generously throughout both works, drawn by Jack Boothe, then political cartoonist for the Toronto *Globe and Mail*. The great majority of these equated the CCF with regimentation, dictatorship, confiscation, and in general with the systems operating in Russia and Nazi Germany. Several of these portrayed CCF National Secretary David Lewis with an exaggerated Jewish profile. Trestrail referred to Lewis' father as a "Russian Jew"[30] and to Lewis himself in these words: "Well, the day may yet come in Canada when a Jewish immigrant boy, whose father saw fit to forsake the Bolshevik Communist atmosphere of Russia, will rise to a position where he writes the ticket for the social and economic program of this nation. . . . "[31] These gratuitous references led some to accuse Trestrail of anti-semitism, but he denied it, pointing out that "I include among my good friends a considerable number of Jews."[32]

Trestrail received funds, as he boasted, to mail *Social Suicide* to "every postal address in Canada"; Eugene Forsey estimated that three million copies were distributed during the campaign.[33] Who his benefactors were cannot be proved, although one inevitably wonders whether those he named as supporters in 1944 remained so. CCF'ers believed they had the answers to several intriguing problems, but could not marshall documentary evidence. The party publicly asked Trestrail for replies to the following queries:

1. Did he not receive recently $200,000 from the Robert Simpson Co. Ltd., that put his fund over the $1,000,000 mark?

2. Weren't huge stocks of "Social Suicide" assembled in the warehouses of the DeHavilland Aircraft Company and Simpson's in Toronto?

3. Weren't the female employees of Simpson's taken off the job of mailing catalogues to work on the free distribution of this pamphlet?

4. Did Simpson's pay for this work, or Trestrail?

5. Did Simpson's place considerable quantities of paper, obtained, presumably, by permit of the Administration of Printing, Publishing and Allied Trades, at the disposal of the Public Informational Association so that there might be no delay in disseminating "Social Suicide"?

If these remained unproved accusations, there were some hard, factual points which the CCF wanted the federal government to clarify. *Social Suicide* nowhere contained the name of its printer and publisher, in direct violation of both the Defence of Canada Regulations (Section 15A) and the Dominion Elections Act. "Why was it allowed to enter the mails?" This fact was drawn to the attention of the Department of Justice by letter on May 10, and to Postmaster-General W. P. Mulock by the Glace Bay *Gazette* on May 22, "in sufficient time to stop what was obviously going to be a breach of the law. . . . Why was no action taken by [those] Departments? Why have Trestrail and the printers not been prosecuted?"[34] No answers were forthcoming from either Trestrail or the Prime Minister. In the decisive showdown, legal niceties ceased being bourgeois luxuries.

In many ways, the Ontario CCF was better prepared for these campaigns than any in its history. Psychologically, it had a confidence generated by optimism; and if this optimism was slowly declining, some neutral source could always be found predicting CCF governments both in Ottawa and Queen's Park.[35] Party finances and memberships, though below expectations, were far larger than ever before. It ran eighty-one federal candidates in Ontario, and eighty-nine in the provincial election, including all its M.P.P.'s; the provincial candidates included thirty-four trade unionists, twelve farmers, twenty-nine business and professional men, and eleven service men. During the campaign, Ontario had at its disposal Coldwell, Winch, Douglas, Gillis, and two Saskatchewan cabinet ministers, all of whom were sent on speaking tours throughout the province.

Welcome support was obtained as well from Labour Councils in Toronto, London and Hamilton (all C.C.L. affiliates), which endorsed the CCF provincial and federal candidates in their respective areas.[36] After the provincial results were known, the C.C.L.-P.A.C. published an emergency leaflet, which was distributed to trade unionists through the Toronto area. It explained that Drew's re-election resulted from a huge vote in "upper-class areas while in working class districts the turn-out was disappointingly small. . . . The pressure of the CCF at Ottawa has brought us social and economic reforms. That pressure must be increased."[37]

At first, party strategy was to emphasize the horrors of the Depression decade. Hence the newspaper advertisements portraying a clean-cut young Canadian declaring, "I'm for the CCF because I want Jobs, not Breadlines!"[38] This approach, however, was soon and wisely replaced by a more positive one, as it became apparent that such anxiety as existed in the province focussed more on problems of the future than on memories of the past. By early May, the CCF began concentrating its resources primarily upon its simple, welfarist "Five-Star Program For Ontario." The five stars represented job security, farm security, home security, health security, and national security, and they came to provide the basis of most advertising, radio broadcasts, leaflets and speeches. As Jolliffe impressed upon all candidates, speakers, and organizers, "our immediate objective is to get everybody in the province talking about the Five-Star Program."[39]

Not until the final week of the campaign did the CCF publicly take notice of the crusade being waged by the devotees of free enterprise, and even then only two inadequate advertisements appeared in the Toronto *Star*. The reason for this grave error of judgement was simple. Most party leaders agreed with Professor George Grube that "the attacks on the CCF were based on such utterly false and obviously untrue premises that I . . . did not take them seriously enough."[40]

Moreover, although the CCF's national election fund was ten times greater than that of 1940, and its Ontario receipts almost twice what they were in 1943, it was derisory to think the party could run a serious national campaign on a budget of $83,800. Half of this sum came from Saskatchewan, one-fifth from British Columbia and only $6,151 from Ontario, less than the contributions of either the Manitoba or Alberta CCF. The national fund was spent on newspaper advertising, billboards, literature, organizers' salaries, and expenses, and some was squandered on subsidies to campaigns in Quebec and the Maritimes.[41]

In Ontario, $46,000 was raised for the two elections. Of that total, all but $9,000 went for publicity and literature, while organizers' salaries and expenses accounted for another $1,600. Advertisements were placed in 35 daily newspapers across the province; 650,000 copies of four different leaflets were printed, as were 50,000 "blotters for businessmen," the same number of gummed CCF stickers, and 5,000 CCF posters. Two thousand dollars was spent on radio broadcasting, $3,900 on billboards. Farm papers received specially-designed advertisements, and a farm broadcast emanated from Hamilton for five minutes each evening during the month of May. A friendly professional advertising agency again helped prepare ads and leaflets.[42]

Such was the basis of the CCF's election campaign in these two crucial contests – that is, at least, until Ted Jolliffe decided to take to the airwaves with a sensational statement ten days before the Ontario election.

References

1. Toronto *Telegram*, May 19, 1945. The Tories played another old game. They used the conscription issue outside Quebec to exploit anti-French Canadian prejudice, while in Quebec Bracken joined with local reactionary chauvinists against the Liberals. Although this duplicitous ploy had worked for Borden in 1911, Bracken had less luck with it. He got nowhere in Quebec, while King and Liberal newspapers elsewhere used it effectively against the Tories. Hutchison, *Incredible Canadian,* pp. 407-8; Toronto *Star,* May 19, 1945.

2. Toronto *Star,* May 1945.

3. *Ibid.,* May 23, 1945.

4. *Ibid.,* May 26, 1945. Letter to the editor.

5. Editorial, *ibid.*

6. Hutchison, *op. cit.,* p.413

7. L. H. Laing, "The Pattern of Canadian Politics – The Election of 1945," *American Political Science Review,* August 1946, p. 765.

8. Toronto *Star,* May 19, May 26, and May 30, 1945; *Maclean's,* June 1, 1945.

9. Toronto *Star,* May 22 and June 1, 1945.

10. *Ibid.,* May 23, 1945. Kelz beat his CCF opponent by 650 votes but came a weak second.

11. The *Canadian Outlook,* published by the Winnipeg South Centre Liberal Association, May 30, 1945, copy in Stanley Knowles Files. Maybank, the Liberal candidate, won easily.

12. McKenty, *Mitch Hepburn,* p. 274.

13. Burt bought a CCF card early in 1944, but played a curious game. According to Walter Reuther, he was "completely in the camp" of the Communist members of the U.A.W. and "always votes with the Communist gang on the international board." Even while he held a CCF card, Burt "made quite an antagonistic speech about the CCF at a [U.A.W.] board meeting." David Lewis suggested the explanation for this behaviour was "simply his political nose." National Office Files, Lewis to Jolliffe, March 9, 1944. Burt probably took enough labour votes in his riding to defeat the incumbent CCF'er. The Conservatives received 7880 votes, Burt 6284, and Riggs, the CCF'er, 5402.

14. Reaume lost in 1945 and 1948, finally winning in 1951 on a straight Liberal ticket. He too helped defeat a CCF incumbent in 1945. The Conservative won with 8487 votes to Reaume's 6981 and the CCF' s 5439.

15. *CCF News* (formerly *New Commonwealth*), May 31, 1945.

16. *Maclean's,* June 1, 1945.

17. Toronto *Telegram,* May 29, 1945.

18. *Maclean's,* May 1, 1945.

19. Toronto *Telegram,* May 26, 1945.

20. Eugene Forsey, *CCF News,* May 31, 1945.

21. Toronto *Star,* May 22, 1945, letter to the editor from a man in Larder Lake, Ontario, who had received such gifts in the mail.

22. National Office Files, photostatic copy of Millar's letter, June 5, 1945, sent by W. J. Sauve, Acting Quebec CCF Provincial Secretary, to David Lewis, June 28, 1945.

23. Cited in Guillet, *Famous Canadian Trials, volume 50,* Chapter VI, Section 5.

24. Cited in *CCF News,* May 31, 1945.

25. National Office Files, Trestrail to (name and company blacked out), St. Catherines St., Montreal, May 1, 1945. Before the 1949 election, when Trestrail attempted to raise funds to finance the sending of a sixteen-page booklet, "Is Democracy Doomed?" to postal addresses across Canada as an attack upon the CCF, he used the added appeal that "It is our understanding that, under the law, such fees are chargeable as an operating expense." *Ibid.,* from letter from Trestrail, May 19, 1949.

26. Toronto *Telegram,* May 18, May 22, May 26, and June 2, 1945.

27. *Maclean's,* June 1945.

28. National Office Files, Public Informational Association's Seven-Point Educational Program, 1949.

29. This was Trestrail's own peculiar devil theory of Canadian politics. The "professional social students" were Frank Scott and David Lewis, whom he regarded as the evil geniuses controlling the CCF. They were using the

party as a "vehicle" on which to "ride into power," then rule the entire nation for their own selfish and brutal ends.

30. Trestrail, *Stand Up and Be Counted*, p. 29.
31. *Ibid.*, p. 31.
32. Vancouver *Sun*, July 3, 1945.
33. Ottawa *Citizen*, June 1, 1945.
34. *CCF News*, May 31, 1945; Glace Bay *Gazette*, May 22, 1945, editorial.
35. See, for example, Ottawa *Citizen*, editorial, May 30, 1945.
36. *CCF News*, May 31, 1945.
37. *Provincial Election Documents*, 1945, copy of leaflet.
38. Toronto *Star*, May 19, 1945.
39. *Provincial Election Documents*, Jolliffe to all riding executives, early May 1945.
40. *Ibid.*, copy of lecture given at Ontario Woodsworth House, November 1945.
41. National Office Files, National Election Finances, 1945.
42. *Provincial Election Documents*, 1945, CCF Publicity Campaign; Report to the Annual Provincial Convention, November 1945.

▌▌ GESTAPO

On the evening of May 24, 1945, in a radio address broadcast across Ontario, the provincial leader of the CCF dramatically unfolded "the most infamous story in the history of Ontario":

> It is my duty to tell you that Colonel Drew is maintaining in Ontario, at this very minute, a secret political police, a paid government spy organization, a Gestapo to try and keep himself in power. And Col. Drew maintains his secret political police at the expense of the tax-payers of Ontario – paid out of the Public Funds. . . .
>
> Now all through this election campaign, you've been hearing that the real issue is freedom versus dictatorship. . . . And I quite agree; there certainly is a very grave danger; and when you've heard all the facts, true facts, supported by affidavits, about Col. Drew's Ontario Gestapo – Well, I'll let you decide for yourselves where the danger of dictatorship is coming from!

Emphasizing that he understood fully the gravity of his charges, and that he would therefore not be making them without full proof, Jolliffe proceeded to relate his strange tale. A few weeks after the Drew government assumed office, he charged, it secretly established a political police office on the second floor of an old police garage at 18 Surrey Place in Toronto, just off Queen's Park. Captain William J. Osborne-Dempster was placed in charge of this office, and, with public money provided by the government though unauthorized by the legislature, began his spying. Periodically, Dempster submitted reports of his findings to his superiors, always signed, in the best traditions of espionage, with the code number D-208. These reports, Jolliffe charged, were often sent to the Commissioner and Deputy Commissioner of the Provincial Police, and occasionally directly to Attorney-General Leslie Blackwell or to Drew himself.

Dempster's task was to try to link as many non-Conservatives as possible with the Communist Party. Much of his spying was devoted to the CCF members of the legislature; he had written reports on Jolliffe, Arthur Williams, Dennison, Agnes Macphail and others. There were reports as well on Hepburn and David Croll, proving to Jolliffe that "this secret police is deliberately designed by Drew to spy on all opposition to his government, and thus to try and keep himself in power." Nor had private citizens who had come to Dempster's attention been ignored in his work; his files contained "a great mass of half truths, misinformation and deliberate lies" about such persons, it was later revealed, as B. K. Sandwell, editor of *Saturday Night*, and R. C. Wallace, principal of Queen's University. Labour unions also fell under Dempster's jurisdiction. He held a union card in order to be able to attend labour meetings when he pleased. "Union offices were rifled, documents taken and photostatic copies made. Spies were sent to union meetings. Blacklists of people of whom the Gestapo disapproved were prepared and Big Business was given the opportunity of checking their [employees] against them."

No mention of the "Special Branch" of the Provincial Police, as Dempster's organization was called, had ever appeared in the public accounts of Ontario, nor had Dempster's name or salary appeared there as was required by law. The only place his name ever appeared was in Provincial Police orders, after he received a promotion by Order-in-Council in June 1944.

Since Dempster's reports were so obviously unreliable, Jolliffe continued, the Drew government refused to use his "rubbish" directly, allowing him instead to give or sell his misinformation to "the paid propagandists of Big Business, especially Gladstone Murray and Sanderson, the Bug Man. These men used the Drew Gestapo rumours to form the basis of advertising in the interests of Big Business against the CCF."

Jolliffe charged that Murray and Sanderson both had a "clear connection" with the secret police office and with each other. Murray often called Dempster's office by telephone, although the number was unlisted and ostensibly secret. Sanderson wrote his notorious January 1, 1944 civic election advertisement, which the courts later declared libellous, from information in Dempster's office and in collaboration with Dempster. Jolliffe claimed as well that when Sanderson was sued for his advertisement, Drew, then in England, wrote him "an intimate and reassuring letter on the letterhead of Ontario House, London." Sanderson showed several persons the letter, which began "Dear Sandy: They tell me that since I left you are getting quite ritzy. . . . "

The letter went on, according to Jolliffe, to assure Sanderson that his expenses would be "taken care of."

On one side, then, Jolliffe asserted, the side which smelled from "the stench of fascism," was "this group of close associates: Drew, Osborne-Dempster, Gladstone Murray, Sanderson and George McCullagh [of the *Globe and Mail*]." On the other side were people who "recognize that stench ... and who did something about it." Specifically, it was later revealed, this referred to Constable John Albert Rowe, who had been Dempster's assistant for several months in 1944. Believing Dempster's activities to be improper, Rowe took his information to his M.P.P., Agnes Macphail, who then reported to Jolliffe.

After investigations by himself and Leslie Wismer, CCF member for Toronto-Riverdale, had confirmed the truth of Rowe's allegations, Jolliffe's "duty became clear, my duty to place the facts before the people of Ontario and denounce this outrage against democracy." Those facts, and many others which Jolliffe had no time to present in his speech, were part of a story which "has no parallel in any British country or in any other democracy in Canada."

> We of the CCF stand now and have always stood ... for freedom and for democracy. If you give us a majority on June 4, one of my first acts as Premier will be to abolish Drew's secret political police and root out every vestige of this evil. With a CCF government there will be no political spying. There will be no secret blacklists. Democracy will come into its own. We shall protect and extend the freedom of the people.[1]

It was a sensational address, and Jolliffe's accusations immediately became the focus of the remainder of the campaign. While the CCF, Liberals, and Toronto *Star* denounced Drew and his "Gestapo" without restraint, the Premier and Attorney-General Blackwell passionately and categorically denied each and every charge made by the CCF leader. Within four days, so violent was the exchange that Drew was forced to appoint a Royal Commission to investigate the subject. The opposition's demand for a postponement of the election until the Commission had concluded its deliberations was, of course, rejected. The Commission's final report appeared several months after the election, when its political ramifications were negligible.

It may be asked, none the less, what effect the issue itself had on the 1945 election results. After the CCF's defeats in the provincial and federal contests, it became – and remains – commonplace to see a simple causal relationship between Jolliffe's accusations and his party's humiliating losses. Such criticism seems unjustified. It likely developed after the election when "Gestapo" could be made a convenient scapegoat upon which blame and resentment for the twin defeats could be laid. The available facts tend to the interpretation that the issue, on balance, lost the CCF very few votes. A Gallup poll taken immediately prior to Jolliffe's broadcast showed the CCF with 21 per cent in Ontario (for a federal election); in the provincial election on June 4, the party actually received 22 per cent of the popular vote. If its federal vote one week later was considerably lower, there seems little doubt this was attributable to the mass defection of many fringe supporters and the demoralization of many members after the Ontario results. On the other hand, it may be suggested that the Gestapo charges were a factor in Drew's phenomenal success in almost doubling his 1943 vote. The vicious irresponsibility of Jolliffe's speech, as many must have judged it, reinforced the monstrous image of the CCF that had been so brilliantly created by the anti-socialist propagandists over the previous two years; it was well calculated to frighten to the polls tens of thousands of cautious, sober citizens who might ordinarily not have bothered to vote.

If the political question has been shrouded in mythology, so has that of truth. Today's accepted version, on the whole, seems to be that the Drew administration was innocent of the accusation hurled against it, and that the culpable party in the affair was Jolliffe for his gross opportunism and irresponsibility.[2] This may be so. Jolliffe's charges, however, were so serious that a thorough examination of the issue seems necessary before a considered judgement can be rendered. It is useful first to examine the evidence as presented before the Commission, and then to consider the Commissioner's own evaluation of the evidence.[3]

As Royal Commissioner, Drew had appointed Justice A. M. LeBel, a former London, Ontario lawyer and a known supporter of the Liberal party. Before he handed down his judgement, Judge LeBel heard testimony and examined documentary evidence which totalled well over five thousand pages and one and a half million words. During the hearings, Jolliffe acted as his own counsel, with the assistance of F. Andrew Brewin, another prominent CCF lawyer. Mr. Joseph Sedgwick occupied the anomalous and unfortunate position during the enquiry of defending the Drew administration as well as being counsel for the Commission; he thus combined what should obviously have been two separate functions.

The Commission's terms of reference, as decided by the government, were to prove crucial to LeBel's final conclusions. Their effect was to restrict his verdict to the question of whether Drew was personally responsible for the establishment of "a secret political police organization, for the purpose of collecting, by secret spying, material to be used in an attempt to keep him in power."[4]

The enquiry centred on the activities of Captain William J. Osborne-Dempster of the Ontario Provincial Police. Dempster was one of fourteen operatives employed in anti-sabotage work in Ontario in the early war years. He told the Commission his duties had in no way changed after the "Special (Anti-Sabotage) Branch" of the OPP was closed by the provincial Liberal administration early in June, 1943: he was still to investigate and prevent sabotage and subversive activities. In mid-June, expecting a staff reduction, Dempster submitted his resignation. In July it was rejected, and he was instructed only "to report to the Deputy Commissioner (McCready)" and "to carry on the work I was doing." The provincial election followed in August.

He found, however, that his files and reports had been moved from his office and his telephone disconnected. He complained to McCready that he could not operate without equipment, and in fact he did nothing but draw pay from July until early November when, suddenly, his files and reports were returned. Although he claimed no further instructions were given him, he began reporting daily thereafter to McCready, and the nature of his work, notwithstanding his own disclaimer, underwent a qualitative change. For as Dempster admitted to Jolliffe, he had submitted no reports on members of the legislature prior to November of 1943. He then began reporting to McCready not only on individual M.P.P.'s but "regarding the political situation in the province of Ontario. . . . " Dempster could not explain why the Deputy-Commissioner of the Provincial Police, a civil servant, should be interested in such matters.

Dempster admitted having six or eight copies of each report made. He usually sent three copies to McCready, and took some "downtown" to Gladstone Murray, the anti-socialist propagandist. Buggsy Sanderson had come to the office two or three times and he had frequently visited the latter's office; he admitted giving Sanderson information from his secret files. Murray had telephoned him "about a dozen times" and he had been in Murray's office "probably half a dozen times," but their mutual interest, he insisted, was books, not the CCF. He had seen Drew twice, he acknowledged, at the Albany and Empire Clubs where they both dined, but only on the latter occasion did they shake hands. Dempster agreed that he might have told Mrs. Freeman, his secretary, that some of his reports went to the cabinet, and also that he gave Sanderson information from his files for the libellous newspaper advertisement. He granted as well that certain material used by an employee of Gladstone Murray and a leading Conservative to heckle Jolliffe at a meeting in Aurora "looks like my stuff." But he denied all other statements which Albert Rowe alleged he had made.

The basis of the CCF leader's accusations was the evidence presented by Constable J. A. Rowe of the Ontario Provincial Police. Rowe told the Commission that during the three months he was Dempster's assistant – from November 1943 to February 1944 – his work for the "Special Branch" of the OPP bore no relation to crime or sabotage. It was strictly political; it consisted of perusing the press for any complaints "against the capitalistic system, free enterprise, international finance." All such items were recorded in a card index under the speaker's name. Dempster told Rowe that the "present task" was to submit reports on all the CCF M.P.P.'s. Rowe typed seven copies of each report, of which, Dempster told him, three went to Deputy Commissioner McCready of the OPP, one was kept for the Special Branch, and one was sent "downtown" – that is, to Gladstone Murray to duplicate for the cabinet or his assistants.

In Dempster's absence from the office, Rowe said he took "several" phone calls from Murray, and one from Deputy Commissioner McCready who asked him to have Dempster call Murray. Rowe described various occasions when Dempster and M. A. Sanderson co-operated, and others when Murray was a party to their proceedings. Some of this evidence was based upon statements by Dempster, some upon direct knowledge such as Sanderson's visit to the Surrey Place office. Dempster told Rowe of a letter Sanderson received from Drew, and Sanderson once read Rowe the letter. Rowe thought it had been written on Ontario House stationery, that it began, "Dear Sandy: I hear you are getting quite ritzy . . . ," and that it promised Sanderson his expenses in the libel action would "be taken care of." Dempster also told Rowe that in 1939 he had planned to run as an Independent Conservative candidate in a provincial by-election in East Simcoe riding against George Drew, the official Conservative candidate. He had finally consented to withdraw, however, a decision that resulted in an acclamation for Drew and in Dempster thereafter having, so he boasted to Rowe, "a certain influence" with the Premier. This statement contradicted Dempster's own claim to the Commission that he had withdrawn in favour of the CCF candidate.

There was one serious discrepancy in Rowe's testimony, disclosed by counsel for the government. No stationery from Ontario House in London had been printed until after Drew was reported to have written his "Dear Sandy" letter, and Drew had, in any event, left England early in 1944, before the libel actions were instituted against Sanderson. Whatever it was that the latter read Rowe, it was not a letter from Drew in England written on Ontario House letterhead.

Mrs. Bertha Freeman, Dempster's stenographer after February 1944, provided testimony corroborating Rowe's. She was instructed to type eight copies of each report which Dempster said he gave "to the Commissioner [of the OPP]" who "distributes them to the Premier and Cabinet." Almost all the reports she made referred to the CCF, one to the Liberals, none to the Conservatives.

M. A. Sanderson admitted visiting Dempster's office, particularly concerning the writing of his notorious advertisement. He knew Drew and Blackwell, but denied any relations with them involving his propaganda work. He admitted that he had sent the Premier "an outburst" of Eugene Forsey's and had received an acknowledgement. Moreover, two innocuous letters submitted in evidence from Sanderson to Drew and Drew to Sanderson were not directly related one to the other, suggesting an unexplained gap of at least one letter each way between August 31 and November 11, 1943.

Sanderson claimed that his payments to Dempster were for assistance the latter had given in the extermination business, but he did not explain why, if this were so, some were made under the pseudonym "Orville Ray." He did admit knowing the secret unlisted telephone number of the Special Branch office. He also revealed that he and Dempster had gone on a combined business and pleasure trip to Kitchener, which was "quite a centre of Communist activities." But he denied stating later that Dempster wanted to report on the trip to Premier Drew personally. Sanderson believed that his ads had helped raise his status in the community, for many people "were quite surprised that a pest-control operator could sign his own name, let alone write an article in which fairly good use is made of English. . . . "

It was Robert G. Hall, one of Sanderson's assistants, who testified that he had heard his employer twice repeat that

Dempster wished to report to Drew directly. Hall further stated that he had once overheard Sanderson telephone Drew's office and apologize for keeping a certain letter too long. Hall also pointed out that Sanderson achieved a sudden prominence in the Conservative party after he had published a newspaper advertisement in 1942 denouncing Mackenzie King. He then attended the national leadership convention in Winnipeg and was accepted as a member of the posh Albany Club in Toronto.

Miss Margaret Carruthers, another Sanderson employee, testified that Sanderson had once told her excitedly that "he had received a letter from Mr. Drew of which he was very proud." She had, however, not seen the letter. She placed it in January 1944, for it related to the libel action. This was unquestionably the same letter Rowe claimed Sanderson read to him in Dempster's office, though it clearly had not been sent from Ontario House in London.

In his testimony which followed, Gladstone Murray agreed that he "might have had" various contacts with both Dempster and M. A. Sanderson, as had several of his employees. Murray admitted knowing Dempster's secret telephone number, but denied having used any influence with Drew or Blackwell relative to Dempster's activities. He stated that he had once discussed the functions of "Responsible Enterprise," his propaganda organization, with the Premier, although Drew categorically denied that any such topic had even been mentioned.

Attorney-General Leslie Blackwell, who followed, repeated what he had consistently claimed during the election campaign. Dempster's name never came to his attention prior to Jolliffe's charges, nor had he ever heard of 18 Surrey Place nor of any investigations of subversive political activities. Yet Blackwell admitted that 41 "Secret and Confidential" reports of "Yours to Command, D-208" had been placed on his desk over a period of time, but he said he did not know D-208's identity nor had he paid much attention to the reports. He was not "awfully interested in them" since he considered their contents concerned "Communist activities" – although many of them, he later admitted, dealt with prominent CCF'ers, including Jolliffe himself, M. J. Coldwell, William Dennison, and Sam Lawrence. Nor did he explain his lack of interest in "Communist activities." His secretary did not know D-208's identity, and Blackwell had never asked him to enquire. Finally, in June 1944, he had his secretary inform Commissioner Stringer of the OPP that he wanted no further reports sent him. He stated that he had never divulged the reports' contents to anyone, including the Premier.

Blackwell admitted knowing Sanderson and Murray, but their contacts bore no relation to the subject of the hearing. His only conversation with Murray, which he agreed sounded so unlikely that "I almost hesitate to say this," was on "the ravages of budworms." But he did receive Murray's various anti-socialist publications through the mail.

Andrew Brewin, who was assisting Jolliffe, asked the Attorney-General what relation his campaign statement that "Mr. Jolliffe dreamed up" Dempster's reports had to the fact that there were forty-one of D-208's reports in his own office files. Blackwell replied: "I saw no reason why I should indicate what I had on my files." Brewin then questioned Blackwell about his knowledge of an anti-sabotage branch of the OPP, the existence of which he had previously denied. The Attorney-General was unable to explain why he had reports from a branch he did not know existed.

In his testimony, Premier Drew agreed he had heard the name Osborne-Dempster before Jolliffe's speech, since he had almost faced a man of the same name in the East Simcoe by-election of 1939. But he had never seen or heard of any reports from D-208, and none had ever been discussed in cabinet sessions when he was present. He denied writing a letter to Sanderson from England, or knowing of the libellous advertisement until he returned to Ontario. He had met Sanderson some years earlier, for both men were members of the same Canadian Corps Association. They later met periodically, but Drew's business dealings with him were only in Sanderson's professional capacity as an exterminator. As for Gladstone Murray, the Premier stated he had never had any conversation with him "even remotely connected" with his propagandist activities; Murray's previous testimony contradicted this statement.

The case of Mr. Cecil W. Peppin was then presented. Peppin was an innocent bystander. In April and May, 1945, he had written to Drew and members of his cabinet several times concerning allegedly unfair treatment he had received from the provincial Workmen's Compensation Board. One of his letters to the Premier, dated April 5, 1945, was received and acknowledged by Drew's executive-secretary five days later, with the assurance that it would "be placed before the Prime Minister at an early date." On April 17, upon the instructions of Chief Inspector Ward of the Criminal Investigation Branch of the OPP, Dempster filed a brief report on Peppin. Dempster said Ward instructed him "to find out all he possibly could about him [Peppin]; if he was a member of any political party or labour union." Why the head of Criminal Investigation should be concerned with such information was not determined. In the event, Dempster found that Peppin had nothing to his discredit, but Drew's clearly implied connection with Dempster in this affair subsequently proved one of the most controversial subjects of the hearings.

The testimony of Commissioner Stringer and Deputy Commissioner McCready of the OPP followed. Dempster reported personally to McCready, his immediate superior, each morning, and the Deputy Commissioner agreed that Dempster was the only constable in the OPP to do so. He claimed he did not know what Dempster was doing other than "carrying on," nor did he enquire. There were no reports from the Special Branch for three and a half months after the Liberal defeat in August 1943, although Dempster was drawing his salary. When finally the first of the new series, on William Dennison, a CCF M.P.P., was given him, he did not question it, nor did he confer with Commissioner Stringer about the qualitative change in Dempster's work. Moreoever, none of these reports were sent to the R.C.M.P. for action, as had often been done before August 1943.

> Altogether [observes Edwin Guillet] it seems incredible that Dempster should have been reinstated without instructions, given a free hand without comment, and his reports accorded but a passing glance. It is unbelievable that these and all the other discrepancies could have been accepted as routine unless Dempster had an unseen influence and a higher control, his work a far more insidious purpose, and his reports another and very different ... destination. To reach any other conclusion would be to ignore all the evidence.[5]

And Brewin reminded the Commission that responsibility for the Provincial Police fell under the jurisdiction of the Attorney-General, Leslie Blackwell.

In his concluding argument, Brewin also emphasized that, by the theory of ministerial responsibility, the Premier had ultimate responsibility for the conduct of all departments of his administration, and each of his cabinet ministers were accountable for every activity of his respective department. He stressed, too, that the distribution of secret material to propagandists contravened the Official Secrets Act, while the fabrication and distortion of reports on members of the legislature was a grave breach of the privileges of parliament.

Jolliffe, in concluding, made the point that no fewer than

thirteen witnesses during the investigation had given evidence which, directly or indirectly, linked Drew or his office with Dempster's activities. Jolliffe noted that the operations of the special anti-sabotage branch of the OPP – a war-time necessity, he agreed – had originally been known to and authorized by the legislature. But after Drew took office, a new unauthorized branch began functioning with largely political aims. Whereas previous anti-sabotage activities had been reported upon regularly by the OPP, there had never been a mention of the new branch or an explanation for its functional changes. Similarly, Dempster's work had been hidden from public view by keeping his name and salary out of the public accounts. Indeed, Jolliffe argued, "one of the great unexplained mysteries" of the entire case was why Dempster's activities continued at all after Blackwell decided, in June 1944, to receive no further reports. Why, he asked, should the Provincial Police, as civil servants, be interested in purely political information if their ultimate superior, a politician, was not? It was noted as well that prior to Drew's victory, D-208's reports were signed "Respectfully submitted," but that the closing thereafter was "Yours to Command." This, it was suggested, clearly implied a change in Dempster's relations with his superiors. Finally, the CCF leader concluded, excepting Dempster himself, only politicians stood to benefit from his activities, "and yet we are asked to believe that the politicians in the case knew nothing about it and had nothing to do with it."

Jolliffe's scepticism may seem reasonable. But the fact remained that only circumstantial evidence had been produced which directly tied Dempster to any politician. Joseph Sedgwick, in his capacity as counsel for the Government, stressed this point, and it was to have great weight in Commissioner LeBel's final judgement. While agreeing that the collaboration of Dempster and Sanderson must be "very severely criticized," Sedgwick emphasized that "no member of the government was making any use of their information."

Justice A. M. LeBel issued his fifty-page report on October 9, 1945, four and a half months after Jolliffe first made his charges. He emphasized at the outset

> the importance of the principles involved in Mr. Jolliffe's charges.... A secret political police organization ... for the purpose of keeping a government in power would constitute a serious departure from the principles ... of our democratic system.... It would mean ... the rule of the dictator.... If

a government merely made use of information [properly] . . . gathered in war time for . . . maligning its opponents, the self-same principles of our democratic system would be violated. And if . . . the Drew government were fearful of making direct use of information received, and for that matter made indirect use of it in the manner Mr. Jolliffe described, the results, in my opinion, would be precisely as iniquitous.[6]

LeBel's first conclusion was that Dempster's reports were frequently misleading and false, but that no intent wilfully to misrepresent the facts had been proved. Further, it was "incredible" to the Commissioner that "big business," through the agency of M. A. Sanderson and Gladstone Murray, would be "in the market for the purchase of palpable falsehoods. . . . Big business did not need the assistance of Constable Dempster if it wanted to embark upon a campaign of libel and vilification." LeBel consequently concluded that "neither Constable Dempster nor any other person mentioned by Mr. Jolliffe . . . ever intended to publish anything which was deliberately false."[7]

This was unconvincing. In the first place, as Guillet notes, "a mere opinion cannot logically be the basis of a judicial conclusion."[8] Furthermore, Dempster's persistent references to the "Communist Controlled c.i.o." and his attempts to link CCF M.P.P.'s with communism[9] may not have been intended "wilfully to misrepresent the facts"; but they did, surely, indicate Dempster's incompetence to deal objectively with the subjects of his investigations. Moreover, as Professor George Grube stated, LeBel's subjective assumption that big business did not have to hire political propagandists was "obviously contrary to the facts of political life. . . . "[10] Indeed, as several documents received by LeBel himself conclusively proved, Gladstone Murray, for one, was the perfect example of a propagandist hired by business to "vilify" the CCF. At best, LeBel seemed incredibly ingenuous.

Turning next to the establishment of the Anti-Sabotage Branch of the OPP, the Commissioner traced its course from a war-time origin under the former Liberal administration. LeBel argued that although the original Secret Branch was abolished in June 1943, the Conservatives, through Dempster, merely carried on the legacy of the former government. Nor would he accept Jolliffe's claim that Dempster's work changed qualitatively under the Drew administration.

Since Blackwell pleaded ignorance of the existence of both the Special Branch and Dempster, LeBel concluded that he could not, therefore, have given any directions for a change in either's

functions. The Commissioner found, rather, that the re'urn of
Dempster's equipment had been authorized by McCready,
although "it is unlikely that the [OPP] Deputy Commissioner
[did so] . . . without first taking them up with the Commissioner
[Stringer]." If so, Stringer must have "considered it of a routine
nature, involving no matter of government policy, and hence
within his own jurisdiction. As a result, he did not refer it to the
Attorney-General or any member of his Department."[11] But
LeBel's judgement about the similarity between Dempster's original reports on subversive activities and his later political reports
is at least debatable. Professor Grube's comment that the
authority for Dempster's changed activities "went perhaps even
further up than Commissioner Stringer"[12] must seriously be considered.

Judge LeBel devoted considerable space to "Reasons for the
Increase of Constable Dempster's Interest in the CCF Party." He
pointed out that Dempster had become acquainted with Sanderson and Murray in April and May, 1943, and that these associations affected Dempster greatly: they increased his antipathy to
the CCF and simultaneously presented him with an opportunity
to better himself financially. The Commissioner accepted that
Dempster clandestinely received thirty dollars a week from Sanderson, in direct violation of police regulations. He did not accept
that these payments were for part-time work by Dempster as an
exterminator. He decided, indeed, that a close relationship
existed between Sanderson and Dempster. They did visit and
telephone one another, and Sanderson did obtain information
from official files for use in his advertisements attempting "to
establish a 'tie-in' between the Communist and CCF parties."
The libellous advertisement of January 1, 1944, was largely
prepared in Dempster's office. (The Commissioner noted *en
passant* that much of the transferred information was erroneous
or entirely false.)[13] He concluded that it was because of Dempster's relations with Sanderson that the former's reports after
November 1943

> displayed a greater political tinge than hitherto, and in my
> opinion accounts for the existence of such reports as the
> following: " The CCF Caucus. . . . "; "Some Aspects of the
> Recent Saskatchewan Election and Its Possible Effect
> on the Impending Federal Election as It Affects . . . Ontario
> . . . "; "Re Ottawa Caucus C.I.O.-CCF . . . "; the reports on
> some nine or ten members of the CCF Party . . . as well as other
> political material.[14]

But while thus reposing responsibility for Dempster's activities upon Sanderson and Murray, LeBel failed to ask why neither Deputy Commissioner McCready nor Attorney-General Blackwell questioned reports based not on governmental policy but on Dempster's personal predilections.

LeBel believed that Dempster had in fact told Constable Albert Rowe all the latter claimed he did, but that Dempster's statements were falsehoods designed merely to impress his subordinate with his importance. Though admitting the possibility of some other explanation, the Commissioner argued simply that Rowe became increasingly "gullible" as Dempster became progressively more boastful. Thus LeBel was able to reject entirely Dempster's crucial assertions that he had influence with both Drew and Blackwell, and that Murray received his reports and passed them on to the government.

LeBel's decision on this point was based upon the denials by Drew and Blackwell of personal contact with Dempster; the Commissioner accepted these denials unquestioningly. And he accepted as true, of all Dempster's many statements, only one: the claim that he withdrew as an Independent Conservative candidate in East Simcoe in 1939 in favour of the CCF candidate, not in favour of Drew. This was an important conclusion. If Dempster had been lying, the possibility existed that a *quid pro quo* had been arranged in 1939: Dempster would quit the campaign in return for later favours. By accepting Dempster's claim, Lebel implicitly rejected this possibility. But in fact the CCF had *not* contested the by-election, and there is no evidence that it had ever considered doing so. Drew alone could and did benefit from Dempster's withdrawal, allowing him to win by acclamation.

In fact, the Commissioner rejected as "fantastic" virtually every claim Dempster made which might injure the Drew government. He decided that Dempster's motive in making such claims to Rowe was his fear that "his increased activities in the matter of the CCF Party would not be countenanced by his superiors if brought to their attention, and that Rowe might report him to higher authority" unless he believed Dempster's work was sanctioned by Drew and Blackwell.[15] LeBel did not consider the alternative theory that Dempster's claims of influence with "higher authority" were designed to intimidate Rowe so that he would not take his information to anyone *outside* the government, as he in fact ultimately did. It could even be argued that Dempster was indeed trying to impress Rowe – with the truth.

The Commissioner then turned his attention to the important

letter Drew allegedly wrote Sanderson concerning the libel action against the latter. Both Constable Rowe and Miss Carruthers, Sanderson's bookkeeper, testified to the existence of such a letter; these two witnesses were in no way acquainted. Drew and Sanderson both denied the existence of any such letter.

LeBel accepted both Rowe's evidence that Sanderson read him a letter once, and Miss Carruthers' assertion that Sanderson boasted of having received a letter from the Premier. Yet "Upon all the evidence," the Judge was "of the opinion that Mr. Drew never wrote the letter . . . and that there was no such letter . . . what Sanderson held briefly in front of Rowe was something which he had prepared for the occasion."[16] He rejected Rowe's evidence as proof of the existence of the letter because of the impossibility that Ontario House stationery had been used and because of Drew's ignorance of Sanderson's advertisement until he returned to Canada. Jolliffe and Brewin had both admitted these facts during the inquiry, but pointed out that this still did not account for the letter Sanderson certainly read Rowe. LeBel rejected Miss Carruthers' testimony as insignificant since she had not seen the letter. He made no attempt, however, to suggest why Sanderson might have wanted to deceive Miss Carruthers with a false claim. The Commissioner's conclusion referred only to the specific letter on Ontario House letterhead to which Jolliffe originally referred. Properly rejecting its existence, he did not consider whether any letter of a similar nature had been written by Drew to Sanderson.

LeBel was critical of Attorney-General Blackwell for taking such an apparently casual interest in the forty-one reports by D-208 sent him by Commissioner Stringer of the OPP. He thought Blackwell should have taken the trouble to learn D-208's identity and methods of obtaining information. LeBel stated that it was "an embarrassment" for Blackwell to have to admit that the OPP was carrying on work without his knowledge. He ignored the possibility that the Attorney-General in fact knew more than he had publicly admitted.

Seven or eight copies of each report had usually been made. Yet the Secret Branch files contained only two or three copies of each. LeBel found that the missing ones were likely accounted for by the "confusion" which prevailed at 18 Surrey Place. He was unable to infer from their loss their possible possession by Drew or any member of his cabinet other than Blackwell, but he made no attempt to account for the missing copies other than suggesting that Dempster had "misfiled or lost" them.[17]

Constable Rowe had stated earlier that Dempster had been in

contact with Murray and his office manager, James Suydam, concerning a meeting in Aurora at which Jolliffe was to speak. Dempster then prepared, and Rowe typed, a list of questions with which hecklers could presumably embarrass the CCF leader. Suydam admitted he was present at the Aurora meeting, along with two friends, one of whom was Major James Baxter, chief advertising agent in Ontario for the Conservative party. The other friend, Richardson, did much of the heckling, and asked Jolliffe two or three questions from Dempster's list. LeBel agreed that Dempster gave the list to Suydam, who showed it to Richardson. Murray was implicated in the incident as Suydam's employer. No significance was attached to the role of Major Baxter of the Conservative party.[18]

The Commissioner found that there was a close relation between Dempster and Murray, but that their only interest in common was opposition to communism. The CCF only entered the picture where it appeared to be closely related to the communist movement.[19] But LeBel knew that Dempster had not made a single report on members of the Labour Progressive (Communist) Party, and the Commission had received in evidence two of Murray's circulars appealing for funds to fight the "CCF Socialists."[20] Thus it in fact appeared that the primary interest of both Murray and Dempster was to combat, each in his own way, not communism, but the CCF party.

While prior to 1943 the Special (or Anti-Sabotage) Branch of the OPP was reported upon in the annual reports to the legislature, Commissioner Stringer made no reference to it in the reports of 1943 and 1944. He gave as reason the abolition of the Branch in 1943, although Dempster continued his activities as a member of the Branch. Judge LeBel found that Stringer accepted full responsibility for his annual reports and that there was no evidence that the Attorney-General or anyone else authorized him to prepare those reports. Nor did he question the omission of the functioning Special Branch from Stringer's annual reports after the Drew administration took office.[21]

LeBel then turned his attention to the important C. W. Peppin incident. Peppin had written Drew about a personal matter on April 5, 1945, and was informed by the Premier's secretary that his letter would "be placed before the Prime Minister at an early date." On April 17, Peppin discovered that he was being investigated by Dempster and twice wrote Drew in protest. The significance of this incident is twofold. There is, first, what Guillet calls "the logical assumption" that Drew had ordered Peppin's investigation after reading his April 5 letter. Secondly, had Drew read Peppin's letters of April 28 or May 18, in which he protested his investigation by "an undercover man" who "has a government office in Surrey Place," he would have known of Dempster's activities. The Premier, of course, consistently denied such knowledge. Drew did not deny reading the April 5 letter, but he denied seeing the protest letter of April 28, and "could not say whether the May 18 letter [sent by Peppin] to his home reached him or not, since he received a great many 'crank letters.' "

The Commissioner attempted to determine two facts: whether Drew had ordered Peppin's investigation, and whether he learned of Dempster's existence from reading one of Peppin's letters. Strangely, however, LeBel based his conclusions on both points upon the letter of April 28, which referred to an "undercover man" at Surrey Place. "If he (Drew) did not see the letter," he wrote, "then of course he could not have" ordered Peppin's investigations. This was inaccurate. Drew had only to read the original letter of April 5, in order to have Peppin investigated, and we know his secretary acknowledged that letter. The April 28 letter would have revealed to him Dempster's activities. The Commissioner never clarified this confusion. Since "No one swore that this letter [of April 28] had been brought to Mr. Drew's personal attention . . . and in view of Mr. Drew's categorical denial that the letter in question ever was brought to his attention, I am satisfied that he never read the letter, and I so find."[22] Thus Drew was exonerated of the charge of calling for Peppin's investigation, and it followed that he could not have known of Dempster's activities as a result of Peppin's letter.

LeBel then, through a factual inaccuracy, failed to establish responsibility for Peppin's investigation. It began within two weeks of the time Peppin wrote Drew and was assured in a letter of reply that the Premier would see his letter "at an early date." George Curlew, who was Dempster's informant concerning Peppin's background, testified that Dempster "told me there was a letter sent to the Prime Minister's Office. . . . "[23] Dempster could have learned this only from Inspector Ward of the Criminal Investigation Branch who instructed him to conduct the investigation. Drew denied ordering Ward to set the investigation in motion. The Premier's secretary, who acknowledged Peppin's letter, did not testify. If Drew did not order Peppin's investigation, who but his secretary could have done so or ordered it done? And even had Drew not been involved, could the Premier evade responsibility for the actions of his own executive secretary? Unfortunately, Mr. Justice LeBel ignored such questions.

Throughout the inquiry, as in his radio address, Jolliffe had sought through evidence and inference to link Sanderson and Murray to both Drew and Blackwell in a secret conspiracy against the CCF. And, indeed, each of the politicians had admitted during the hearings having many contacts with each of the propagandists, but claimed that business and social matters, never politics, brought them together. Professor Grube thought "it is hard for anyone who knows the facts of political life" to believe that Conservative party politicians and professional propagandists avowedly favouring that same party could have such frequent contacts without the subject of common interest to all of them ever being raised.[24] Judge LeBel, however, accepted all of Drew's and Blackwell's disclaimers without qualification.

At the conclusion of his report, the Commissioner declared, in fact, that

> There is nothing in the evidence that directly connects Mr. Drew even remotely with Constable Dempster or the work he carried on . . . other than the Peppin incident with which I have dealt . . . and likewise *nothing other* than the receipt of some 41 of Dempster's reports that might serve to show that Mr. Blackwell knew his identity or the nature of his work. . . . I am convinced Mr. Drew knew nothing about these matters, and that Mr. Blackwell dismissed the reports as of no importance. However . . . I believe that Mr. Blackwell should have found time to discuss the reports with Commissioner Stringer before dismissing them as of no interest to him.[25]

After this mild reproach to Blackwell, LeBel turned to Dempster's relations with Sanderson and Murray. He declared that Dempster's collaboration with the two men in their propaganda activities was

> highly improper but in my opinion there is not a jot of evidence to indicate that [it was] openly or tacitly authorized by Mr. Drew or any member of his Cabinet, or that Mr. Drew or any of his Ministers knew of the association between Dempster and Sanderson or of Dempster's acquaintanceship with Mr. Murray and Mr. Suydam [Murray's employee who used Dempster's information to heckle Jolliffe]. I am therefore unable to conclude on the evidence that the Drew Government allowed Dempster to "work

hand in glove with the propagandists of big business" who were said by Mr. Jolliffe to be Murray and Sanderson especially.

As for the principle of cabinet responsibility for all activities of an administration, the Commissioner felt this matter to be beyond his powers as Royal Commissioner, as well as outside the scope of Jolliffe's charges, which were specific, based on no constitutional principles. They concerned "deliberate and wilful acts of wrong doing" on the part of Drew and his government. And no such acts, concluded LeBel, had occurred.[26]

Such were the essentials of the Royal Commission Report. Several occasions have been noted above where Mr. Justice LeBel's conclusions seemed at least questionable in view of the available evidence; these included his error in the matter of the East Simcoe by-election, his confusion in the Peppin incident, the alleged letter from Drew to Sanderson, and the many ostensibly innocent meetings of Drew and Blackwell with Dempster, Murray, and Sanderson. A more general criticism of the Commissioner's report was made both by the *Canadian Forum* and by Edwin Guillet. Although LeBel was a known Liberal supporter, the *Forum* pointed out that his report found against Drew and his government "only to the extent that points were proved beyond the possibility of doubt, and to have interpreted all other evidence in the government's favour."[27] And Guillet noted "a tendency [on LeBel's part] to soften the culpability of those in responsible positions by making 'goats' out of smaller fry."[28] This referred particularly to LeBel's conclusion that Deputy Commissioner McCready alone was responsible for Dempster continuing his activities after November 1943.

Moreover, although all the evidence connecting Drew with Dempster was indirect and inferential, the cumulative effect of no fewer than thirteen witnesses presenting such evidence was, at least, suggestive. Yet LeBel hardly gave these testimonies serious consideration.

Still, all the relevant evidence was circumstantial. This was crucial. The most unfortunate error in Jolliffe's original charges was the one which precluded his vindication by the Commissioner, for the weakest link in the chain of evidence proved to be his personal charge against Drew. Not only could Drew's alleged connection with Dempster not be proved conclusively, it was not even essential to do so for Jolliffe's important charges to be proved. His entire case should have been based upon "the illegality and enormity" of the existence of a state of affairs which was, as Guillet points out, proved to the satisfaction of (almost) all: Dempster, a public servant, had distributed or sold information to Sanderson, a Conservative propagandist. This information, noted George Grube, was deliberately used "in campaigns against the opposition party, and therefore in support of the party in power, and thus played some part in keeping it there."[29] Furthermore, added Guillet, by the theory of cabinet responsibility, which LeBel considered outside his terms of reference, "The culpability of the Cabinet and the Prime Minister follow automatically, irrespective of how directly their connection could be proved to the satisfaction of a court of law."

Mr. Guillet, to be sure, had developed some rather passionate sentiments about the Gestapo affair while reviewing its history. If Drew was the villain of the piece, Jolliffe was manifestly its hero. The CCF leader, he declared, "has obviously proved the basic substance of his charge beyond the shadow of a doubt, and to him, to Constable Rowe, . . . and to the other informants, posterity will accord an honourable place in the history of human freedom."[30]

Posterity, in fact, has not done so, and, some will think, justifiably. There are grounds for questioning both Jolliffe's motives for and method of introducing the issue into the campaign. Was he in fact using Rowe to gain power in the same way that he alleged Drew had used Dempster to retain it? Jolliffe learned of Dempster's activities in November 1943. Why did he delay making public his evidence until eleven days before the election? He claimed that it was only in early May 1945 that Miss Carruthers, Sanderson's bookkeeper, appeared with the evidence of a letter from Drew to her employer.[31] But this testimony was only hearsay, and in any event, there was enough evidence to link Dempster with Sanderson and Murray even without it. Jolliffe never raised the issue in the 1944 or 1945 sessions of the legislature, yet he had learned of Dempster and his activities in November 1943. He did not question the omission of Dempster's name and salary from the official report on the Provincial Police. He never attempted to get the approval of the CCF's Provincial Election Committee for injecting this new issue into the election, although it alone had authority to initiate such a radical change in the planned pattern of the party's campaign. He did not discuss his plans with any of his closest colleagues.[32] Moreover, the manner of presenting his evidence in his original radio broadcast was unfortunate. Jolliffe wrote his speech with the assistance of Lister Sinclair, then a popular dramatist.[33] The result of their combined effort suggests that they decided that, rather than a restrained, legalistic statement of the evidence, a more sensational presentation would have the greater impact upon the public.

All this suggests desperation and expediency. It does not seem utterly unfair to suspect that Jolliffe withheld his information until there appeared a political need to reveal it. With two weeks of the election campaign remaining, such a need clearly existed. The CCF had entered the campaign with a certain amount of confidence. Yet the Gallup poll now gave the party only 21 per cent in Ontario. The attempt to identify socialism with totalitarianism was, apparently, proving successful. What better method of counter-attack than using the enemy's own weapons? "Now all through this election campaign," Jolliffe had stated in his broadcast, "you've been hearing that the real issue is freedom versus dictatorship. . . . And I quite agree; there certainly is a very grave danger; and when you've heard all the facts . . . well, I'll let you decide for yourself where the danger of dictatorship is coming from." Jolliffe's choice of rhetoric in the speech was well calculated to support his contention. It conjured up in the public mind a terrifying spectre. But that spectre was grossly exaggerated. Although there can be little question that Dempster's activities constituted a perversion of democracy, surely there was a difference in kind between Ontario's political police and a Nazi-like "Gestapo"; that is not a comparison to be made frivolously.

Nevertheless, Jolliffe must be judged by the same standards applied to Drew. The case for questioning his motives, while persuasive, is, in the last analysis, unprovable. More important than his motives were his accusations. The evidence marshalled before the Commission in the main supported those accusations. There was "a secret political police" in Ontario, it did function as a "paid government spy organization," it was used to help keep the Conservative administration in power. However posterity remembers E. B. Jolliffe, it should recognize Dempster and his activities on behalf of George Drew's government as an unhappy episode in the history of the Province of Ontario.

References

1. *Report of Royal Commission appointed May 28, 1945 to Investigate Charges Made by Mr. E. B. Jolliffe, K. C., the Hon. Mr. Justice A. M. LeBel, Commisioner* (hereafter *LeBel Report*), Appendix A., pp. 49-55.

2. See, for example the article on George Drew by Ralph Hyman, Toronto *Globe and Mail,* September 21, 1963. "The so-called Gestapo," Hyman writes, "was nothing more than the anti-sabotage branch of the Ontario Provincial Police, established before Mr. Drew came to office [in 1943]." And when Drew died in 1973, the Toronto *Star's* obituary stated flatly that Drew "had nothing to do with the [Gestapo] file which had been the work of Provincial Police and private investigators." January 4, 1973.

3. The following summary is taken in part from the *LeBel Report*, in part from E. C. Guillet, *Famous Canadian Trials*, volume 50, "Political Gestapo" (Toronto, 1949). Guillet was formerly the Ontario Archivist. Fortunately, his unpublished manuscript presents a detailed report of the Commission's hearing, because, curiously, neither the legislative library nor any departmental library – including those in the offices of the Premier, the Attorney-General, and the Provincial Secretary – includes a copy of the complete transcript. It is peculiar indeed that the Provincial Government has no copy of the hearings of a provincial Royal Commission.

4. Guillet, "Political Gestapo," chapter 1. Guillet's manuscript is unpaginated. He reproduced whole chunks of the original report, and all subsequent quotations are from that source unless otherwise noted.

5. *Ibid.*, chapter 7, introduction.

6. *LeBel Report,* pp. 9-10

7. *Ibid.,* p. 11.

8. Guillet, *op. cit.,* chapter 10.

9. *Ibid.,* Appendix E, Dempster's Reports, No. 2, "CCF Caucus," November 29, 1943.

10. G. M. A. Grube, "The Lebel Report and Civil Liberties," *Canadian Forum,* November 1945.

11. *LeBel Report,* pp. 11-19.

12. Grube, *op. cit.*

13. *LeBel Report,* p. 24.

14. *Ibid.,* p. 34.

15. *Ibid.,* pp 22-3.

16. *Ibid.,* pp. 26-8.

17. *Ibid.,* pp. 28-9.

18. *Ibid.,* pp. 32-4.

19. *Ibid.,* p. 35.

20. Guillet, *op. cit.,* Appendix G, Murray's circulars of August 4 and September 29, 1943.

21. *LeBel Report,* pp. 36-8.

22. *Ibid.,* pp. 39-40

23. *Ibid.,* p. 38.

24. Grube, *op. cit.*

25. *LeBel Report,* p. 41. Emphasis added.

26. *Ibid.,* p. 42.

27. *Canadian Forum,* November 1945.

28. Guillet, *op. cit.,* chapter 11.

29. Grube, *op. cit.*

30. Guillet, *op. cit.*

31. Interview with Jolliffe, 1961.

32. Interviews with Brewin, Lewis, and Grube, 1961.

33. Interviews with Brewin and Lewis.

12 MYSTIFICATION AT WORK

The first post-election issue of the *CCF News* carried the banner headline: "CCF'er BEATS KING."[1] It happened to be true. But it was also true that King's personal humiliation was the single reason for joy after two grim elections. June 4 and June 11, 1945, proved to be black days in CCF annuls: socialism was effectively removed from the Canadian political agenda. In Ontario, the Conservatives were re-elected by a minority vote; they took sixty-six seats, the Liberals eleven, the CCF a mere eight. Hepburn, for the first time in six campaigns, was defeated, as was Jolliffe; although the CCF leader polled 3000 votes more than in 1943, the Tory increase was even more spectacular. Yet Jolliffe came closer to victory than any other CCF candidate in Toronto or the Yorks. The majority against Drew was about ninety thousand, his party polling 774,982 votes, the Liberals 474,817, and the CCF 390,910. With the significant exceptions of Bellwoods and St. Andrews, where Salsberg and MacLeod were re-elected for the L.P.P., Drew swept the seventeen seats in the Toronto area.

After June 4, CCF supporters in Ontario were shattered. This reaction, while understandable, was excessive. In fact, given the campaign against it, the party did remarkably well. While it won only eight per cent of the seats in Queen's Park, it got twenty-two per cent of the total provincial vote. True, while in 1943 it had received almost a third of the total vote, there had been a smaller number cast then. The CCF polled only 27,610 votes fewer than in 1943; in traditionally Conservative Toronto, while the party lost its three best members in Jolliffe, Charles Millard, and Agnes Macphail, it actually received 667 more votes than two years earlier. Moreover, in eight ridings an L.P.P. candidate so split the labour vote as to allow a victory for the older parties. This cost the CCF the official opposition.

Four-fifths of the CCF vote came from the fifty non-agricultural ridings; two thirds came from the twenty-seven most highly industrialized constituencies; all eight victors were from labour ridings, one in Hamilton, the rest from northern Ontario. The CCF received twelve per cent of the rural vote, twenty-seven per cent of the total urban vote; its·urban support was one per cent greater than the Liberals, eleven less than the Conservatives.

Rural Ontario wrought havoc on the CCF even in urban centres. It is also likely that urbanization added to city electorates a large rural group whose baggage included anti-CCF and anti-union political tendencies.[2] Although there is no final tabulation of the soldiers' vote, an incomplete Toronto record gave the CCF 3859, the Conservatives 2997, and the Liberals 1690.

It is thus clear that the total CCF vote remained generally constant. But the vote of the old parties soared, and therein lay the difference. The Liberals increased their 1943 vote by 65,000, the Conservatives by a staggering 305,000 votes. The conclusion was irresistible: the anti-socialist crusade had proved supremely effective.

For the CCF, the consequence of the Ontario disaster was an even greater debacle one week later. As usual, Mackenzie King was the prime minister of Canada. True, his popular vote had declined from 53 to 39 per cent in five years, and only because of Quebec did he retain a bare majority in the Commons. Still, the Tories were crushed while the CCF dream was shattered. The party that one year earlier appeared destined to form the next government of Canada won 28 federal seats and 16 per cent of the total vote. It was true it had doubled its national vote to 800,000 in just five years; but it was planning to *win*. Moreover, the election decimated the party east of Manitoba. All but one of its 28 seats came from the west: eighteen in Saskatchewan, five in Manitoba, four in British Columbia; Noseworthy lost badly in Toronto, Gillis hung on in Cape Breton. West of the Great Lakes, the CCF polled the largest vote of any party, and elected as many members as the old parties combined.

In the five eastern provinces, the CCF's civilian vote increased from 87,000 in 1940 to 300,000 in 1945, but this was grossly inadequate; it was considerably less than half the party's total national vote. Most striking of all were the Ontario results. There the Conservatives polled 750,000 votes, only a few less than the week earlier. The Liberals raised their vote dramatically from 475,000 on June 4 to 745,000 on June 11. The CCF vote, in that one short week, plummeted from 390,000 to 260,000, from 22 to 14 per cent. Clearly a large number of CCF bandwagon supporters, discouraged by the losses in the provincial election, had deserted the sinking ship. Moreover, as in the Ontario election, the Communists successfully split the vote in eight close urban contests.

The service vote had little effect on party standings in Ottawa, and in only one important constituency was it the decisive factor. In the Saskatchewan riding of Prince Albert, a CCF'er defeated Mackenzie King. The socialist polled 934 service votes, the Prime Minister of Canada 542; this made the final total 7928 to 7799. Besides providing a traumatic experience for King personally, the service vote in Europe perhaps reflected the thinking of the only group of Canadians spared the machinations and propaganda at home. The CCF polled 61,000 votes, the Liberals 47,000, the Conservatives 41,000.[3]

To orthodox political commentators, the overriding significance of the two elections was the "trend" they indicated back to the two-party system. All the third parties had been contained, but above all the CCF, "the greatest threat in recent years to the old parties," had made "no gains which can entitle it to recognition as a national party."[4]

This was palpably true. But it was no less true, as some pointed out, that the victors had weighty obligations to fulfil. The old parties, admonished the Toronto *Star*, must "adequately meet the needs of the masses [and] put into operation whatever reforms are necessary for that end."[5] Business and industry, added *Maclean's*, had "a challenge in the next few years to prove that free enterprise is better – and is better for all groups – than complete State Control."[6]

For Mackenzie King, after all, his New Social Order notwithstanding, had not amassed a particularly proud victory. He received 39 per cent of the national vote, Bracken's Tories an unimpressive 27 per cent. But the several third parties collectively got 34 per cent. The 1945 election was the only' one in Canadian history in which third parties received a larger percentage of the total vote than one of the traditional parties; moreover, their total was 12 per cent larger than in 1935, the election many consider the most radical in the nation's history. In Ontario in the 1945 federal campaign, the result was similar if less record-shattering. In 1921, third parties polled 29 per cent of the provincial vote, the greatest ever; in 1935, they received 20 per cent and in 1945, 22 per cent. Whatever else the 1945 results indicated, they proved that Canadians were far from satisfied with the achievements and promises of the traditional parties. At the same time, there was a widespread belief that a great many old party votes had not gone to the CCF because of the unprecedented welfare and social security legislation offered by both Liberals and Conservatives.[7]

To be sure, there were serious tensions and problems within the CCF which circumscribed its full organizational potential. Unlike Saskatchewan's, Ontario's political tradition was one of quiescence and passivity; democracy meant nothing more than voting, not active participation in the political process. As a result, the Ontario CCF never rose to the level of an entity integral to the life of the community, which in turn resulted in a small membership base and consequent inadequate financing. In Ontario, the CCF simply never developed into a mass political movement.

At the same time, however, there was a substantial increase in membership during the "golden age." Yet this too had certain counter-productive functions. The old guard who had maintained the faith during the grim days before Noseworthy's victory was inevitably suspicious of the motives of the newcomers. The latter, equally inevitably, were embittered by this distrust, and definite factions emerged within the membership. In the Windsor area, for example, few candidates had the wholehearted support of all groups within the party.[8]

This tension was exacerbated by the continued ambivalence of the party's two main constituencies towards each other. The trade unionists saw the middle class radicals as naive, utopian, ivory tower dreamers; the radicals feared the unionists as power hungry right-wingers.[9] They also irrationally resented the failure of the union leaders to bring their rank-and-file with them into the CCF, although no one in the party had the remotest idea of how this might be achieved. The C.C.L.'s P.A.C. acknowledged the failure. At the 1946 convention of the C.C.L., Pat Conroy, the Secretary-Treasurer, explained that "Despite my efforts to make this programme work, it has been sabotaged from beginning to end . . . [by] those who opposed it. . . . "[10] He meant the Communists, but the disappointing performance of the Congress nevertheless fired the hostility of the middle class members of the party.

CCF'ers generally agreed on the reason for their party's disappointing showing. They believed the old parties "gulled" voters by their promise to achieve all the attractive goals proposed by the CCF with none of the drastic methods commonly attributed to it.[11] And they unanimously agreed that the Toronto *Star's* post-election editorial headline was precisely accurate: "Fear of Socialism," it declared, "Strong in the Election."[12] This fear, together with Jolliffe's Gestapo charge, was responsible for the tremendous increase in Drew's vote. For weeks it had been widely predicted that the results would show "Drew for Ontario, King for Canada." On June 4, the large number of persons who dreaded socialism reasoned that the surest way to prevent its triumph was to support the party conceded the best chance of defeating the CCF, namely Drew's Conservatives. The same logic prevailed, if not as widely, on June 11, when King and the Liberals were expected to triumph, albeit with a minority government. King thus received the support of many Liberals who, in their hatred of the CCF, had voted for Drew; of indifferent Liberals who had little incentive to cast their ballots for Hepburn but who turned out to support King against a possible CCF victory; of at least a few Conservatives who agreed that only King could forestall a socialist victory; and, ironically, of CCF sympathizers who were so shattered by the Ontario results that they determined to make their votes "count" federally.

It is evident that business's deliberate attempt to foster a fear-psychosis in the electorate was highly successful. Because its propaganda campaign brought out such vast numbers of anti-socialists who had rarely voted in the past, the CCF had to increase its vote merely to stand still; it failed to do so, and thereby, relatively speaking, fell far behind.

The party's great mistake was to believe that the revered Common Man would not be deceived by what socialists saw as self-evident lies and misrepresentations. Its normal attitude to adverse criticism was, first, to assume a pose of high-minded self-righteousness and, secondly, to stigmatize critics as unscrupulous, self-interested apologists for an immoral capitalist system. The validity of this position is irrelevant. Trestrail's and Murray's audiences were swayed by their arguments, and the CCF failed to respond effectively enough to remove the doubts planted by the propagandists.

In fact, the CCF was unprepared organizationally to assume the task of counter-propaganda. But the problem was greater than that. The truth was that the CCF in these years suffered from delusions of grandeur, from enervating over-confidence and optimism. This was due in part to the fundamental tenet, held equally by Marxists and Christian socialists, that History was on the side of socialism, and that History would inevitably triumph. "The stars in their courses are fighting for the cause of socialism"; so stated the executive of the Ontario CCF in 1936, when the party was virtually moribund.[13] The delirium of the early forties was also of course attributable to the spectacular successes in Ontario, Saskatchewan, and the various by-elections. Hence there was in the CCF, by early 1945, "an almost complete lack of urgency, an unwillingness to take great pains or make great sacrifices."[14] This was the reason the party could not convince itself to take seriously the propaganda crusade being directed against it every day of every week of every month for two entire years. CCF over-confidence and the anti-socialist campaign together help explain why, in the elections, the comfortable residential sections of city and town turned out a huge vote, while balloting in working class areas was comparatively light: Forest Hill Village in Toronto sent ninety per cent of its residents to the polls, most industrial areas only fifty per cent.[15]

Most important, perhaps, the belief in inevitable victory explains why CCF leaders lost almost completely their rational perspective on the existing political situation. They knew party organization was woefully inadequate. They knew natural forces had created a climate of opinion favourable to the CCF. They sensed that many of those forces – gratitude to Russia, disillusionment with unfettered laissez-faire and the politicians who upheld it, the desire for a better post-war world – had, one by one, been diminished in impact. They were aware that a great number of people supported the CCF not because they were socialists but because it appeared to be the "coming thing." CCF leaders should have known that failure was quite as conceivable as success. Their strategy was to mobilize their members to action by sweeping promises of inexorable triumph. It had exactly the opposite effect; there developed such unthinking optimism that supporters saw little need to give of themselves unsparingly in a task they considered superfluous: their party, after all, was destined for victory.

The 1945 election ended an era in the history of Canada and of the `CCF movement. After that time, the possibility of the party winning power in a sudden nation-wide sweep became wholly unlikely. The postwar period, with its unprecedented and unexpected prosperity, muted the intensive wartime demand for social reform. The resurgence of the CCF in Ontario in 1948 can be more easily explained than that of 1943: it was the result of unprecedented labour support above all in Toronto, combined with a growing alienation from George Drew personally in many sections of the province. In 1951, the CCF polled its smallest vote in Ontario in a decade, less than one-fifth of the total. After that, it continued to be a factor but not a threat in provincial politics.

Nationally, some observers spoke of the prospect of the CCF superseding the Conservatives as the official opposition as late as 1948. It is unlikely that such a possibility really existed, but if it did the federal election of 1949 shattered such a hope. Perhaps because Trestrail and his backers began another mighty "Stop Socialism" effort, perhaps in reaction against the British Labour Government, perhaps because of the hysterical anti-Communism developing in the United States – whatever the reasons, the CCF suffered a crushing and irreparable defeat. The tide of history had conclusively subsided, and the efforts of man proved inadequate to the task; the CCF never again provided a major threat to, although it remained the nagging conscience of, the old parties.

The CCF, it is evident, suffered from a number of internal weaknesses which prevented it from realizing its maximum potential support. Yet in the end, this is an insufficient explanation for its electoral failure. The reality seems to be that even at best, its realistic potential amounted to a minority of the electorate. The majority, including those who favoured much of the CCF programme, was instinctively susceptible to the elementary strategy of the old parties: "Let a third party once demonstrate votes are to be had by adopting a certain programme, then one or the other of the old parties can be trusted to absorb the new doctrine."[16] Such "pragmatism" is, of course, of abiding benefit to the Canadian people. As one reporter summed it up after the 1945 elections, "There is no gainsaying that the progress of the CCF has been responsible for much progressive legislation provincially and federally by the older parties, designed to head off the new threat to their domination."[17] Such moral victories, however, were politically fatal to the CCF.

But this was not merely because the CCF was another third party. It is possible to be more precise than that. The CCF described itself, and was considered to be, a socialist party. This accounts for the overwhelming success of the old parties and the anti-socialist propagandists in mobilizing a large majority of the Canadian electorate, including those in the working class, to repudiate it at the polls. The public perception of socialism and socialists was the variable which intervened between large-scale political disaffection and the re-election of George Drew and Mackenzie King.

Voting behaviour is determined less by one's objective class position than by the status to which one aspires. In Canada almost as palpably as in the United States, the vast majority of citizens are socialized to accept "the major premise of unlimited upward mobility for those with energy and initiative."[18] The ideal is not social equality but equality of opportunity. Agnes Macphail wanted to rise *with* her class; most Canadian workers

aim to rise *from* it. "Making it" in Canadian terms is diametri-
cally opposed to the concept of levelling down with which socialism is associated.

"The average North American," B. K. Sandwell of *Saturday
Night* once observed, 'is too good at thinking of himself as a
boss to hate bosses as a class.'"[19] The CCF's constant attacks on
bosses were predicated on "the existence of a Canadian working
class. Objectively, such a class existed, but the members of that
class did not, for the most part, accept their position as such."[20]
To the majority, socialism was seen as an ideology outside the
mainstream of Canada's political culture, alien and in opposition
to the cherished Horatio Alger myth. This, surely, accounts for
the success of the propaganda campaign against the CCF. "I
don't believe in a law to prevent a man from getting rich." This
statement of Lincoln's, quoted often by Trestrail, must have
evoked an immediately sympathetic response from most Canadians. When bank ads stressed the virtue of profit-making, when
Hiram Walker's proclaimed that any Canadian boy could rise to
be prime minister, they were simply reminding the public that
several of its most passionately held ambitions were threatened
by the "CCF socialists." If most Canadian working men considered themselves incipient entrepreneurs, it stands to reason that
they would feel threatened by what they were told about the
CCF. In the 1945 federal election, the CCF received 28 per cent of
the votes of manual workers, the highest in the party's history.
King, however, won 43 per cent. Walter Young's comment
seems eminently sensible: "One possible explanation . . . is simply
that manual workers saw the Liberal party as corresponding
more closely than the CCF to their status aspirations."[21]

Young pursues this argument to a second important dimension. Following Zakuta, he points out that it was not the CCF's
ideology alone that was alien: as well, "the people who espoused
and promoted it were clearly the 'wrong' kind of people." The
party's activists were not, outside of Saskatchewan, typical of the
wider community. They were the marginal members of society,
the alienated, outsiders, rebels, malcontents, those who rejected
the prevailing norms, "in a sense deviants, devoid . . . of respectable attributes."[22] Party leaders worked consciously to portray
themselves as reasonable, forward-looking, humane men. But
given those who were most vocal among its membership – plus
occasional gaffes like the Gestapo charges – the propagandists
had little difficulty making even conventionally respectable individuals like Coldwell and Jolliffe appear almost as crypto-
revolutionaries. In short, as Walter Young neatly wraps it up,

"The party image was one of social and economic deviation."[23]

On the other hand, it is, of course, self-evident that Canadian socialism has achieved levels of success undreamed of by socialists in the United States. Canadians do not dismiss socialism so facilely or so contemptuously as do Americans; Canadians have been consciously influenced by the socialist position as Americans have not. Daniel Bell's useful phrase that the American socialist movement was *in* but not *of* the community[24] is simply not applicable to the CCF. In America, socialists have traditionally been relegated to the status of a futile, even subversive, lunatic fringe group. In Canada, notwithstanding the perception of socialists as more or less deviants from the norm, serious attention has been paid to the party and its leaders.

Gad Horowitz has attempted to explain this phenomenon by adapting Louis Hartz's analysis to Canada. The ethos of "absolutist liberalism" which Hartz isolates in the United States is modified in Canada, according to Horowitz, by a fragment of British toryism which gives rise to its dialectical correlate, socialism.[25] The hypothesis is ingenious, provocative, and seriously flawed.[26] Nevertheless, the reality of the socialist influence in Canada is empirically demonstrable.

Canadians vote for socialist candidates, often in relatively large numbers. But to say this is to return again to what has, until recently, seemed to be the limitations of socialist legitimacy. There has existed a certain definable point at which the voter has pulled back. It was no accident that only in Saskatchewan did the CCF party ever win an election. In Ontario, British Columbia, and Manitoba, official opposition was as close to power as the party was allowed to get. In Canada as a whole it was never even in sight of second place. For socialism could not be permitted to capture control of those jurisdictions which are seen as most crucial to the continuing stability and prosperity of the nation. Socialism in Canada had to be halted at precisely the point where real power begins.

After about a decade of existence, however, the CCF's successor is apparently getting around this impasse. Besides regaining Saskatchewan, it has since 1969 won quite unexpected victories in Manitoba and, most significantly, British Columbia. With the goal of federal power still a chimera, Ontario remains the great and most elusive target. It is by no means clear, however, that the reasons which account for the success in Manitoba and British Columbia are of a kind to offer sustenance to the morale of the Ontario party.

There are a host of secondary reasons which help account for the electoral failure of the CCF in Ontario: its financial difficulties; its ties to organized labour, which alienated many voters without delivering the labour vote; the public confusion between communism and socialism; fear of experimentation during a depression and complacency in a time of prosperity; the tendency of the working class to be politically passive; the absence of natural working class leaders in urban centres; the religious and ethnic affiliations of many workers which often cut across their class loyalties.[27]

Ultimately, however, the problem for Ontario socialists has been both simpler and more intractable than such a catalogue implies. It is this: most Canadians have viewed socialism as an ideology designed to stifle their most precious basic aspirations. Because it never successfully challenged this perception, the CCF, at least in conventional electoral terms, died a failure. Its successor, at long last, appears to have made inroads in overcoming this vexing dilemma. As a result, the Ontario party is justified in indulging in a modicum of cautious optimism. Prudence dictates that undue expectations should be eschewed. But who, after all, anticipated three social democratic islands in a sea of affluent Canadian capitalism? For the Ontario New Democratic Party, the future is not yet closed.

References

1. *CCF News,* June 1, 1945.

2. Ian MacPherson, "The 1945 Collapse of the CCF in Windsor," *Ontario History,* Vol. LXI, No. 4, December 1969, p. 199.

3. CCF National Office Files, Margaret Thelford to Corporal Burwood in Germany, July 16, 1945. Miss Thelford, David Lewis' secretary, included these results in her letter.

4. Toronto *Star,* June 12, 1945.

5. *Ibid.*

6. *Maclean's,* July 15, 1945.

7. Hutchison, *Incredible Canadian,* p. 406; editorial, *Saturday Night,* June 9, 1945.

8. Macpherson, "The 1945 Collapse of the CCF in Windsor," *op. cit.,* p. 206.

9. Horowitz, *Canadian Labour in Politics,* pp. 83, 150.

10. *Ibid.,* p. 102.

11. *CCF News,* June 21, 1945.

12. Toronto *Star,* June 5, 1945.

13. *New Commonwealth,* April 18, 1936.

14. Andrew Brewin, *Canadian Forum,* February 1946.

15. *Ibid.,* July 1945.

16. J. D. Hicks, "Third Party Tradition in American Politics," *Mississippi Valley Historical Review,* June 1933, pp. 26-7.

17. Toronto *Star,* June 12, 1945.

18. Young, *Anatomy of a Party,* p. 289

19. *Saturday Night,* May 18, 1935.

20. Young, *op. cit.*

21. *Ibid.,* p. 207.

22. *Ibid.,* pp. 183-4, 186-7, 290-1.

23. *Ibid.,* p. 186.

24. D. Bell, "Marxian Socialism in the United States," in Egert and Persons, *Socialism and American Life,* volume 1, p. 217.

25. Louis Hartz, *The Liberal Tradition in America* (New York, 1955); Horowitz, *Canadian Labour in Politics,* chapter 1.

26. See Ramsay Cook, letter to the editor, *Canadian Dimension,* Volume 2, No. 5, 1965, commenting on Horowitz's review of George Grant, *Lament for a Nation,* in *ibid.,* Volume 2, No. 4, 1965.

27. Martin Robin: *Radical Politics and Canadian Labour* (Kingston, 1968), p. 5; Lipset, *Agrarian Socialism* (1968 ed.), p. 261; Young, *op. cit.,* p. 208; Gerald L. Caplan and James Laxer, "Perspectives on Un-American Traditions in Canada," in Ian Lumsden (ed.), *Close the 49th Parallel etc: The Americanization of Canada* (Toronto, 1970), pp. 311-14.

SELECTED SOURCES

A. Archival and Private Collections

Reverend Salem G. Bland Papers, United Church of Canada Archives, Victoria University, University of Toronto.

CCF National Council Minutes, 1937-1945, Woodsworth House, Ottawa.

CCF National Office Files, Woodsworth House, Ottawa.

W. C. Good Papers, Public Archives of Canada.

Stanley Knowles Files, Private, Ottawa.

Donat M. LeBourdais Papers, Private, Toronto.

Bernard and Alice Loeb Papers, Ontario Woodsworth House, Toronto.

Agnes Macphail Private Papers, Mrs. Margaret Stewart Collection, Toronto.

Agnes Macphail Public Papers, Public Archives of Canada.

Ontario CCF Provincial Convention Reports, 1937-1945, Ontario Woodsworth House, Toronto.

Ontario CCF Provincial Council Minutes and Documents, 1941-1945, Ontario Woodsworth House, Toronto.

Ontario CCF Provincial Executive Minutes, 1941-1945, Ontario Woodsworth House, Toronto.

Toronto District Trades and Labour Council Minutes, 1926-1938.

J. S. Woodsworth Papers, Public Archives of Canada.

(Note: All Ontario Woodsworth House documents have been transferred to the archives of Queen's University, Kingston.)

B. Personal Interviews

Mr. and Mrs. F. Andrew Brewin
Prof. George Grube
Harry Hatfield
Edward B. Jolliffe
Donat M. LeBourdais
David Lewis
Mr. and Mrs. Walter Mann
William Ewart Gladstone Murray
Donald W. Sanderson
Margaret Stewart
Frank H. Underhill
Irving J. Weinrot

C. Official Publications

Debates and Proceedings of the Legislature of the Province of Ontario.

Report of the Royal Commissioner Appointed May 28, 1945 To Investigate Charges Made by Mr. Edward B. Jolliffe, K.C., The Hon. Mr. Justice A.M. LeBel, Commissioner (Toronto, 1945).

D. Periodicals, Magazines, Newspapers

Canadian Annual Review of Public Affairs, 1932-38 (Toronto).

Canadian Congress Journal, 1932-1945 (Ottawa).

Canadian Forum, 1932-1945 (Toronto).

Canadian Unionist, 1932-1945 (Ottawa).

Farmers' Sun (Weekly Sun), 1932-1933 (Toronto).

Financial Post, 1932-34, 1943-45 (Toronto).

Maclean's Magazine, 1932-45 (Toronto).

New Commonwealth (CCF News), 1934-39, 1943-45 (Toronto).

News, 1941-1945 (Toronto).

Rural Co-operator, 1941-1945 (Toronto).

Saturday Night, 1933-1945 (Toronto).

Time Magazine, 1932-1945 (New York).

Toronto *Globe*, 1932-1936.

Toronto *Globe and Mail*, 1937-1945

Toronto *Mail and Empire*, 1932-1936.

Toronto *Star*, 1932-1945.

Toronto *Telegram*, 1932-1945.

Winnipeg *Free Press*, 1933-1935, 1943-45.

E. Unpublished Secondary Sources

Richard M. Alway, *Mitchell F. Hepburn and the Liberal Party in the Province of Ontario, 1937-1943*, M.A. thesis (University of Toronto, 1965).

Myrtle M. Armstrong, *The Development of Trade Union Political Activity in the CCF*, M.A. thesis (University of Toronto), 1959.

Dudley A. Bristow, *Agrarian Interest in the Politics of Ontario: A Study With Special Reference to The Period 1919-1949*, M.A. thesis (University of Toronto), 1950.

Edwin C. Guillet, *Famous Canadian Trials*, volume 50, "Political Gestapo," typewritten manuscript (Toronto), 1949.

J. D. Hoffman, *Farmer-Labour Government in Ontario, 1919-1923*, M.A. thesis (University of Toronto), 1959.

Larry Zolf, *The Emergence of Hepburn Liberalism in the Thirties*, graduate dissertation (University of Toronto), 1960.

F. Published Secondary Sources

E. Wight Bakke, *Citizens Without Work: A Study of the Effects of Unemployment Upon the Workers' Social Relations and Practices* (New Haven, 1940).

John Bracken Says (Toronto, 1944).

Tim Buck, *Thirty Years, 1922-1952* (Toronto, 1952).

Jack L. Granatstein, "The York South By-Election of February 9, 1942: A Turning Point in Canadian Politics," *Canadian Historical Review*, vol. XLVIII, No. 2, June 1967.

George M. Grube, "The LeBel Report and Civil Liberties," *Canadian Forum*, vol. 25, November 1945.

Gad Horowitz, *Canadian Labour in Politics* (Toronto, 1968).

David Lewis and Frank Scott, *Make This Your Canada* (Toronto, 1943).

Seymour M. Lipset, *Agrarian Socialism* (revised edition, New York, 1968).

Harold A. Logan, *Trade Unions in Canada* (Toronto, 1948).

Grace MacInnis, *J. S. Woodsworth, A Man to Remember* (Toronto, 1953).

Neil McKenty, *Mitch Hepburn* (Toronto, 1967.)

Kenneth McNaught, *A Prophet in Politics* (Toronto, 1959).

Gladstone Murray, *Private Property: A Guarantee of Freedom* (Toronto, 1944).

Ontario Conservative Party Election Pamphlets, 1934, University of Toronto Library Collection.

J. W. Pickersgill, *The Mackenzie King Record*, vol. 1, 1939-1944 (Toronto, 1960).

Margaret Stewart and Doris French, *Ask No Quarter* (Toronto, 1959).

Burdrick A. Trestrail, *Social Suicide* (no information).

Dennis Wrong, "Ontario Provincial Elections, 1934-1955: A Preliminary Survey of Voting," *Canadian Journal of Economics and Political Science*, vol. XXIV, No. 2, May 1958.

Walter D. Young, *The Anatomy of a Party: The National CCF, 1932-1961* (Toronto, 1969).

Leo Zakuta, *A Protest Movement Becalmed: A Study of Change in the CCF* (Toronto, 1964).

INDEX

205

208   *The Dilemma of Canadian Socialism*

Ontario Provincial Police –
Special Branch, 168-188
Osborne-Dempster, W. J., 119,
168-170, 172-174, 177-186

Parent, Alex, 157
Parker, Percy, 70
Peppin, Cecil B., 176-177, 183-184
Philpott, Elmore, and CCF, 25,
26-27, 29, 31, 35n, 41, 42-43,
44, 52-53,
and Liberals, 56, 57, 73
Plaunt, Allan, 11
Proctor, Samuel, 31
Progressive Party, 120

Reaume, Arthur, 160
Reconstruction Party, 72-73, 75,
76
Regina, Manifesto, 36-38, 39
Robinson, Bert, 22, 57, 64
Roebuck, Arthur, 32, 64, 69, 93
Rowe, John A., 170, 173, 174,
181, 182-183
Royal Commission to Investigate
E.B. Jolliffe's Charges
(LeBel Commission) 171-188,
189n

Saint-Laurent, Louis, 92, 135
Saturday Night, 89, 96, 98, 99,
100, 106, 120, 127, 141
Salsberg, J. B., 74, 86n, 105, 150,
191
Sanderson, Monatgue A., 102, 119
Special Branch OPP, 170,
172-174, 179, 180, 182, 185
Sandwell, B. K., 89, 169, 197
Scott, R. J., 45, 52, 53
Scott, Frank, 111
Sedgewick, Joseph, 178, 171
Shaw, Lloyd, 127
Sifton, Clifford, 125
Simpson, James, 22, 34n, 50, 68,
70, 81
Sinclair, Lister, 186-187
Smith, A. E., 18, 22, 43, 50-52
Smith, Stewart, 73
Socialist Party of Canada, 15,
23-24, 53, 61

The Society for Individual
Freedom, 14-125, 129
Spence, Reverend Ben, 68
Soviet Communism,. 42, 83, 90,
123
Spivak, Sol, 91
Spray, Graham, 11, 26, 60, 70
Stevens, H. H., 72, 73, 75
Strange, Charles, 115
Stubbs, Judge L. S., 46
Stanley, R. C., 123
Stringer, Commissioner, 180, 177,
183
Sullivan, Pat, 117, 148
Syndam, James 183

Temperence, 11
Temple, William, 68, 105
Toronto Labour Party, 22, 24
Toronto Star, 39, 71, 78, 101, 106,
193, 194
Toronto Telegram, 16, 30, 64, 118
Trades and Labour Congress of
Canada, 19-20, 22, 41, 83, 91,
95, 114, 116-117, 156-157
Trestrail, Burdrick A., 124, 132n,
159-163, 166n, 196, 198

Underhill, Frank, 14, 36, 86n
United Church, 36, 68
United Farmers of Ontario, 10-14,
28, 36-37, 44-46, 55, 75 (*see also*
CCF-rural relations)
Unionist (Canadian Unionist), 21,
46, 104

Wallace, R. C., 169
Walter, John, 26-28
Ward, Inspector, 184
Watson, George, 24, 34n
Weinrot, I. J., 86n
Williams, Arthur, 34n, 60, 61
Winch, Ernest, 38
Winch Harold, 129
Wismer, Leslie, 170
Workers' Association, 5 (Workers'
Party, 23)
Workers' Unity League, 43
Woodsworth, J.S. – 1932-1933, 8,
13, 22, 25, 28, 29, 30 1934 – 41,
55, 56, 58, 70, 76.

The Dilemma of Canadian Socialism
The CCF in Ontario

GERALD L. CAPLAN

"Most Canadians have viewed socialism as an ideology designed to stifle their most precious aspirations. Because it never successfully challenged this perception, the C.C.F., at least in conventional electoral terms, died a failure."

Here, set in the context of the national movement, is the history of the Cooperative Commonwealth Federation in the crucial arena of Ontario politics. From small beginnings in the West of the 1930's, the C.C.F. grew to a position of imminent power in Ontario and in the nation. Yet it never recovered from the resounding defeats incurred in the 1945 federal and Ontario provincial elections, and gradually disintegrated as a viable political force. Focusing on the internal and external causes of its demise, including a highly organized hate campaign financed by opposing political and business interests, author Gerald L. Caplan has traced the varying fortunes of the Ontario arm of the party in clear and well-documented detail. His book has exceptional merit as a valuable work of history and as a solid basic study. It is also a strikingly relevant work, with an implicit and pertinent message for today's New Democratic Party, the political successor of the C.C.F. and inheritor of the dilemma of Canadian socialism.

Gerald L. Caplan is a political activist and a noted specialist in Canadian history and politics. He also writes on African history and politics and has appeared in *Canadian Forum*, *Canadian Dimension* and various historical journals. He is a member of the Executive of the Ontario N.D.P. and an Associate Professor in the Department of History and Philosophy of the Ontario Institute for Studies in Education.

McClelland and Stewart Limited
The Canadian Publishers

0-7710-1896-7